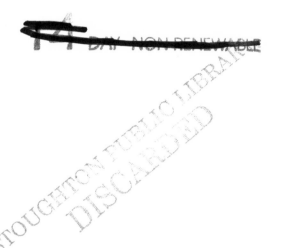

14 DAY - NON RENEWABLE

VOICES

OF THE

PLAINS CREE

by Edward Ahenakew
edited by Ruth M. Buck

Canadian Plains Research Center
University of Regina
1995

Copyright @ Canadian Plains Research Center

Canadian Plains Research Center
University of Regina
Regina, Saskatchewan S4S 0A2
Canada

Canadian Cataloguing in Publication Data
Ahenakew, Edward, 1885-1961
    Voices of the Plains Cree

    (Canadian plains studies, ISSN 0317-6290 ; 28)
    Originally published: Toronto: McClelland & Stewart, 1973.
    Includes bibliographical references and index. ISBN 0-88977-083-2
1. Cree Indians - Saskatchewan - Folklore.
2. Legends - Saskatchewan.   3. Tales - Saskatchewan.
I. Buck, Ruth Matheson, 1905-   II. University of
Regina.   Canadian Plains Research Center.   III. Title.
IV. Series.

E99.C88A34 1995   398.2'089'97307124   C95-920003-7

Cover Design: Agnes Bray/Brian Mlazgar
Cover artwork by Allen Sapp
Cover photo courtesy of Don Hall, Audio-Visual Services, University of Regina
Text illustrations by Calvin Sand

Printed and bound in Canada by
Hignell Printing Limited, Winnipeg, Manitoba
Printed on acid-free paper

CONTENTS

Publisher's Preface.. vi
Foreword vii
Introduction to the 1995 Edition.. ix
Introduction to the 1973 Edition.. 1
Introduction to Part I... 9
Part I: The Stories of Chief Thunderchild 13
1. A Winter of Hardship 14
2. Indian Laws... 17
3. Revenge Against the Blackfoot 20
4. Thunderchild Takes His First Horses from the Blackfoot 22
5. It is *Pu-chi-to* Now Who Tells His Story 24
6. Thunderchild Takes Part in a Dangerous Game.. 26
7. Encounter With the Blackfoot in the Eagle Hills 28
8. A Fight With the Sarcee 30
9. A Story of Friendship 31
10. Truce Making and Truce Breaking.. 32
11. Buffalo Pounds 36
12. The Buffalo Chase 38
13. The Grizzly Bear 39
14. Walking Wind Tells His Story of the Grizzly 40
15. Thunderchild's Adventure With the Bears... 41
16. The Foot-Race.. 42
17. A Faithless Woman... 43
18. The First Man... 45
19. The Sun Dance... 46
20. The Thirst Dance.. 48
Thunderchild's Conclusion.. 50
Introduction to Part II 51
Part II: Old Keyam... 53
1.. 54
2.. 58
3.. 61
4.. 64
5.. 71
6.. 76
7.. 80
8.. 86
9.. 89
10.. 93
11.. 100
12.. 104
Notes Relating to the 1973 Introduction... 109
Notes Relating to Part I: The Stories of Chief Thunderchild 112
Notes Relating to Part II: Old Keyam.. 120
Appendix: Account of the Signing of Treaty Number Six:.................................... 123
The Treaty at Forts Carlton and Pitt, Number Six... 124
Bibliography 130

PUBLISHER'S PREFACE

As the twentieth century draws to a close, the conventional portrait of human life on the Canadian Plains prior to the coming of Europeans is being challenged and revised.

Part of this challenge comes from oral histories and stories told among the Plains Indians. There was a time when social scientists regarded such histories and stories merely as cultural artifacts. Today, a growing number acknowledge what Plains Indians have always claimed — these oral histories and stories offer building blocks to reconstructing and understanding the past.

It is in this spirit that the Canadian Plains Research Center has undertaken to republish Edward Ahenakew's classic *Voices of the Plains Cree*.

James N. McCrorie
Executive Director
Canadian Plains Research Center
November 1994

FOREWORD

In the last several decades, literature related to all facets of North American Indian life has become popularized and prolific. Worthy to note, however, much of it is now being written by Indian people.

The late Dr. Edward Ahenakew, who was my uncle, wrote extensively throughout the 1920s. He also attempted, repeatedly, to have his work published. After his death in 1961, his papers came into the care and attention of Ruth Matheson Buck, who through her own determination and personal effort, to the task of deciphering and editing them. Her efforts, twelve years after Edward Ahenakew's death, resulted in the publication of *Voices of the Plains Cree* in 1973. Again, with the assistance of Ruth Matheson Buck, the Canadian Plains Research Center at the University of Regina has agreed to undertake a second reprinting of this book.

The Indian way of preserving and passing on knowledge from one generation to the next was through story-telling or oral history. Most stories were told in a circuitous manner. This technique challenged the listener to be both imaginative and alert to the lesson in the tale. Stories invariably started with *Kayas*, which in Cree means "long ago." Each retold some aspect of history, teaching traditions, values or mores of the culture. The children's stories used humour and startling consequences to illustrate a point. Unfortunately, not all of these stories translate well. Those that do, however, are found in Edward Ahenakew's "Cree Trickster Tales."

Uncle Edward understood what the future held for Indian people — how the Indian identity would be shaped by the inequity of their history and how difficult it would be for Indians to assert their place in the society of the future in their own land. He also realized that the oral tradition, which was the vehicle for passing down our history, was seriously threatened by European settlement. Preserving the history therefore meant that its transmission would of necessity have to change. He foresaw this as reality, without debate or judgement.

Edward Ahenakew's written work illustrates the manner in which the oral historian would transfer knowledge through story-telling. His unpublished, unedited notes are particularly amusing to the Cree ear as they fully capture the essence of Cree humour and its picturesque, situational aspects. In the Chief Thunderchild stories, Uncle Edward followed the old way, *Kayas,* that things were done, listening to a respected Elder and then passing on the stories.

Keyam means, "I do not care." Those of us who remembered Edward Ahenakew also remember that this gentle man, as "Old Keyam," personified not only himself, but the Indian people of his generation, people who were part of the struggle to harmonize competing cultures and survive with spirit intact. Uncle Edward's farsightedness in collecting the stories and committing them to print has given the Plains Cree a tangible record of their past.

It is a truism that in order to define one's self or, "to know who we are," we must also know from whence we came.

Old Keyam,

Kitatamihinan oma ka acimoyan ka-ki-kiskeyihtahmak oma e neyiyawiyak.

"Thank you for telling these stores that we may know that we are Cree."

To the editor of *Voices of the Plains Cree*, Ruth Matheson Buck, whose perseverance resulted in the publication of my uncle's work,
  Kitatamihinan "We thank you."

Christine Wilna (Willy) Hodgson, 1994
Daughter of Agnes Ahenakew Pratt
and niece of Dr. Canon Edward Ahenakew

Footnote: The Ahenakew and Matheson families have experienced more than a century of friendship. Ruth Matheson Buck's generosity of spirit fired her efforts to reach for the dream of my uncle, Edward Ahenakew — the writing and publication of stories he heard in the "voices" of the Plains Cree.

INTRODUCTION
TO THE 1995 EDITION

I remember being delighted to find Edward Ahenakew in the "Indian Village" at Saskatoon, sitting on the running board of his old car, polishing his shoes. We had both come down south to see the king. I had come down on the train with my high-school class from Prince Albert for the Royal visit of 1939. He had come down from Fort à la Corne[1] in his dusty old Chevrolet to pay his respects when King George VI and Queen Elizabeth came to Saskatoon.

I left my high-school group to go to the "Indian Village" because the king was supposed to pass by twice in the course of visiting the Tuberculosis Sanatorium. In those days there were no houses out there along the road to the Sanatorium, just bushes and fields. The Indians had lined their trucks and cars along the road and changed into their regalia in anticipation of the visit. In an open area, we waited with some people from Red Pheasant Reserve, a group of school children from *Atahkakohp* Day School and *Mistawasis* Day School. After I found Edward Ahenakew, I stayed with him for the rest of the day. We stood together and watched the king and queen pass by on the gravel road which is now Avenue K. They came along in an open car, and we waved as they passed by on the gravel road. They came back; we waved again. There were hundreds of people in Saskatoon to see them. Edward Ahenakew told me that when he saw King George going by, "I could feel the hair sticking up on the back of my head and I felt proud to be part of the British Empire." He didn't say he felt "a thrill" but he said he could feel "the majesty of the King." After that he said, "Well, let's go home together." He was a generous man. We drove home to Prince Albert and had supper together. We had a good time and that's when he told me what he felt when he saw the king. He said he reacted to the king that way because, unlike the Americans, our country had a living constitution represented by a living person, the king.

Although at the time I wondered about what he said, I later came to understand his feelings. He, and eventually I, were both educated at Emmanuel College, the Anglican Theological School in Saskatoon, and there we received a thorough education in the rightness of all things English and the virtues of the Anglican way of life. We were both taught the history of the Church from Augustine through Thomas à Becket to the latest Archbishop of Canterbury. Some of our teachers were men from England who wore black academic gowns now found only at places like Oxford University. In fact the students still wore academic gowns for meals, lectures and chapel when I attended from 1940 to 1944. (I even remember playing soccer in gowns between classes.) We learned that the king was the temporal head of the Church. Everything was English.

These attitudes are an important part of Edward Ahenakew's story. Edward Ahenakew was 54 years old when the king visited Saskatoon. He had been living and working in near poverty on the Fort à la Corne Reserve along the northern fringe of the prairie in Saskatchewan for twenty years. His world was full of "Indian Villages" and people who polished their shoes to show respect for authority figures and thought nothing of travelling many miles for a chance to glimpse the king of England.[2] Many of them were like Edward

Ahenakew. They never publicly voiced any misgivings about these things. The stories in *Voices of the Plains Cree* came about in this context.

Edward Ahenakew was born into a Christian family. He was proud that he was a second-generation Christian. He came into this world on June 11, 1885, at the Sandy Lake Reserve in Saskatchewan. He was sickly and frail and his mother, Ellen Ermine Skin, told me that at the time she made a solemn vow. If he lived, she would present him to the Church for the ministry.

Edward Ahenakew had three brothers — Shem, Samson, and Jehu — and three sisters — Agnes (Pratt), Flora (Beeds) and Sophia (Robinson). He and his brothers and sisters were what I call "second-generation" reserve Indians. This is important because it shaped their attitudes to many things, particularly deference to authority, and even Edward's feelings for the King. Many of that older generation respected religious authority and were very impressed by it. I think it was because of their strong Cree upbringing. Their attitudes toward Christian religious authorities were shaped by their respect for medicine men and powerful Cree leaders. That respect took the form of deference. You never asked questions of the real old-timers. You just waited and watched. That was how they were. I know Edward Ahenakew's attitudes to authority were different from mine because there were times when he used to find me disrespectful, especially in my youth, although I didn't mean to offend. However, I am a "fourth-generation" reserve Indian and my family encouraged me to ask questions and stick up for myself in a way that he and others of his generation found impertinent.

The reserve which Edward Ahenakew's family helped to establish is at Sandy Lake about seventy miles west of Prince Albert. The land was selected by *Atahkakohp*[3] and the Reverend John Hines on land they mutually agreed was good for farming.[4] Edward's father, Baptiste Ahenakew, was among the first to establish a home on the reserve. Baptiste's father was David Ahenakew,[5] whose brothers *Sasakwamos, Napeskis* and *Atahkakohp* were also considered grandfathers by Edward. Edward's great-grandfather, Charles Chatelaine, came from France and married a Cree woman whose name is not remembered now. Edward's paternal relatives connected him with many families living on the eastern side of Saskatchewan while his mother's family had connections in the west. She was the daughter of *Notowewikamik*, the sister of Poundmaker.[6]

Edward attended *Atahkakohp* Day School at Sandy Lake. Here he was taught English history, the English language and to be loyal to the king. I imagine in many ways his experience would have been like mine at the day school on Little Pine Reserve thirty-one years later. We had to salute the flag every morning before we went into the classroom. Of course that was the style in most schools. And then Miss Cunningham would lead us in singing, "Three Cheers for the Red, White and Blue," "The Maple Leaf for Ever" and "God Save the King." We used to sing first thing every morning, then attend religious instruction for half an hour and after that we started studying mathematics and other subjects. Edward Ahenakew's experience at day school might have been a little different in one way. When he was at the *Atahkakohp* Day School his teacher was his own uncle, Louis Ahenakew, who was said to be a good Christian. What they meant by a "good Christian" was that he was a real conformist. He conformed to what the church expected him to be. In his later years Louis Ahenakew could easily have been mistaken for a distinguished Frenchman. He had grey hair and a neat pointed beard. Edward believed that what he learned in day school "stood me in good stead when I arrived at the school in Prince Albert."[7]

The "school" in Prince Albert was Emmanuel College Boarding School. It was established in the early 1880s by the Church Missionary Society of the Church of England to train teachers and pastors who would expand the missionary movement among the Indians.[8] The school was later moved to Saskatoon where it became the Anglican Theological College of the new University of Saskatchewan.[9] But when Edward Ahenakew attended the school, Emmanuel College was an unprepossessing collection of shacks in Prince Albert.

He and his parents arrived at the school in a horse-drawn wagon. Edward's mother talked to me about that moment many years ago when I was visiting Sandy Lake. "After we left Edward at the school we went back to our tent, and that evening even Baptiste was crying!" she said, looking at her husband. Baptiste, leaning over towards me, said humorously, "I was a little drunk." Edward was not generally a very reflective person but he did recall this moment. He wrote about it many years later. "I shed no tear, but the pain in my heart was great, as I watched my father walking away. He did not look back once. I was much depressed, and scarcely noticed the boys kicking a football around the school grounds. Then two of my cousins ran over and took charge of me."[10] As they would in later years, this web of family relations connected him with a larger community and eased his transitions from place to place.

In 1903, at the age of 18, Edward passed his Junior Matriculation. Leaving Emmanuel College Boarding School, he went back to his father and worked with him for a year. He then taught at John Smith's Day School for a year. During that year he began to write a newsletter in Cree syllabics. The handwritten newsletter he started then was the precursor of his *Cree Monthly Guide*, which was produced with the help of the Missionary Society of the Church in Canada (MSCC) (Anglican Church) from 1925 until Edward's death in 1961.

He was called to the ministry as his mother had hoped and went to Toronto to attend Wycliffe College, where he began his studies in Theology in 1905.[11] His mother really encouraged him and she did the same to me, too. She said to me once, when I was a young man, "You work hard too and get through and don't ever give up." Because of that encounter, I have an idea of what she might have said to encourage her son.

Edward was joined at the University of Toronto by his cousin, Alec Ahenakew, and together they participated in many athletic competitions at the university. Edward won the pole vault competition several times. However, although Edward persisted, his cousin did not complete his theological training. Alec quietly left the College one day and for a long time Edward did not know where he had gone. He later learned that Alec had joined the Hudson's Bay Company and begun a lifelong career as a trader. Edward continued his studies in the winter and taught school and preached at Sturgeon Lake and John Smith's during the summer. In 1910 he transferred to the newly established Anglican Theological School, Emmanuel College at the University of Saskatchewan. Edward graduated in 1912 with a degree of Licenciate in Theology; a Bachelor of Arts was later conferred on him. He was appointed on a temporary basis to serve Cedar Lake Mission in Manitoba.[12]

After his ordination into the priesthood in 1912, Edward Ahenakew was appointed to assist the Reverend John R. Matheson at Onion Lake. He always respected Canon Matheson. Once, when he was irritated with me because I seemed impertinent, he said to me, "When I was working with Canon [Reverend] Matheson, I was always careful the way I behaved myself." And that struck me. Why was he so careful? What was he afraid of? He used to puzzle me. I think he deeply respected the non-Indian church leaders and to him, Reverend Matheson was special. He maintained a close connection with the family and it was Reverend Matheson's daughter Ruth Matheson Buck, who eventually sorted, edited and typed Edward Ahenakew's Cree stories so that they could be published.

Not all the stories Edward Ahenakew wrote are included in this volume. In her role as editor Ruth Matheson Buck chose some and left others out, and the choice to some extent reflects her bias. I know this because in the 1970s I translated several stories or parts of stories for Mrs. Buck. One story which was left out was typical of Indian humour, but may not have "translated" well in her eyes. It was the story of a man who believed that his protecting spirit — his *pawakan* — was the spirit of the louse. He was a very lousy man and he didn't want to kill one louse. He thought that they gave him spiritual power but after I had spent two or three days translating it, Mrs. Buck told me, "You know, that's silly," and she left it out. That is the kind of story she left out. It's humorous. It doesn't necessarily mean that there was such a man who was that lousy. I think it's just a story which symbolizes that some people will believe anything, or that maybe you shouldn't be too proud about who your spiritual power comes from. It needs to be explained but it should be in there. Edward Ahenakew collected it for a reason. He understood Cree thinking. He spoke Cree fluently and he had a good sense of humour. When he came to our house, my father would tell him a funny story and he would appreciate it. The people knew this. He spoke to them and they understood him. He had that Cree ethos; he told Indian jokes.

Soon after Edward went to work with Reverend John Matheson, the Reverend suffered a stroke and Edward was thrown into taking responsibility for many of the missions under Reverend Matheson's charge.

After World War I, there was an outbreak of influenza which had been brought home by the soldiers returning from Europe. The people to whom Edward Ahenakew ministered suffered terribly and many died as a result. Sid Keighley, whom I later knew in Stanley Mission, was in Onion Lake shortly after the epidemic struck. As he described it, "All the deaths had taken place within a two week period, and the church was piled high with bodies. The epidemic was striking everywhere. On the reserves so many people were dying that mass funerals and burials were being held."[13] Other diseases also took their toll on the Indians of the Onion Lake area. In fact, the population of Indians in Canada was at its lowest during the 1920s. According to the Indian Department's Annual Report, March 31, 1923, there were "about 105,000 for the whole Dominion."[14]

It was during these hard times with so many funerals that Edward Ahenakew decided to study medicine and become more useful to his people. He took a leave of absence from the Diocese of Saskatchewan and went to the University of Alberta in Edmonton. He completed three years of study and applied to have his leave extended by another two years in order to complete his medical course. But medical school was terribly hard for him and he became so ill that he was unable to complete his studies.

In an article in the March 30, 1950, edition of the *Western Producer*, W. Bleasdell Cameron related Edward Ahenakew's own explanation of his illness:

> "I had very little money," he said, "and was obliged to practice the most rigid economy. I had a small room in an apartment block over the river and I used to buy a good size piece of beef ready roasted: this I placed on the sill outside my window where it froze solid. I lived on this frozen meat and little else. When one piece was finished, I bought another.

Well after a time I began to feel not too well and it wasn't a great while after I was down and out. One of the doctors examined me. "Young man," he said, "you're trying to kill yourself. What do you think you are, a polar bear trying to live on frozen meat!" He said my stomach was almost paralyzed so I left the university and did not go back. I was ill for a year though I never stopped working."

He explained his illness somewhat differently in a letter to his friend, Professor Paul Wallace in Pennsylvania. Writing on August 25, 1922, he said, "I have been in hospital here (Lloydminster) since I came back from Edmonton (nervous breakdown) and am only getting on my feet again."

One thing he always said to my father was, "No Indian should go into medicine. It's just too tough." Well, Edward Ahenakew found it tough because he was underfed. He was reluctant to ask for help. He should have asked for more money but he wouldn't. He was too accepting of non-Indian church leaders. He had his pride and he suffered as a result. I think he always felt he was a failure because he was unable to complete his medical degree.

In the meantime, he went to Thunderchild's Reserve to convalesce. He was nursed back to health by Mrs. Annie Brown, the widow of another Cree clergyman, the Reverend James Brown.[15] Edward wrote from Mrs. Brown's house on December 9, 1922, and told Wallace that he was "still hors de combat and slowly mending and regaining my nerves. I am in a nice quiet home." On January 18, 1923, he wrote to Wallace that he was "feeling much better now although, I cannot read very much, my head bothers me if I read much more than a page or two at one time — I can write however without much effort. It is strange." It wasn't until July 17, 1923, that Edward Ahenakew reported to Wallace that he was finally feeling "very well indeed, almost back to my old self again, I think. I do a great deal of travelling and the outdoor life is doing wonders for me."

It was during this period when Edward Ahenakew was recovering from the rigours of medical school that the stories in this book were written. Before the first letter to Wallace in August 1922, Edward had already submitted the "Old Keyam" manuscript to a Mr. Button, who took it to Ryerson Press in Toronto. It was not published by Ryerson, but he remained hopeful that eventually it would be. Years later, on June 4, 1948, he wrote to Wallace about its possible publication, stating that Dr. Lingelbach of the American Philosophical Society and Dr. William Fenton of the Bureau of American Ethnology at the Smithsonian appeared to be "vitally interested."

Paul A.W Wallace (1891-1967), Edward's correspondent, was a friend from his days at the University of Alberta. While in Edmonton they were both members of the University of Alberta Literary Club. Wallace, a professor of English at Lebanon Valley College in Pennsylvania, seemed to have an interest in encouraging authentic aboriginal voices. Edward wrote to him of his ambition to write "*as things appear to the Indian himself*, in Saskatchewan more particularly but I am sure to other provinces in the west at least."[16]

Wallace consistently encouraged Edward Ahenakew to write and did his best to get the stories Edward sent to him published. Edward seemed very willing to allow Wallace to edit and improve his manuscripts, saying in one letter with reference to "Old Keyam," "Please use the greatest freedom in arranging the book and I shall be pleased to abide with what you advise."[17] His openness to editing may have been related to the fact that "Old Keyam" was fiction — a fictionalized account of Edward Ahenakew's personal vision. I think Edward Ahenakew's model for "Old Keyam" was himself and, since he wrote it in his younger years, it represented his vision of himself in the future, his vision of the person he became.

In many ways Edward Ahenakew was fortunate when he created the fictitious character, "Old Keyam," to be the teller of some of the tales he recorded. "Old Keyam" is not a typical Cree storyteller because they usually tell about adventures, battles and their participation in great events. "Old Keyam" is more interested in philosophy, politics and the working of institutions than most storytellers, and as "Old Keyam" himself once said, "Sometimes, I talk too much."[18] However, "Old Keyam" allows Edward to reflect on contemporary problems. "Old Keyam" is a philosopher whose reflective character allows Edward to do as he had hoped and show how an Indian thinks about the world. This literary vehicle allows Edward to tell the stories from a Cree point of view and describe Cree philosophy in a positive light, with a minimum of comparison between this philosophy and Christianity. The prevailing Christian/pagan dichotomy and the judgmental nature of writing about Indians in the early part of this century presented problems for other aboriginal writers at the time Edward wrote, such as Joe Dion and Mike Mountain Horse. Edward's framing of his writing in Indian terms allowed him to avoid making such judgments.

In their correspondence about the "Old Keyam" manuscript, Wallace encouraged Edward to add humour and romance to increase its appeal to readers. Edward wrote this story with the idea of making money. His poverty had made medical school impossible and this story seemed to offer some possibility of providing him with royalties. He corresponded with Wallace about the manuscripts and in one letter to Wallace he wrote, "I am sorry that the new chapters I sent were not so satisfactory but I did them too hurriedly and [they] were more for the material in them than the form."[19]

Voices of the Plains Cree has two distinct parts. The longer section is the story of "Old Keyam" but the book begins with a retelling of the stories of Chief Thunderchild, better known as *Kapitikow*. He was a well-known storyteller then living on the Onion Lake Reserve who had experienced the tribal wars in the late 1800s.[20] In 1923, when Edward interviewed him, *Kapitikow* was in his late seventies. Edward Ahenakew explained to Wallace the process of recording the stories told to him by Chief Thunderchild: "I go daily now to hear Chief Thunderchild tell them [the stories] & I write them down as he tells them. I have left out much of the detail and have I am sure lost much of the beauty through desire for brevity."[21]

Kapitikow had been a follower of Big Bear in his resistance to Treaty 6 in 1876, but later signed the treaty a few years later. Chief Thunderchild is well known for his stand on the terms of the treaty, insisting on one school and one missionary for every reserve. He was not a Christian but agreed to let the first missionary to his reserve build a church. He then tried to avoid a second church. Ultimately he had to fight the Indian Department and lost out; the government let another church move in.

I saw Chief Thunderchild at a sports day on Little Pine's Reserve sometime in the early 1930s. He was wearing his chief's uniform, surrounded by white people looking at his Treaty medals. *Kapitikow* stood there with dignity and was generous with his person. During the 1870s, when he was a young man, the buffalo herds had diminished so extensively that some of the bands went as far south as Montana to hunt. They were destitute and starving and the Canadian government did all in its power to settle them on the reserves. There was a longing for the return of the "good old days" and many Cree people believed that the buffalo would return from under ground — they had witnessed mud-covered buffalo coming from a spring where they left deep wallows.

Edward Ahenakew was anxious to record this history and oral literature before it was forgotten. In this he was encouraged by Wallace, but Edward did not take the time to rewrite his stories nor did he ask anyone else to help him edit his works. He was such a private person that later in life he never talked about the stories. He corresponded with Wallace about them and eventually the stories of *Wisakecahk*, the Trickster, were accepted for publication.[22] The other stories remained unedited and unpublished, and were not discovered until after his death.

After Edward Ahenakew recovered his health in 1923, he began to work in the Diocese of Saskatchewan again and it was sometime soon after this that I first saw him. I was just a small boy, but I recall that some sort of church ceremony was being held in the day school building. The ceremony was very well attended. There were so many people that the young men had to wait outside and look through the windows. Archdeacon John Mackay was there. He was an old, old man with a long beard and he was helped by a young man named Edward Ahenakew.[23] They were taking a service and Archdeacon Mackay spoke Cree fluently. He did a lot of talking and they did a lot of singing and the place was packed.

I got to know Edward when he came back again to live at Little Pine in 1927. I was at school and I must have been about nine or ten years old. He used to come to school to give us our religious instruction. He lectured us about feasts, holy days, and movable feasts and non-movable feasts, and he went on and on about it. It had nothing to do with our daily life. I'll never forget that.

We didn't have a mission house at Little Pine at the time, so, for the two years he was there, Edward Ahenakew lived in the little shack that Archdeacon Mackay had built years before. That's where he used to run the machine to mimeograph copy after copy of *The Cree Monthly Guide*. He used the newsletter to promote Christianity. When he lived at Little Pine he had been writing the *Guide* for several years. He had published the first edition in February, 1925, and in June of that year his fledgling publication was featured in the *MSCC Bulletin*. It showed the cover of the first volume with the title, drawings of the sun, a bible, a crown and an Indian chief, teepee and mountain scene. (A copy of the cover is reproduced on the following page). At the bottom of the page was a note in English saying " 'The Guide,' a monthly paper published in the interests of the Cree Nation by the Church of England in Canada." The title, in Cree syllabics, was "*Nehiyaw Okiskinotahikowin*."[24] Edward's choice of Cree phrasing in the title showed his intention that the people be guided spiritually by the contents of the paper and that it be a source of information to guide them as Christians. The cutline under the illustration explained the symbols drawn on the cover:

> Above is a cut of the cover of our new monthly magazine for Cree People. The significance of its design is understood by the Indians, is explained as follows: "The Indian in his natural state worshipped the sun — the Word of God gave him a better light to worship and showed him the Cross of Redemption and taught him to seek the Crown of Life; so he has now turned his back on the old ways and seeks to walk by the true light."[25]

The article in the *MSCC Bulletin* describes Edward's plan of the *Cree Monthly Guide*. He intended to have an editorial, "talks" on spiritual matters, lessons on the catechism, and teachings by various colleagues who could write syllabics or who would allow him to

BULLETIN

CANADA & OVERSEAS.

The Cree   Monthly Guide

VOL. NO. 1.

"THE GUIDE" A MONTHLY PAPER PUBLISHED IN THE INTERESTS OF THE CREE NATION BY THE CHURCH OF ENGLAND IN CANADA.

translate their words. He intended to include newly translated hymns, for which he believed there was a great need, and information about health and other practical topics.[26]

He also wanted to bring the words of his church superiors to his Cree-speaking readers. The first few words of *The Guide*, reproduced in the MSCC article are a translation of a message from S.P. Matheson, Archbishop and Primate of the Anglican Church in Canada:

ᒥᐣᑕᐦᐃ ᓂᒥᔕᔨᐦᐅᑊ ᑭᑕ
ᐃᐧᐦᑳᐧᐊᒪᑕᑯᐢ ᓂᐟᑕᒥᐦᐠᐤᖅ ᐃᐧᐅ
ᑭᔕᐊ·· ᓂᒥ ᐅᑕᔨᒥᐦᐊᐠᐟᕽ ᑭᔕᐊ··
ᑐᐦᐃᔭᖏᐟ

which means: "I am very glad to write to you my greeting, my fellow Christians. You are Crees..."[27] Unfortunately, I have not been able to find any back issues of *The Cree Monthly Guide* and none were saved in the Anglican Church Archives in Toronto where I went to look, so this is one of the few indications of what this publication was like.

I remember reading *The Cree Monthly Guide* years ago, and there were no Cree stories in it of the type recorded in this book. My father asked Edward one time, "Why don't you write Indian stories in the newsletter? There are lots of stories." And Edward Ahenakew said, "No. I have to abide by the Missionary Society." They sponsored the paper and he was receiving some money from them for publishing it. He didn't want to do anything contrary to their wishes. I doubt if he ever asked them about it. I think he had an idea that Indian stories would hurt their feelings. He didn't want to rock the boat of the church. He was a very cautious man. He never used Cree stories in his preaching, either. If he had done so, he would have been a very great man. I never knew he wrote these stories or was interested in them until after his death. He never talked about it.

Edward Ahenakew and my father were great friends. My father had a car and used to drive him to town to catch the train. They had many talks and he told my father that he believed that white people discriminated against Indians. He felt that the only job an Indian could have was to be a minister in the church because in the church there would be no discrimination. He recommended that Adam, my elder brother, and I go into the ministry. My father agreed that we might as well go to school because that was in 1929 and the price of wheat had dropped to 10¢ a bushel. It was a really rough time for our family and at one point my father had to sell his Model T car for a team of horses. He sold the chickens because there was no feed, and it was at this period that Edward Ahenakew worked on my father to convince him that we should go to high school and then to Emmanuel College, which we both did.[28]

In 1935, as World War II loomed, the Bible Churchman's Missionary Society (BCMS) in England, which had supported Edward as the Superintendant for Western Missions, pulled out of Canadian missions. Edward became a missionary for the Diocese of Saskatchewan. He was assigned responsibility for the mission at Fort à la Corne and he worked there for twenty years until he retired in 1955.[29] When he worked under the auspices of the BCMS he had been relatively well paid. He had a new car. But when he began to work for the local diocese he became a poor man. He must have worked hard to sell the stories he wrote because he needed money. He was too generous with what little he had. I remember on one occasion he was asked to teach a lay readers school. All they gave him was a few dollars for his gas; nothing for his time. After that he said in Cree, "*Ni'kitimahikawin*" — "They make me poor."[30] They should have given him some remuneration for teaching. As it happened those students, who came from farther away than he did, received more than he did. That's one time he was really angry.

Canon Ahenakew's poverty became a kind of joke with Bishop Henry Martin. He used to tell stories about visiting Edward in his mission house, an old recycled Hudson's Bay house, at Fort à la Corne. The bishop would bring him cigars and Edward would serve dinner. The bishop often told about one dinner during which a mouse crawled into Edward's bag of rolled oats. "Canon Ahenakew, there's a mouse crawling into your rolled oats," the bishop said. So Edward grabbed the bag, pounded it, took the mouse by the tail and tossed it outside. Again it happened and again Edward took the bag, hit it, and threw the mouse out the door so the next morning he could have porridge. The bishop was amused by this and amused by the telling of it, and sadly, Canon Ahenakew was pleased that the bishop was amused. To me it was a real insult to the poor man. Why didn't the bishop build him a good house? Why laugh at his misfortune? Why did he accept Indians living in very poor, mouse-infested buildings? I guess they both thought it was good enough for an Indian. In those days bishops were powerful people and Edward Ahenakew never criticized him.

On one occasion Edward Ahenakew privately told my father that he was very angry at another bishop. It was at the moment when Bishop Walter Burd insisted that Edward quit his work as vice-president of the League of Indians for Western Canada.[31] He had been on a trip to Ottawa to speak to the Department of Indian Affairs on behalf of the League. The Indian Department urged the bishop to tell him to attend to his duties as a churchman and not to meddle with the affairs of the state. Bishop Burd offered him no choice but to discontinue his work with the League. He came to the meetings of the League at Poundmaker's Reserve in 1933 and stayed for a while; then he disappeared and the people said he looked sad. I remember James Wuttunee saying, "We should make him an honorary vice-president so we can keep him with the organization." Publicly, Edward said he was resigning because of his health. His health was never very good, but he told my father in the car on the way from the train station that the truth was that the bishop forced him to quit the League.

Privately, Edward Ahenakew was very pessimistic about the government's handling of Indian Affairs. He felt the department was malevolent and manipulative. Smith Atimoyoo and I spent the summer of 1938 with Canon Ahenakew to learn his philosophy and his style of leadership. He felt that "the Indian can only go so far as the Privy Council and would fail to get a hearing with the Crown."[32]

During that summer we talked to him about his life. I was naturally drawn to him because he was very informal with me and there were certain things he said that he wouldn't say to other people. But he had a negative side. Sometimes he would ask us roughly, "Who are you?" And we were supposed to answer him, "I am nobody." He seemed to think that way about himself. He sometimes spoke of himself as a failure because he failed to become a doctor, failed to get a wife and failed to get a promotion. His bishop had insisted when Edward Ahenakew quit the League that he devote himself to the church. This Edward did. He was loyal to the Anglican Church to the end of his days. But the church did little to reward his long service. When Archdeacon John Alexander Mackay died in 1923, Edward Ahenakew had reason to expect to be promoted to Archdeacon of Indian work. He was the one who spoke at the funeral, he had the language and the culture. and he was a devout, second-generation Christian. The bishop chose an

Irishman named W.E. Jeffrey Paul for the job, and Edward Ahenakew went on serving the people at Fort à la Corne.[33] That must have hurt him quietly inside, but as far as I know he never said anything to anybody.

Although Edward Ahenakew was deferential to the bishop, he was a strong man in many ways. He was quick tempered and he spoke forcefully from the pulpit. He was determined that his Indian congregation was going to follow what he himself had experienced to be the true way. Why didn't he have any doubts? Why didn't he say, "There are certain things I question"? He may have been cautious because we were immature or because he didn't want to mislead us. He looked down on people who practiced Cree beliefs and rituals. He never talked about this to me, but I sometimes think he had a real struggle inside himself. On the one hand he was writing stories about the past so they would be preserved for posterity, before they were forgotten, while the old men were still alive. At the same time he was preaching the gospel, so there were two sides to him. One was hidden from us because we were too young to see.

In 1947, Emmanuel College honoured Edward Ahenakew with a degree of Doctor of Divinity, which he humbly accepted in the name of his people. He deserved the honour, but "I was more elated," he said, "when the boys [as he called us theological students] wrote to congratulate me." He was proud of us and when we met him he would give us a treat. His favorite bit of pleasure was to enjoy ice cream.

Canon Edward Ahenakew's greatest accomplishment was to enrich and update the Cree-English part of *A Dictionary of the Cree Language* in collaboration with Archdeacon R. Faries. It was printed in 1938. Canon Ahenakew was a humble Christian and took an active part in community celebrations. His gift was patience and an understanding heart and these attributes made him influential among his fellow aboriginal clergy and lay readers. He was noted for his anecdotes which, when told in Cree, fully exploited the humorous possibilities of the language.

In early July of 1961, Canon Edward Ahenakew had been teaching at the Lay Readers School at Emma Lake. He was on his way to Dauphin, Manitoba, to teach the lay readers there when he suddenly had a stroke while on the train. He was transferred to Canora and died at the local hospital on July 12, 1961, at the age of 76, alone as he always was.

Edward Ahenakew would probably find it ironic that in death he is remembered for his Cree stories and praised for recording Cree cultural beliefs, when in life he vigorously championed the Anglican faith. But he is not alone in this situation. Mike Mountain Horse, a Blood Indian from Alberta, and Joseph Francis Dion, a Cree from Long Lake (*Kehiwin* Band) were also writing at about that time. All three were well-educated men. Ahenakew had the most formal education but Joseph Dion was also well educated. Dion went to the Onion Lake Mission School north of North Battleford, Saskatchewan, where he finished grade nine and earned the prerequisites to teach school. This he did on his home reserve, *Kehiwin*, for twenty-four years.[34] Mike Mountain Horse went to St. Paul's Mission School and then to the Indian Industrial School in Calgary. After graduation he served in the Canadian army, worked for the RCMP, and became a fireman in Lethbridge, Alberta. He published a regular column in the *Lethbridge Herald*.[35] All three were politically active although Joseph Dion was by far the most successful in this arena, both in his work with the League of Indians and with the Metis Association of Alberta.

Like Edward Ahenakew, these two also died before their books were published. Edward Ahenakew's book, *Voices of the Plains Cree*, was the first to be published — in

1973 — twelve years after his death. His League of Indians colleague, Joseph Dion, tried to get his own manuscript published for many years but died shortly before *My Tribe, the Crees* came out in 1979. Mike Mountain Horse's manuscript, like Edward Ahenakew's, was discovered after his death. Edward Ahenakew's manuscript was found by his niece, Kate, in the log cabin where he lived at Sandy Lake. In Mike Mountain Horse's case the manuscript was in the files of a Lethbridge lawyer. Hugh Dempsey of the Glenbow Foundation, who edited Joseph Dion's book, also edited Mike Mountain Horse's book and it was published in 1989 under the title *My People, the Bloods*.

All three of these writers had the sense that they were chronicling the feelings of their people at a moment when, as Mike Mountain Horse put it, Indians "put aside their native garb and began to take up life as civilized beings."[36] I think these men wanted to record the ideas behind the old rituals because the times were changing fast. Young people who were attending boarding schools had become dismissive of their own culture, and because they were losing their language they had lost respect for the old people who might have eductated them. These writers knew enough of the cultural context of the old times to respect them, and although they were Christians they did not want the beliefs of their fathers to be forgotten or discounted. They were Christians and had all attended mission schools. Edward Ahenakew was a canon in the Anglican church, Joseph Dion was a devout Catholic, and Mike Mountain Horse was first an Anglican, then a Mormon, then a traditionalist, then a member of the Salvation Army, and finally an Anglican again.[37] Yet they still spoke their languages, had an instinctive feeling for their people, and had a profound respect for the values of their own communities. They saw themselves defending their communities against ugly stereotypes and condescension through their writing. In the case of Edward Ahenakew, his mentor Paul Wallace provided him with an immediate audience, someone concrete to write to and to consult about writing. Mike Mountain Horse had a column in a newspaper so he developed a sense of audience through that experience. These three men aimed to tell, as Joseph Dion hoped, of "history as seen through the eyes of the Indians, revealed at long last by the Indians themselves."[38] Their writings showed their conviction that an explanation of Cree and Blood philosophy would elicit respect from non-Indian readers. These early Plains Indian writers were personally frustrated in their effort to publish aboriginal oral literature and history. They never realized in their lifetimes the contribution they had made by just getting the stories down. Publication came too late for them but not too late for us.

Let us give Edward Ahenakew the last word, because he was the voice of many people during his term as Western President of the League of Indians. He repeated some of those concerns through the voice of "Old Keyam," who held an ancient red stone pipe and said:

> This was given to me many years ago by one who had been a great Warrior and a wise man, in the tradition of the past; one who spoke to us of courage and of mercy, of love for our fellow men, and reverence towards God. These teachings are the heritage of our past. They are for all time: they belong to all ages, to all people.

Stan Cuthand
Saskatchewan Indian Federated College
University of Saskatchewan
Saskatoon, January 1995

NOTES

Special thanks go to Maureen Matthews of Winnipeg, Manitoba, for her assistance in editing this "Introduction" to the 1995 edition of *Voices of the Plains Cree*.

1. Fort à la Corne is called *Nicawkicikanis* by the Cree. The word is a dimutive term for "good gardens." The Hudson's Bay post was called *Nicawkicikanis* because the Bay employees had a garden where they grew vegetables. The area where the Cree now live is called James Smith Reserve.
2. This was a sentiment shared not just by Anglicans, but by all treaty Indians because Treaty 6, which bound the Indians in this area, was signed in 1876 by representatives of Queen Victoria, King George VI's great-grandmother.
3. Star Blanket, *atahk* = star, *akohp* = blanket.
4. Treaty 6, the original signing at Fort Carlton in 1876. The Christian chiefs really pushed for the treaty. The chiefs who held back were the non-Christians like Little Pine, who eventually signed in 1879 on behalf of my family.
5. Edward Ahenakew wrote a family genealogy in which he explained that *Ahenakew* did not have any meaning in Cree. He wrote that it was just a name. He said that David *Ahenakew*, his grandfather, was injured in a fall from a horse and had a permanently damaged knee which crippled him for life. He was the first person in *Atahkakohp*'s band to accept Christianity, hence the Christian first name, David.
6. Ruth Matheson Buck, "Story of the Ahenakews," *Saskatchewan History* 17, no. 1 (Winter 1964): 12-23. *Notowewikamik* means "Old Woman's House," a name she received as the result of a prophecy that she would live to an advanced age — which she did. *Sasakwamos* means "Adherer" and *Napeskis* means "Manlike."
7. Ahenakew papers, American Philosophical Society, Philadelphia, Pennsylvania (hereafter Ahenakew papers).
8. Frank A. Peake, in "Church Missionary Society: Policy and Personel in Rupertsland," *Journal of the Canadian Church Historical Society* 30, no. 2 (October 1988): 70, refers to the school as having been started by the Bishop of Saskatchewan, John McLean, specifically for the training of Cree, Blackfoot and Chipeweyan students, and that it had thirty-four students by 1883.
9. They actually floated the lumber of the old buildings up river from Prince Albert and rebuilt it all in Saskatoon. I once saw a picture of these buildings.
10. Ahenakew papers.
11. W.F. Payton, *The Diocese of Saskatchewan of the Anglican Church of Canada, 100 Years 1874-1974* (Prince Albert: Diocese of Saskatchewan, 1974), 102.
12. Cedar Lake was just below The Pas. This community no longer exists because of the flooding caused by the dam at Grand Rapids. The people were moved to Easterville.
13. Sidney A. Keighley, *Trader, Tripper, Trapper, The Life of a Bay Man* (Winnipeg: Rupert's Land Research Centre, 1989), 38. I was born in 1918 and when I was born they had the minister come to the house to baptise me right away because they were so afraid I would die. One of my elder sisters did die in that epidemic.
14. Canada, Department of Indian Affairs, *Annual Report* (March 31, 1923).
15. Mrs. Annie Elizabeth Brown had worked at Onion Lake Mission from 1895 until 1904, when she married James Brown, who had been ordained. They served at Grand Rapids, Lac La Ronge and Stanley Mission, where Reverend Brown died in 1912.
16. "Letter to Wallace, September 5, 1923," Ahenakew papers.
17. Ibid., August 11, 1923. *Okiyam* means "oh, never mind" or "it doesn't matter."
18. This volume, page 106.
19. I think the stories were still in this fairly rough form when Mrs. Buck began to look at them.
20. Keighley, *Trader, Tripper, Trapper*, 39.
21. "Letter to Wallace, March 23, 1923," Ahenakew papers.
22. Edward Ahenakew, "Cree Trickster Tales," *Journal of American Folklore* 42 (October/December 1929). Twenty-six of the *Wiskecahk* stories were published here. Three were reprinted in Carlyle King, ed., *Saskatchewan Harvest: A Golden Jubilee Selection of Song and Story* (Toronto: McClelland and Stewart, 1955).
23. Keighley, *Trader, Tripper, Trapper*, 64.
24. *Nehiyaw* means the Cree people and *kiskanota* is to guide him or her — *kiskino* is the root of the word which would be used to describe the act of leading people to a particular destination but it is also the root

for words used to describe aspects of education and teaching *kiskinohamaw* — teach him/her *okiskinohamakew* — teacher).

25. Missionary Society of the Church in Canada, *MSCC Canada and Overseas Bulletin* 8 (June 1925), front page. Anglican Church Archives, Toronto.

26. Ibid. I think he hoped that others would contribute articles but in the papers I saw, he was the primary writer and when he died, so did *The Cree Monthly Guide*.

27. They are accompanied by this note: "On the left are the first words of this message as printed in the Guide. The securing of sufficient type has been quite a difficulty, as the outfit at The Pas which was being counted upon was destroyed by fire. The extract showing the characters used will explain that this has to be specially supplied."

28. I graduated and was ordained in 1944.

29. Payton, *The Diocese of Saskatchewan of the Anglican Church of Canada*, 103.

30. This is really an idiom with the literal meaning "they don't pity me" or "they don't care for me." It shows how his Cree mind was working. The poorer he seemed the more they should have given him according to Cree thinking. There was an obligation on his superiors, if they cared for him, to share more equitably with him and to treat him fairly.

31. Burd was a good man. He was in fact very kindly but in those days bishops, even kindly ones, had considerable influence and authority to discipline their clergy.
   The League of Indians was started by a Mohawk World War I veteran named Frederick Ogilvie Loft (1862-1934). Olive Dickason writes about him: "His proposals included giving Indians the vote without losing their special status and allowing them greater control over band properties and funds… The department branded him an agitator, placed him under police surveillance, and sought to nullify his efforts by enfranchising him against his will. The League came to nought, but the need for a pan-Indian organization was recognized." Olive Patricia Dickason, *Canada's First Nations* (Toronto: McClelland and Stewart, 1992), 328.

32. He was telling me this as he reflected on Loft's experience.

33. Paul was a very highly educated but somewhat naive Baronet from Ireland. After the death of his elder brother he became Sir Jeffrey Paul and when he retired he returned to Ireland to look after the estate he had inherited.

34. Joseph, Dion, *My Tribe, the Crees* (Calgary: Glenbow-Alberta Institute, 1979), v.

35. Mike Mountain Horse, *My People, the Bloods* (Calgary: Glenbow-Alberta Institute and the Blood Tribal Council, Standoff, Alberta, 1979), v-vi.

36. Ibid., preface.

37. I knew him when he was old and dying of cancer. He wanted to become an Anglican again and asked me what he should do about taking communion. I told him, "just go ahead as if you had never left the church." The old people on the Blood reserve were very happy he had come back to the Anglican faith because they wanted him with them.

38. Dion, *My Tribe, the Crees*, x.

INTRODUCTION
TO THE 1973 EDITION

The papers in this collection deal with the traditions and past history of the Plains Cree, and with the effects, fifty years ago, of a changing way of life.

The notes of Chief Thunderchild's stories and the rough draft of *Old Keyam* were written in 1923. It was after the death of Edward Ahenakew in 1961 that the papers were found in a tattered and neglected state by his niece, Katherine Ahenakew Greyeyes, who sent them to me because of my own interest in western history and the long association and friendship between our families.

No material other than Edward Ahenakew's is used in the assembling of this work; and in framing Thunderchild's stories from the original notes his words have been largely retained. Even the impulse to supply explanations within those stories has been resisted. There was no need for Thunderchild to explain any of his references when he talked to Ahenakew of their own customs. When he spoke, for instance, of "the shaking of the lodge" that he had helped to build for an old conjurer, the notes tell little more than that; in *Old Keyam*, however, Ahenakew gives a more detailed account of the ceremony. A few such instances occur — but, for the most part, Thunderchild's stories remain only as flying notes made in the early spring of 1923.

Edward Ahenakew had come to Thunderchild's Reserve the year before that when serious illness had terminated his studies in medicine, and he was sent to regain his health under the capable charge of the mission worker, Mrs. James Brown. It was a period of deep discouragement for him, and he was urged to use the opportunity that his convalescence offered to collect the legends and stories of his people. That proved sound therapy. He brought his *Cree Trickster Tales*[1] to completion; and he planned *Old Keyam*, outlining more than twenty chapters, revising drafts of earlier ones, sketching others, and framing brief articles drawn from the over-all plan.

The return of his health, however, had brought with it all the demands of increased responsibility in the mission work of the diocese. Unmarried, he had no settled home of his own, and his duties involved almost constant travelling. Only for a few years, at Little Pine's Reserve, did he have both a place where he could write, and friends who encouraged him to continue. Then, all his notes and his unfinished manuscripts were set aside.

That was not surprising, under the circumstances of his life; what is remarkable is that his papers survived. Fortunately, when he was prompted to collect the stories of Chief Thunderchild, he used a hard-cover ledger-book in which he had begun a casual journal. His entry for February 17, 1923, reads: "Made arrangements with the Chief to tell me Indian traditions at $1.00 per night." And for March 6: "Paid Chief $5.00 on account for story-telling. Am writing as he speaks, just to remind myself. Unintelligible to anybody else."

At that point the journal became a writer's book, and it is Thunderchild himself who seems to speak — the voice of the Old Man of the tribe, in all the ancient meaning of that term. To the Plains Cree, through centuries without a written language, an honoured Old Man was both historian and adviser, "the repository for the annals of his people, a worthy medium through whom the folklore of previous generations could be transmitted."

It was winter still on Thunderchild's Reserve, and the place of meeting was the Chief's log-house and not a teepee; but it was crowded with listeners, and all of them Cree — the speaker an Indian, talking to Indians alone, in their own language and imagery, telling Cree legends, traditions, stories — while Ahenakew's vivid notes raced through page after page.

In 1923, Thunderchild (1849-1927) was a man in his early seventies. In 1876, as a young man, he had been one of the followers of Big Bear[2] in resistance to the Treaty[3] that many of the Plains Cree Chiefs signed either at Fort Carlton or Fort Pitt. The Indians who were resolute in their independence continued their former way of life, following the diminished buffalo herds far down into Montana; but by 1879 they were destitute and starving, and the Canadian Government did all in its power to induce them to settle on reserves.

In order to be nearer the plains and those "treaty Indians" who were still buffalo hunters, annuity payments were made that summer at Sounding Lake; and Edgar Dewdney, Commissioner of Indian Affairs for the North-West Territories, was present. Big Bear attended the discussions, but still refused to sign. Thunderchild's band, however, had endured a winter of desperation, and he severed his connection with Big Bear, signing his adhesion to Treaty Six.

His band comprised some thirty families, so his chiefship was confirmed by the Government, and he was settled in 1880, west of Battleford, between the Saskatchewan and the Battle Rivers, on a reserve that he shared at first with *Moo-so-min*, until his band could be moved to an adjoining reserve of their own. Then in 1905, the Canadian Northern Railway was built, crossing the reserve at Delmas. By agreement with both bands, their land was surveyed for homesteading in 1909, and the Indians moved to larger reserves across the Saskatchewan River, Thunderchild's about forty miles north-west, near Turtle Lake.

These people were all plains hunters, the "River People" who were at the forefront of that steady movement of the Cree from their original forests and woodlands; a movement which began with the acquisition of firearms from traders — the Cree driving the Blackfoot west, and gradually taking to horses themselves. This migration had accelerated in the later years of the nineteenth century with the passing of the buffalo, but was finally arrested by the reserve system.[4]

Thunderchild's stories of his youth, before the Plains Cree were "fenced into reserves," were of the fierce wild freedom of the plains, of the buffalo chase, of horse-stealing, of raids and warfare.

Ahenakew knew that any true account of Indian life on reserves had to be given in relation to these former ways, in order to explain the effects of the radical change that had overtaken all his people, and within a period of years that the memory of an Old Man could still span in 1923.

He would always assert proudly that he was himself a Plains Cree. Although distinctions had developed among these Crees during their movement to the plains, and although the numbers and range of each of the major divisions varied, inter-marriage did maintain a strong kinship.

Ahenakew's own ancestry,[5] within the three generations that he traced, included River People of the Battleford area, and Upstream People of the Edmonton district, as well as Cree-Assiniboine, and an infusion of French blood on both his father's and his mother's side. The division to which he belonged, however, was not the free-ranging and independent River or Upstream People, but the House People, so designated because they had long clustered about the houses of the Hudson's Bay Company.

Ah-tah-ka-koop (Star Blanket), an outstanding Chief of the House People, was the older brother of Ahenakew's grandfather, and the family continued as members of that band, on the reserve north of the Saskatchewan River, not far from Fort Carlton where *Ah-tah-ka-koop* had signed Treaty Six in 1876. Carlton was the post for which he and his brothers had hunted. They trapped furs in the northern bush during the winter, and hunted buffalo on the plains in the summer, reconciling both the old and the new environment of their people. They had learned as well to accommodate themselves to the white man's ways, and their transition to reserve life was easier in many respects than for the River People.

Thunderchild had spoken for the River People, recalling a past that had vanished with the buffalo. Some of this material found its way into Ahenakew's manuscript, dealing with Indian life in general, its customs, its traditions, its problems. Ahenakew required, however, another speaker as well; one who would look to what lay ahead, urging his people to accept the necessity of change, and to adapt to it without losing their identity as Indians.

The concept of another Old Man as speaker appealed to Ahenakew, though the speaker would have to be one who knew English as well as Cree, who had some formal education, and some experience of changing conditions beyond his own reserve. To have had such opportunities, he would need to be at least twenty years younger than Thunderchild, "old, not so much in years as in the sense of tradition because, in this relationship to our past, he is the successor of those Old Men whose role was a responsible one in the life of the tribe or band."

It might have seemed logical that this speaker should command such respect as Thunderchild, and even exercise a measure of authority. Instead, Ahenakew saw him as "poor, inoffensive and genial," and he named him "Old Keyam," a Cree word with many shades of meaning. Ahenakew interpreted it simply as "I do not care"; but he added, "Old Keyam had tried in his youth to fit himself into the new life; he had thought that he would conquer; and he had been defeated instead. If we listen to what he has to say, perhaps we may understand those like him, who know not what to do, and, in their bewilderment and their hurt, seem not to care."

In 1923, such withdrawal was the only alternative if an Indian could not agree to Government or Church policy, and Edward Ahenakew knew that well. Although Old Keyam might be excused or simply ignored, and his opinions always disclaimed, he had to speak with caution nevertheless.

The manuscript, in fact, represented a painful and even hazardous process of thought for Ahenakew, and it was never finished. Much of the material is drawn from his own experiences in the counselling of his people, and is sometimes autobiographical. It expresses his deep concern for his people, but it reveals also the humour and understanding that won friendship for him wherever he went, that made it possible for him to accept rebuffs, and that enlivened his calm stoicism.

In Part II, the beautiful Plains Cree reserve which Old Keyam describes feelingly is that of *Ah-tah-ka-koop* at Sandy Lake, where Edward Ahenakew was born in June of 1885. He was named for Edward Matheson, who had come from Kildonan Settlement at Red River to teach the mission school at Sandy Lake before he began his studies in theology at Emmanuel College,[6] Prince Albert, in 1879.

Edward Ahenakew's first teacher at the mission school was his uncle, Louis Ahenakew; at the age of eleven the boy was sent to Prince Albert to the boarding school into which Emmanuel College had been converted. Archdeacon John Alexander MacKay,[7] the principal, was to remain a strong influence in Ahenakew's life.

The boy had a lively mind and a strong, swift body, and he led in every activity at the school; yet his notes, recording those years, make the simple statement: "Gradually I fell into the ordinary round of school life, winning a few minor honours both on the playgrounds and in the classroom."

He passed his junior matriculation and returned to Sandy Lake, where he worked for a time with his father. He then taught at mission schools on reserves in the area until he was accepted as a candidate for the ministry and entered Wycliffe College in Toronto. During the summers he worked in the Diocese of Saskatchewan and was ordained deacon in 1910. Emmanuel College was re-opened as a theological college in Saskatoon when the University was established in 1909, and Edward Ahenakew transferred from Wycliffe, graduating in 1912 as Licentiate in Theology.

He was ordained priest and was sent to the mission at Onion Lake to assist his namesake's brother, the Reverend John Matheson, whose strength was failing. Ahenakew's ability and understanding, his unfailing kindness, his young liveliness won him an immediate place in the friendship of our whole family. John Matheson died in 1916, and we left Onion Lake to live in Winnipeg, but our association with Saskatchewan continued, as did our friendship with Edward Ahenakew.

Late in the winter of 1918-19, the dreadful epidemic of influenza swept the reserves, and the suffering of Ahenakew's people affected him deeply. He resolved to undertake the study of medicine, and was accepted in Edmonton. He was then a man of thirty-five, and he found himself separated from all that was familiar to him, competing with classmates some fifteen years younger than he and fresh from such training in science as had never been possible for him.

He had only a small bursary to meet expenses, and had to practise the most careful economy. Years later, he told how he had tried to manage. "I had a small room in an apartment over the river, and I used to buy a good-sized piece of beef, ready cooked. This I kept on a sill outside the window, where it froze solid; and I lived on that frozen meat and little else. When one piece was finished, I would buy another. After awhile, I felt none too well, and finally I was down and out. One of the doctors examined me. 'What do you think you are? A polar bear?' he wanted to know; and he told me that my stomach was partly paralyzed. So I left university, and I did not go back.''

Ahenakew was a sick man, and it was more than a year before he could resume full duties. In the meantime, he lived in the mission house at Thunderchild's Reserve, in Mrs. James Brown's care. He had experienced the bitter taste of failure and was most deeply discouraged. This was a matter for concern to his namesake, the Reverend Canon Edward Matheson of Battleford, who was himself an invalid and retired from active work. Out of his own interest in western history, Edward Matheson urged the younger man to use the opportunity that was particularly his: to collect Cree legends and stories that were passing even then from memory. To do this would be a true service to his people.

The stories of *We-sa-kā-cha'k* were an obvious starting point, and Ahenakew had known many of these from his earliest childhood. In the person of Thunderchild he could have access to a richly-stored memory, and the old Chief would talk freely to this grandson of his old associates. So it was that for February 17, 1923, a journal, that had begun with only random idle notes to pass the time, had the entry: ''Made arrangements with the Chief to tell me Indian traditions. ...''

As the meetings continued, other Indians crowded into the Chief's house to listen, or to speak in their turn, and the talk ranged through every subject that concerned them. They had grown accustomed to the recording of rapid notes, and were no longer curious or self-conscious. But now the ledger-book was often put aside, most of the stories and legends having been set down. Ahenakew might take part in the general discussion, but more often he simply listened while Thunderchild and the others spoke of all the disturbing changes in their lives; and, as he listened, the plan for ''Old Keyam'' began to take shape in his mind.

As summer came, however, he had less opportunity to write. His health was restored, and Archdeacon Mackay assigned to him much of the responsibility that had been Edward Matheson's as Superintendent of Indian missions in the north-western area of the diocese. It was a wide area, extending along the northern side of the river from Battleford to Frog Lake at the west end of the diocese, a distance of well over one hundred miles, with Island Lake, Big Island Lake (Ministikwan) and Loon Lake (Makwa) on the northern fringes. Yet when he bought a car to take him at least as far as roads permitted, he was sharply reproved by the Bishop.

This appears to have been Bishop Lloyd's general policy towards the clergy whose work was less dispersed than Ahenakew's and who might still depend upon horses. It was recognized, however, that the Right Reverend George Exton Lloyd had little understanding of the Indian work, nor much respect for ''the native clergy'' — a grouping which could be extended to include Archdeacon Mackay of a Hudson's Bay Company family, or the Mathesons, who were grandsons of Lord Selkirk's settlers.

Lloyd's stand against any aspect of Canadian life that was not directly British, and his vituperative attacks upon the immigration policy of that day made headlines in the press. His bigotry was undisguised, but he was an able and forceful man, and he had made his views known and his power felt from the time of his arrival at the diocese in 1903 with the Barr Colonists. As Archdeacon, he had directed much of the work in recruiting and training clergy for rapidly expanding settlements; as Bishop, the entire work of the diocese came under his direction.

Ahenakew's position was a difficult one, and his journal contains a draft of the letter that he composed in evident distress of mind, defending not only his purchase of the car, but the termination of his course in medicine and the effects of ill-health upon his work for more than a year after that. That matter must have been resolved, for Ahenakew continued his supervisory work in those scattered missions. Archdeacon Mackay probably saw to that, for the fiery old Archdeacon feared only God, and during his long life had known every bishop of Rupert's Land and of Saskatchewan.

Years later, Ahenakew was to say of John Alexander Mackay: ''The Archdeacon was unique to the time and circumstances of his life, specially raised for a special work. The Indians found in him their truest friend, champion and counsellor. He was a father to our race, not indulgent, but kindly and wise, ever burning with zeal, tremendously effective in his work, a true and honest man. When need arose for determined action, he was far from wanting. He had such moral fortitude that he never allowed to pass unchallenged any wrong done in his presence. I have seen him in action quite often, eyes flashing under bushy eyebrows, a reincarnation of one of the fiery prophets of old who were sent to earth to thunder forth rebukes and warnings to sinful men.''

In this last year of his life, at the age of eighty-five, Mackay was actively involved in a project to which Edward Ahenakew had been able to give the first impetus. That it was the development of a school was entirely fitting, for church and school had been inseparable elements of the Archdeacon's whole experience in Indian work. For years, Ottawa had given some support to day-schools, allowing three hundred dollars per annum for the teacher's salary under certain conditions, but providing no residence for the teacher, and often no suitable schoolhouse. In 1920, the school on Little Pine's[8] Reserve had failed to meet requirements and had been closed.

The reserve was a comparatively small one, situated on the Battle River, just west of Poundmaker's. It was a poor reserve, and considered one of the most backward when Edward Ahenakew visited it in the summer of 1921, on a tour of western reserves as

Saskatchewan and Alberta president for the League of Indians of Canada. After a meeting at which he presented the aims and objectives of the newly formed organization, some of the headmen asked him to stay to discuss another matter with them, and they took him to the buildings that had been their school, but were being used as granaries instead.

"I had never seen a more desolate looking place," he wrote years later. "Here was the pitiful ruin of a government educational enterprise — the result of inefficiency, indifference, and want of inspiration. The people acknowledged their mistake in not sending their children to school regularly, and promised that this would be corrected, but as I stood there, recalling my effort that day at the meeting to encourage them to organize and to strive for their own improvement, I felt a deep sense of frustration. ... At first I thought that I should go to Ottawa myself, as president of the League in Saskatchewan; but I wrote instead to the Archdeacon, that same night, laying the whole matter before him."

Mackay appealed in person to the Deputy-Superintendent of Indian Affairs at Ottawa, Duncan Campbell Scott, and he was able to persuade the Government to support the school — on one condition — that it should be successfully operated for one year before any grant was paid. To prove his point, the Archdeacon, with no means beyond his salary, agreed to advance the costs for that year himself, and he personally supervised the restoration of the school and house at Little Pine's. By September of 1922, the school[9] was in operation, and before the summer of 1923, Ottawa was convinced. The Archdeacon had won his last battle, though much of the credit went quite justly to the teacher whom he had engaged, Anne Letitia Cunningham, and who remained in charge until her retirement in 1944. Edward Ahenakew played his part, not only in the initial skirmish, as he had in the re-establishment of a day-school[10] at Thunderchild's, but also in maintaining the support of the people during the first years of the school's successful operation, when he made his headquarters at Little Pine's.

These were his most active and productive years. He continued as general missionary in the western division of the diocese, and he was representative for his people at diocesan, provincial and general synods. In addition, he assisted in the completion of the Cree-English dictionary that Archdeacon Mackay's death in 1923 had left unfinished, and he resumed publication of the *Cree Monthly Guide*.

The issue of this bulletin for September 1923 consisted of sixteen pages and included articles on agriculture, health, the Indian Act, the League of Indians of Canada, the work of the University of Saskatchewan, and world news. Some of these articles Ahenakew wrote, others he had to revise in simpler form; all of them he translated into Cree syllabics, and then set into type himself. Copies were distributed to Indians throughout the diocese, again largely by his own effort, on visits to reserves.

In 1932, the division of the dioceses of Saskatchewan and Saskatoon was effected, and Ahenakew's work no longer included the reserves in the Battleford area. He was named General Indian Missionary for the northern Diocese of Saskatchewan that year, and in 1933 was appointed honourary Canon of St. Alban's Cathedral in Prince Albert.

These were, however, the bitter years of the depression, and, for the Anglican Church in western Canada, there had been the additional shock of the Machray misappropriations of $800,000. Then World War II brought its overwhelming troubles everywhere.

In 1948, Ahenakew could write of his own situation: "I was General Missionary for many years, and then, owing to our financial position in the diocese, and the shortage of men, Bishop Burd asked me to take a mission. Since 1935, I have been on this reserve, in charge of the Fort à la Corne mission." He was to remain there for more than twenty years, even past his official retirement at the age of seventy.

6

He continued to be a familiar figure at synods, and, in 1947, Emmanuel College recognized his contribution to the mission work of the Church, and conferred on him the honourary degree of Doctor of Divinity.

The province of Saskatchewan celebrated its fiftieth year in 1955, and Dr. Carlyle King prepared his Golden Jubilee Selection of Song and Story, *Saskatchewan Harvest*, requesting permission to include some of the stories in the *Cree Trickster Tales*. Edward Ahenakew wrote to me: "Will you lend me your copy of the *Tales*? I think the mice got mine."

That was indicative of his casual existence, for he never married, and the comforts of a settled home were not part of his life. When he left Fort à la Corne, he served in one small mission or another, wherever his help was needed; he gave his encouragement to the schools for Indian catechists and lay-readers that had been established; and he was on his way to the one at Dauphin, in the summer of 1961, when he died.

During the last few years of his life, he had returned to live near his brother, Shem Ahenakew, at Sandy Lake Reserve. It was a place for which he had the deepest affection, and he described some of his boyhood recollections when he put Old Keyam on a reserve "centred about a lake where ducks nest and the weird cry of the loon echoes in the summer evenings. Spruce and birch grow about the lake, poplars in the hollows and ravines of the hills that command a view from the north over all the gently rolling, sparsely wooded country that stretches south to the Saskatchewan. The members of the band built their first log-houses near the shore of the lake, and from the beginning had their mission school and their church on rising ground that overlooks the lake, so that the tower is visible from all around." It is in that churchyard that his body lies.

Once, Edward Ahenakew had thought to interpret the experiences of his young manhood, and all the concern that he felt for his people, through the voice of an Old Man of the band. He was thirty-seven then, but the idea had its appeal because he was regaining his strength only slowly, and the vigour of his youth seemed lost. The manuscript was to lie neglected, and, with the passing of the years, Ahenakew must have recognized that discouragement and the sense of failure had made him in all reality "Old Keyam" himself. "That word," he had written years before, "expresses the attitude of many Indians who stand bewildered in the maze of things, not knowing exactly what to do, and hiding their keen sense of defeat under the assumed demeanour of 'keyam!' — while in fact they do care greatly."

Because Ahenakew did continue to care, his manuscripts survived. They are all in English; and it was into English that he had translated his rapid but clearly legible notes of Thunderchild's stories, though often he introduced Cree names, or resorted to syllabics as a convenient shorthand.

For the translation of these, I have relied upon the Reverend Stanley Cuthand, a Plains Cree himself, from Little Pine's Reserve originally, and now with the Department of Indian Affairs and Northern Development. He teaches classes in Cree, to promote the acceptance and appreciation of linguistic differences, and is revising a language course in the Plains Cree dialect. His interest and his help are gratefully acknowledged.

No fixed policy of translation has been followed in composing stories from the notes. For some of the Indian names there is no translation that would easily render the meaning, and the Cree has been retained. For others, Ahenakew used the English translation, and the Cree has been supplied. In some words or names his spelling has been retained though it differs slightly from the recently revised form.

Lacking the present interest in such writing, the publication of his work was practically impossible during Ahenakew's life-time. It was not until seven years after his death that the Department of Indian Affairs and Northern Development established its cultural development division to promote such work, and I wish to acknowledge the assistance and encouragement that they have given to the publication of this book.

In 1923, Edward Ahenakew believed that the Indians' view of matters affecting their lives should be known; and it was the struggle that he maintained for years to overcome the apathy and discouragement of his people that has made it possible for Indians today to express their views readily and clearly.

For that reason alone, his writing of fifty years ago would have relevance; but its significance is deeper than that, in an historical sense. Old Indians, when they tell the stories of their people, begin with the Cree word ''Kayas,'' which means ''Long ago.'' In Edward Ahenakew's writing, long ago is only yesterday.

Ruth Matheson Buck

Introduction to Part I

The time has come in the life of my race when that which has been like a sealed book to the masses of our Canadian compatriots — namely the view that the Indians have of certain matters affecting their lives — should be known.

To the superficial observer, we may often seem to be ungrateful to those who are endeavouring to work for our good. Perhaps, in some cases, we are. The whole matter, however, rests upon the viewpoint taken. Ours is necessarily of a peculiar nature, and the key to its understanding lies in the past centuries of our life in the freedom of the prairies which offered no obstruction to the keen eye of the warrior as it swept the spaces before it.

Ours is a different life now. Is it any wonder that, confused by increasing changes and difficulties, we look back with longing to the days that our Old Men still remember, to the familiar scenes of their youth made real to us in story and legend? For they remember the days when teepees against a prairie sky marked the Indian encampment, when buffalo were without number, when horses, carts, and our own skills served our needs.

The sun has set upon those days, but the heart of our nation still mourns for them, still weeps behind the closed door-flaps of the teepee. The council fires have gone out, the voice of the Indian is not heard, the ploughshare of the settler has long since turned the over-grown paths that the buffalo followed.

Once our life and our ideas were simple, our relationships uncomplicated, even primitive. We loved or we hated. Today all these are complex. Modifying phrases have crept into our language. ''Yes'' may not mean exactly ''yes''; ''no'' is not directly ''no.'' If right is at the centre of this confusing web, ours is not yet the discerning eye that can pierce through.

We have our own view of the life that has been imposed upon us, and these pages are written that others may glimpse what we feel and experience. It is not my personal opinion that I intend to present. I serve only as recorder of what I have learned during my life-time, first among my own people, the Plains Cree of *Ah-tah-ka-koop*'s Reserve, where I was born in 1885, and where I spent my boyhood, then on other reserves in that same area when I was a teacher, and finally in these years since my ordination in 1912, when I have ministered to Plains and Woods Cree on reserves from Battleford to Frog Lake and north from the Saskatchewan River to Island Lake, Big Island Lake and Loon Lake.

It was with the hope of serving my people as a doctor that I began the studies in medicine that were terminated by my serious illness more than a year ago. During these months on Thunderchild's Reserve, as I have slowly regained my health, I have had time and opportunity to reflect upon my experiences, and to write.

At first it was my intention simply to collect and preserve the Indian legends and traditions that have been part of my heritage. Chief Thunderchild is a rich repository of these, and I was able to make definite arrangements to have him tell me the legends in all their careful detail. Then, as our meetings continued into the spring, he went on to recall the experiences of his young manhood.

The role that he had readily accepted, that of Old Man, has been an institution of Indian life through the centuries. The fact that the Indians used to have no written language compelled them to rely upon memory for the recollection of things from the far past, as well as for those of more recent date. Because of this the accuracy of an Old Man's memory can be surprising. Two or three Old Men together will recall the minutest details of events that took place in their childhood, sometimes comparing notes, for instance, about the surface markings of a horse that lived forty or fifty years before.

Old Men have had a responsible and important position to fill with the band. In a sense, they have supplied our moral code, taking the place both of historians and legal advisers. Theirs has been the task of firing the spirits of the young men through stories of daring deeds in times past. The religious dances of the Indians have had little moral effect. It is true that, in them, the people were exhorted to be kind and to live at peace with one another, for tribal loyalty was essential; yet, beyond this, the dances had no really elevating influence. It was the Old Men who were the influence for good, who sought to right wrongs and to settle disputes; it was the Old Men who were qualified to speak, for they had passed through most of the experiences of life, and their own youthful fires were burned out.

Young men were often ready to have a little fun at an Old Man's expense, and yet their high spirits could change to quiet deference when he was moved to give them serious advice. That might be on a hillside in the summer evenings; or, as this winter, when they listened silently, almost in awe, crowded into a dwelling where the flickering lamplight lent its own haunting imagery to the shadows, and the long winter nights permitted the Old Man to tell the ancient legends of *We-sa-kā-cha'k* and the beginnings of all things.

To such listening groups, Old Men would speak with earnest eloquence, warning of the dangers that beset youth, exhorting them to be kind and friendly with members of the tribe, to show justice tempered with mercy in all their relationships. They would speak as fathers of the race, having tasted all that was of Indian life, its bitter and its good; they would speak with authority, for they knew all that they needed to know; and they used this privilege wisely, knowing their responsibility and the need that they filled in Indian life.

An Old Man often had the gift of eloquence, enhanced by a descriptive language and by superb mastery of gesture. He used his skill with natural simplicity, weaving into stories of everyday events the great primary meanings of life. This genius was most evident in the narration of past events, of raids and battles and the chase. He might bring a bit of comedy into a tragic story, touch it with pathos, or sweeten it with love and loyalty — and do all this in a language highly figurative, and yet suited to the subject; and his listeners would sit entranced, imagining that they saw and heard the events enacted before them — tales of struggles almost super-human, of endurance, of perilous adventure, of long hazardous excursions into enemy country, of love, of anything indeed that was ever of any consequence in Indian life. All these stories were hoarded in the minds of Old Men; they were kept intact, unchanging, entrusted through the years by one generation to the next.

An Old Man dared not lie, for ridicule that was keen and general would have been his lot, and his standing as a teller of authentic events would have suffered. He dared not lie, for there were always other Old Men on the reserve or in the encampment who would contradict him readily, and who would delight in doing that. Of necessity then, his veracity had to be unimpeachable, and this, together with well-developed powers of observation, made him an authentic repository for the annals of his people, a worthy medium through whom the folklore of previous generations could be transmitted.

Even the least of the Old Men might have something of wisdom to impart, and there were some who in the course of their lives had acquired skill as medicine-men, who had a knowledge of medicinal herbs and roots. If to this skill they could add the art of conjuring, the demand for their services was further increased. It was not unusual for an anxious father to lead a horse or two to the dwelling of such an Old Man, imploring his help for a sick child, and paying in advance. These Old Men were treated with deference always, and could go from one dwelling to another, sharing in the best that was available of food and shelter. No one would question their right.

But Old Men who had been great warriors and hunters in their youth, these the band revered. And such a one in 1923 is Thunderchild, the last of all the Chiefs who signed Treaty Number Six. Other Chiefs whom I remember signed that treaty at Fort Carlton or Fort Pitt in 1876, but Thunderchild resisted until 1879. This is his own account of his meeting with Commissioner Edgar Dewdney at Sounding Lake that summer:

Before I signed the Treaty, I came to talk with Dewdney at Sounding Lake. ''Are you *O-ke-mow* (the Leader)?'' I asked him. ''Tell me yes or no.''

I asked him three times over, and he answered me each time, ''Yes. I am *O-ke-mow.*''

Then I said, ''If I understand your words, is it that you can do for me as God had done for me?''

And he answered, ''No. There is no two-legged man can do so.''

''Then why do want to take that power away from God?''

And he said to me, ''What I can do, I will do humbly. You will not starve under me. Before I took the work, I looked at this paper (the Treaty) and I saw that it was just. I show it now before God, believing that it is true. This is Victoria's word.''

But I asked him, ''What is five dollars a head for this mighty land?'' And we talked all that day.

Then he called out to the camp, ''Wait, ye people. If I were an Indian, I would have this man for Chief. If you make him your Chief, you can use him well, for he is wise and he is young. Answer me.''

And all the camp answered, ''He will be our Chief.''

I had a dream — but I did not believe my dream — that there would be white men everywhere, overwhelming this land. Today I see it. I love this land greatly, and what is still the Indian's I am resolved to hold fast. For that I pray much.

Edward Ahenakew
(Written in June 1923)

PART I

THE STORIES OF
CHIEF THUNDERCHILD

1.

A Winter of Hardship

When I was still young and my father was alive, we came through a winter of great hardship. My brother took me with him on many long hunts, but the buffalo were scarce that year, and there was hardly any food. Everyone looked for old bones to make grease,[11] but it was rancid.

At first there were plenty of foxes. We caught many in deadfall traps,[12] and traded their skins for tobacco, shot, tea, and sugar, when traders came to our camps; but when we tried to buy pemmican, they would not sell us any.

We had travelled far out onto the plains, and there were no more trees to make traps. We were told that there was food at Fort Pitt, and we started in hope towards that post. We still had five horses and many dogs, but wolves followed us, and when we camped our dogs would chase them. Sometimes the dogs killed a wolf, but every day wolves killed some of our dogs. We had to kill dogs too, for we had nothing else to eat; then, we had to kill our horses for food.

One day *Na-pa-ke-kun* (Night Scout) came to our camp. He told us that the people we had left at the encampment had also tried to reach Fort Pitt when they learned that there was food there, and they had died along the way. He and his wives were the only ones left. They had five horses, and they killed one for food, but would give us none. We took the skin, and we boiled that and ate it, but we were too weak to follow *Na-pa-ke-kun* north when he went on with his wives and the other horses. We could go no farther.

The winter was ending. Our women seemed to be stronger than the men. Though they were not eating, they kept moving, if it was only to make fires to keep us warm. The three little children with us were only skin and bones, and their mothers cried over them. We found it hard even to breathe.

One night I dreamed that someone came to me and said, "You can save yourself. Look to the south!" And looking south, I saw that the country was green, but to the north there was only darkness. I tried to flee to the south. The dream was vivid, and when I awoke it was almost morning. I lay thinking about the dream, and then I told it to my father. "Maybe it is only hunger that made me dream," I said. But my father told me, "Dreams count, my son. Try to go south, all of you; and if I cannot follow, leave me. I will do my best."

The thaw had begun. The women went ahead of us, carrying all they could. I had a gun and I tried to hunt, but I had to rest often. Gophers were appearing, and we killed some and made fires with buffalo chips to cook them. We camped four times before we came to any bush. Then early one morning, my aunt suddenly cried out that she had seen an "old

14

man buffalo.'' We thought that she had gone crazy but we looked where she pointed and there stood a buffalo, about two hundred yards away. "*A-a-hay-a-ay*. It is going to be hard. Who can go?''

My brother took his loaded gun and moved slowly down the valley, resting often, for he was very weak. We stayed and watched. Sometimes he was out of sight, and then we would see him again, crawling towards where the buffalo had been, but it had moved on and we could not see it.

After a long time, we heard the sound of my brother's gun, and I went to meet him. He told me that he had hit the buffalo, and it would surely die, but we would have to move our camp and follow its trail. It took us a long time to pull down the tent and move slowly after the buffalo. It was not far, but we were weak. My aunt took the gun. "I will follow the trail,'' she said, "and I will kill the buffalo if it is still alive.'' The other women went with her, all except my mother.

Night came, and it was bright moonlight when we heard the women returning, dragging great loads of meat. They were able to bring most of it back to where we had camped. The buffalo was old and its meat was tough. The women boiled it to make soup, and that was easier for us to eat, but after long hunger my mother and my brother almost died. *A-a-hay*, we were poor, but now we could fatten ourselves a bit, and we began to feel life in our bones once more.

When I was stronger, I wandered through the bushes where we had pitched our tent, and I saw an old camp, with the tracks of foxes and wolves around it. There was a mound of melting snow, and when I kicked it I saw a corpse, a man dead from hunger. I went back to our camp and we moved to the river, hoping that we might meet some Stoneys,[13] my aunt's people.

Each day, we were able to walk a little more, and the snow was almost gone when we reached the river. Away to the west, we could see people moving in single file. We knew they might be Blackfoot and so we loaded our guns in readiness, but when they saw us they turned towards us, moving slowly, for they had no horses and were carrying heavy loads. They were Stoneys, and they greeted my aunt affectionately as a daughter.

There were eleven families, and everything they had was in the loads on their backs, for they had killed and eaten their horses. But they had buffalo meat, and they fed us grease and dried meat. When we had eaten they wanted to go on, though my father asked them to camp with us by the river, at the old Sun Dance place.[14] We gave them tobacco and tea, and they gave us meat; but the next day they crossed the river. We were sorry to see them go.

We camped at the old Sun Dance place, where there was plenty of wood. The women found a buffalo head and neck in the snow, and they made a fire to boil it. I climbed the bank of the river, and as I sat there I saw something that moved and disappeared again with the wind. I went to find out what it was, and I came to a big snowdrift with a pole at the top, from which a bit of cloth blew in the wind. It marked a cache.

I took off my coat and began to dig through the hard crust of snow. Down inside the drift I found hides that covered the meat of two buffalo, cut in pieces. I had to sit down then, for I remembered my dream and was overcome with feeling and with thankfulness to the spirits who had guided us.

I tied the meat into one of the hides and pulled it down the bank as far as I could, and then I left it and went on to our camp. I found the others eating the head that the women had boiled, and my sister-in-law called to me to come and eat. I ate, and when I was finished I said to my father, "We will have another meal, a good one," and I told him what I had found. "Dreams count, my son," he said to me. "The spirits have pitied us and guided us."[15]

The women hurried to bring the meat to our camp, and we stayed at the Sun Dance place until they had dried much of it and made pemmican, and had scraped and tanned the hides. When all that was done, we moved on. It was spring, and we went to where there were maple trees, and made sugar. Truly a change had come, for now we had sugar; and the hunting was good, with a kill every day. It was pleasant in that valley, just to be alive and well, all of us; and yet we felt ashamed to be so poor, without any horses. It was lonely too.

I had begun to feel that I must have things of my own, and I was restless. I said that I would go to see if I could find some of our people, and I had not gone far when I saw a rider, a Stoney whose name was *Chō-ka-se*. I told him all that had happened to us, and he said, "Come with me and I will lend you horses and carts." He came back to our camp with me. My father was surprised that I had come back so soon, and he was pleased that *Chō-ka-se* would lend us horses and carts; but that is the Indian way.

Then *Chō-ka-se* took us to his camp and he gave us what we needed to travel. Scouts who had gone ahead had found the women who had been with *Na-pa-ke-kun*. He had died of starvation and yet they still had the horses that they had refused to share with us. The scouts came on Big Bear's band too, those with horses helping to carry the others. All through the country north of the Saskatchewan River there had been many deaths from starvation, and the Crees were moving west along the river, hoping to make a truce with the Blackfoot. The scouts said that the Blackfoot had not starved, for they had many horses and could follow the buffalo herds.

We travelled west until we came to a Blackfoot camp. They knew of the hardship we had suffered and we were invited into a big tent. At first we could use only signs, and then one of the Crees came who could interpret. My brother made the Blackfoot his namesake; the old man gave him a fine horse and cart. He gave me a two-year-old to ride, but I made up my mind after all the troubles of that winter that I would never again be dependent upon others.

2.

Indian Laws

There were more than a hundred families in our band[16] when I was young, and I saw much hardship. When we moved camp, many of the families had only dogs to pull their belongings, piled on a travois. Some families had horses, but only a few. The men who had horses chased the buffalo for the others and everyone got some of the meat, which would be hauled into the camp by the dogs. There was no selfishness. It is an Indian custom to share with others. That has always been so; the strong take care of the poor; there is usually enough for all.

Those who were great hunters[17] and could look after many were known as the Providers. They were the captains of the buffalo chase, and no one hunter was allowed to begin the chase until all were ready, for the animals could be frightened away. In the camp, the men who enforced law were greatly respected. They belonged to the society of Dancers, and they permitted no one to separate from the band and make his own camp, because trouble could come from that and could involve many.

Sometimes a man had to leave the encampment with his family, and hunt alone, but it was never safe in the days of warfare with the Blackfoot. When my friend, *Na-ne-so* (Twice two), was a small boy, his father went to hunt alone. He took his sisters with him, and his wife, *We-ke-ka-sa-wa-nuk*, and their baby and two children, *Na-ne-so* and his little sister.

It was early in the fall, but the snow came, and one day when he was hunting the man saw the tracks of other men and knew there were strangers close to his camp. He did not want to frighten the women, but he told them to take the children and sleep that night in a sheltered place a little distance away, and he stayed alone in the tent.

It was not a cold night, and the sky was clear, the moon shining. He kept watch, and when he saw heads appear above a snowdrift a little way off, he prepared to shoot, but first he called out to them in Cree, to be sure they were not friends. Two shots answered him, and he knew they were Blackfoot. Then he shot and killed one man. They kept firing at his tent, and his family heard and were filled with fear, but *Na-ne-so* lay in the shelter with his mother and counted the stars above him so that no one would know that he was afraid.

Then *We-ke-ka-sa-wa-nuk* put her baby to her breast so that it would not cry out, and she crept out of their shelter on the far side, away from the Blackfoot, and she ran and walked all night, until at daylight she came to the Cree encampment. Meanwhile, her man had killed another Blackfoot, and his people heard just two shots more, and then his voice calling to them, "They shot straight this time." But the Blackfoot heard the sound of racing horses as the Crees came, and they fled. The man who had fought all night alone was dead.

Hunters often had to take that chance, and that was accepted. The trouble that came through *Ē-pay-as*, the nephew of *Mis-ta-wa-sis*, broke the peace between members of the band. He had made a raid deep into the Blackfoot country and had brought back many horses. The Blackfoot followed him, and they killed a woman and a boy in the Cree encampment. Such raids were common but the boy's father blamed *Ē-pay-as*, saying he had provoked the Blackfoot to retaliate. Grief can make people unreasonable, and this man kept bothering *Ē-pay-as* to give him horses. *Ē-pay-as* said that he had no more to give, and the man went to the Dancers and the Providers, and they asked *Ē-pay-as* to give him the poorest horse he had, but still he refused. He was tired of being bothered, and he went off to make his own camp, with two of his brothers, and their women.

Then the Dancers and Providers gathered together, about fifty of them, and they came to his camp. The three men sent their women away, but they stayed in their tent, and even when the Providers fired their guns above the tent, the three refused to obey the camp law. Then old Bad Hand went forward alone, armed only with a knife, and he called out, "You will not like this, my grandson." *Ē-pay-as* stepped from the tent and said, "I am waiting to see what you will do."

"A Provider does not back down," Bad Hand answered, "and I have been a Provider for most of my life, since first I became a man. I have seen many wrong things done in my life-time, and I will not back out. You are angry, but I am angry too."

Now, I was young then, and I was afraid of what might happen. I heard the Old Man say to a Saulteaux who had just come up to him, "Do what you must do"; the Saulteaux began to cut up the possessions of the three men. They stood watching him, though one of them threatened at first to shoot him. Then the son of *Mis-ta-wa-sis* came with a big six-shooter. His name was *We-ya-te-chu-paō* (Laughing Man) and he was not like that, but close-mouthed. Now the three who rebelled were his cousins, and one of them suddenly pointed his gun at *We-ya-te-chu-paō* as though he would shoot, and *We-ya-te-chu-paō* started to run away and was much ashamed.

He yelled at his cousin, "*Yey-wa-ho-aw*, you did that to startle me!" and the other said, "I didn't know who you were with that big gun. I thought you were a white man." Everyone laughed except *We-ya-te-chu-paō*. He smashed his gun across his cousin's head. The man fell stunned, but he recovered quickly, though the blood was streaming down his long braids, and he said, "The one who did that will pay two horses to me."

We-ya-te-chu-paō stepped back, and all the others retreated with him, in silence, but one of them picked up the wounded man's rifle. *Ē-pay-as* had not seen what happened, and when he turned, he shouted, "Who hit my brother?" and loaded his gun swiftly.

Bad Hand was nearest to him. The Old Man had turned to watch the others as they slowly retreated, and *Ē-pay-as* struck him across the neck with his gun. "This is your fault," he shouted, and then he shot the Old Man, who was armed with only a knife.

The three men were my uncles, and I was standing near them. *Ē-pay-as* saw me, and he said, "Go away, my nephew. We have no relatives now. Go away."

I went. Everyone had run except *We-ya-te-chu-paō* who was walking slowly away. Again and again, *Ē-pay-as* aimed and fired at his cousin. He missed twice, but the third shot hit *We-ya-te-chu-paō* in the leg, a flesh wound only, but he fell.

Then *Ē-pay-as* shouted, "No one is to come to see us. We are not relatives of yours. You have hit my brother." We could hear the wounded man singing his song,[18] and we knew that he was still alive.

Then *Mis-ta-wa-sis* called the people together, and he said, "I have called you to hear my decision. I had no thought that my son could do such a thing — not among Crees should this thing have been done. I am deeply sorrowful. I would that there should be no more trouble. You know that I have horses. Two of the best that I have I will give to *Ē-pay-as*, that he may give them, or two of his own, to Otter-child, the little son of Bad Hand. Tell *Ē-pay-as* that. Ask him if he will consent."

The people asked, "Who will take the horses to *Ē-pay-as*?" and they named my father, for he was brother-in-law to *Ē-pay-as*. My father said, "I will go, and I will take my two sons with me."

My brother and I went with our father, each leading a horse, one with a fine beaded saddle. My father walked ahead. The night was dark, and we could see a light from the camp, but there was no sound of singing, and my father said, "The brother is weak."

When we were close to the camp, he called out, "*Neestaw*, (brother-in-law), I have come with my two sons to see you." And *Ē-pay-as* answered, "Come."

We tied the horses to a cart, and went into the tent. The wounded man lay very still. He was handsomely dressed in his fine beaded clothes and ornaments, and there was no longer any blood on his face and hair. He was still breathing, but near to death.

My father said, "*Neestaw*, I have brought two horses. They are a peace offering, two of the best that *Mis-ta-wa-sis* has, the best in this country. I implore you that there should be no more trouble. Take these horses and give me two of your common ones for the Old Man's son, Otter-child. Do this for the sake of your people, our band."

As my father finished speaking, the wounded man died. *Ē-pay-as* said, "Do not cover his face." And he kissed his dead brother. Then he turned to my father, "I will do as you have asked me to do," he said, and he clasped our hands.

3.

Revenge Against the Blackfoot

One winter, when it was very cold, the Crees came from all over the plains to meet near the place where high platforms had been built for the bodies of their dead. They gathered there to take revenge against the Blackfoot[19] who had killed fifteen women of the Crees that past summer, when they went for water. One of these women was Broken Wing and another was her sister, and their father had gone through all the camps of the Crees, crying for his daughters and stirring up the people to avenge them.

It was January when all the people gathered in a great encampment, and there were women there and many young boys. I was one of these. It was my first expedition and I felt like a man, but the men said to us, "You are not old enough to fight,[20] and if the Blackfoot surprise us, you must run away."

The northern lights were bright above the encampment and for three nights the people danced, before we moved out in long, long lines through the deep snow. Scouts went out before us, and on both sides, and there was a general shout when three riders appeared. Two of them were scouts, the third was a Blackfoot woman, very pretty. The scouts had killed her husband, and they gave her to Short Tail, the brother of Ermine Skin.[21] But they warned us that one Blackfoot had escaped and would give the alarm, and that there might be an attack that same night. We would have to be ready.

It was cold, cold. Everyone was running, some of them on snow-shoes; everyone was watchful. Some went ahead of the main body, and those who reached the Blackfoot camp stole horses and brought them back to our encampment late in the night. We camped in the centre of wooded hills, and across the creek there were stands of poplar, and the Blackfoot camp. With all the other boys, I was made to take my place well back in the circle of our encampment.

When the shooting began, it was as though fire was thrown in streaks into the camp, and shots answered from the tents. I made my way forward towards the lines of firing, and I heard someone moan and strike the ground in his pain. This was *Ma-che-num*,[22] and he was one of us, though his name was Blackfoot and means Good-looking Man. He had been hit in the leg, a bad flesh wound, and he thought that he would be left alone to die. My father said to him, "That is not the way to act, my son. You are a man." And he was ashamed to the quick. My father took him back out of the cold and the snow to where there was a fire.

By now the Blackfoot had fled back to their camp, and there were war yells, and the cries of women and children. I ran forward to the line of Crees facing the Blackfoot camp. One of the Crees ran into the camp and hit a Blackfoot tent, shouting out, "I am called the son of *O-ka-mai-ka-na-wa-sis.*'' Then the others ran forward too, one after the other, and I ran with them.

They began to cut the tents open and pull them down, but the Blackfoot had run in amongst the trees, where there were more tents, and they were digging pits in the soft ground of the fire places. They shot and killed some of the Crees at the edge of the bush.

I saw one man rush forward, and when he was hit, he shouted, ''Come for me. I am killed.'' Two of our men went forward while the others covered them, and they dragged him back. Those two were *As-kā-chas* and *Ka-ya-sa-yis*, a Stoney. *Ka-ya-sa-yis* said to me, ''Come, boy, and bid me good-bye.'' He had been hit in the stomach. He was a man who had always been kind to me, and I felt sad.

Someone began to yell, ''If anyone can take that shield near the tents, he can have all these women.'' And another sang, ''I am *O-pe-po-noik.* Cover me, fellow- children. I will take it.'' And he walked over and took it; but it was a drum, not a shield.

Again there was much noise, for someone had found Father Lacombe's robes in a tent.[23] His horse was taken too, as it was known later. No one would tell where the priest was, and *A-chim* put on the robes, and called out, ''Here is the priest.'' Then there was a cry that a Cree was being scalped, and men rushed to the rescue.

The battle raged all that night; Crees were killed and wounded; the women wailed for their dead.

One of the Crees — he was *Mi-sa-ti-mois* — had been looking for horses all night, and he called out, ''Cover me, and I will try to get them from the corral at the centre.'' He moved slowly towards it, and he had a hard time lifting one big log. At last it was off, and he led out three horses, one of them a beautiful grey racer.

The morning was coming, and the wounded and dead were carried back to our encampment, though the dead who were close to the Blackfoot tents we had to leave. I walked beside my wounded friend and wet his lips with snow. The Blackfoot followed us, but they were afraid to come near, and their shots fell short.

Mi-sa-ti-mois raced part way back on the grey horse that he had taken, crouched low on its back, his robe flying; the Blackfoot shot at him again and again, but they could not hit him. Then a Blackfoot did the same, and was not hit; as he rode, he sang, shouting out to us, ''Crees, go back home quickly. We have two other camps close by, and we will fight you to them.'' But the Crees shouted back that he was lying, and we went on to our camp.

There my friend died of his painful wound. His father said, ''My son has been in the games, and has been beaten. We will leave his body here.'' And we dressed him in his finest clothes and stood him up to face the Blackfoot proudly.

The Cree who had been scalped and stabbed also died at the camp. Before he died, he gave his three horses to his aunt, and he asked her to care for his dog which had waited at the camp for him, and had stayed beside the dying man. Then the woman sang of her nephew, of his manliness, and of the love that his dog had for him. She wept for him, and the women mourned aloud. And the dog searched the camp for the man he had followed faithfully.

We returned the way we had come, having taken our revenge and killed many Blackfoot.

4.

Thunderchild Takes His
First Horses from the Blackfoot

I had only one horse when I first hunted buffalo. I remember how hard that made it for me in the summer of 1869 when we hunted in the country south of Fort Pitt. Our hunters had been chased by the Blackfoot, and we rode back and forth along our line of carts, watching the mirror signals that they flashed from the hills. Our Chief said, "Don't run at them. Don't run at them yet."

Then *Mis-ta-wa-sis* (Big Child) rode out from the line, singing a horse song: "*Ha-ha-ha-how*, why are you watching? We will keep these. Why do you watch?" And he crouched low on his horse and raced about, shouting, "Mount, mount, you horse-fellows, mount. This is no child[24] who goes. He will not stop. After him!" And the hunters all raced after *Mis-ta-wa-sis*, who was far in the lead.

A Blackfoot riding a white horse came in sight and turned to flee, but we were close upon him, and *Wē-zo* shouted, "Go on, go on!" The Blackfoot jumped off his horse, and the hunters all shot at him but could not hit him in the confusion of riders as the Crees swept past. His horse raced on with the others, and one of our party grabbed it. Someone else got his blanket and shield, and all I got were two arrows. The Blackfoot was killed, and I got there too late. My horse had played out, and I had to stop, and could only watch how the fight went in the sandhills below.

Then someone suddenly shouted, "Stop! Stop! The Blackfoot have smallpox. Get away. Get away." But those of us whose horses had played out could not go on, and we stayed together. We saw five men appear from the north, and we watched them riding back and forth. We thought they might be Blackfoot, but we could not tell. Afterwards we knew it was Gabriel Dumont[25] and some of his hunters. They shouted at us in the Blackfoot tongue, telling us to come to them, but one of our party was sure that they were Blackfoot and he tried to run away. They chased him, and it was Gabriel Dumont who killed him and took his horse. We could do nothing to help.

When I got back to camp, I stayed there, for I had only that one poor horse.[26] Then *Ka-ma-cha-was-kis* — he was the father of *Cha-che-ses* — said that he could go with me to the Blackfoot country for horses.

An Old Man who was a conjuror told us to wait while he prayed for a blessing. We built a lodge[27] for him out of young green trees, and we lashed and braced it firmly. Then we tied the conjuror securely with ropes, carried him into the lodge, and left him there alone. He began to chant a song that his spirits had taught him, and we heard other sounds as we waited outside. The lodge began to shake, and it shook until the green poles were loosened and the whole structure leaned. Then the ropes that had bound the conjuror were thrown out, with the knots intact. There was silence until the conjuror walked out. He said, "In my dream, Thunderchild told me that if I want a horse, he will give it to me."

Nine of us started for the Blackfoot country, and one evening we looked down upon a camp, a great circle of Blackfoot tents, with all the best horses inside the ring. It was the time of the full moon and there was too much light; but big clouds came up, as the conjuror had said, and we knew that was our opportunity.

Cha-che-ses and I went around to the other side of the camp and got ready, for there was need to hurry. My gun was big and heavy and I left it, taking only a club with me. As I went down among the tents I felt afraid, and then the fear left me, though the moon was bright again. I saw a white horse near the centre tent, and I cut his rope and began to lead him away. He pulled back at first, but I put my robe on him and rode him out of the camp. He smelled good — a springy horse — his head high. Two other horses followed us.

When *Cha-che-ses* made his try, some Blackfoot went past, and he hid among the horses until they had gone. Then he led a horse in the other direction, out of the camp, and more horses followed him.

We had just the right number to give one horse to each of the men who had none, and there were two for the Old Man. I had three for myself.

That was the beginning of owning things.

5.

It is *Pu-chi-to* Now Who Tells His Story[28]

"We were camped at the place where a stream cuts through, on the south branch of the river, near where Saskatoon is now. There was singing in all the tents as we got ready for an expedition into the Blackfoot country. That was why I was asked to go with the others — to sing. I was a good singer; and before we left I sat in my wife's tent and sang.

"One of the men came to the tent, and we smoked together — not for peace, but for readiness to go to war. He gave me his gun.

"The next day we started out, going first along the south branch of the river. We killed some deer, and looked for buffalo. It was a warm autumn day and the leaves were turning colour. We camped a little way from the river, and went down to bathe in the shallow water.

"Suddenly I felt afraid, and I climbed up from the river, and dressed myself and went back to our camp. I sat there and combed my hair. An old man who was a scout sat near me, mending his moccasins. Then he put them on and the two of us went to the river again to look.

"Below us we saw some of our men running back to the camp. There was great confusion. The Blackfoot were there, they told us; I had only my quiver and bow, for I had given my gun to my brother. I was young and I was trembling.

"A man appeared at the river. He called to us in Cree, 'Who are you?' and we told him. These were Crees, after all, a large party of more than thirty hunters. Thunderchild was one of them; and *Na-toos*, their leader, who had predicted trouble. And there was *Ki-no-sāo* (Fish) too, a black, crooked-nosed, coarse-haired man of terrible looks, but famous as a fighter, both splendid and ugly; and Wandering Spirit[29], who was always reckless, a man not to be trusted.

"We joined parties and went on up the river, and wherever we camped we had sports. Then one day we saw riders again, on the other side of the river. There were seventy of us, and we were ready for attack; but first we watched some Old Men who sat together, *Me-chā-wa-yē-s*, *Se-se-kwa-nis* (Little Rattle), *Me-kwā-kin* (Red Blanket) and others, wondering what they would counsel. Suddenly they jumped apart as though scared, and a rattlesnake slid out from where they had been sitting. One of the young men killed it, and then we all laughed — only a snake, and just when we were talking of war.

"When it was night, some of us went down to the river and made rafts of skin to carry our stuff across. The others swam, but I am no swimmer and I held onto a raft and was nearly drowned, but we all got safely across. I joined my partners. It was cold, and we rested and slept until the scouts returned. They had seen nothing, but the valley was heavily wooded, with a creek running through it.

"We moved on and suddenly came upon tents. Someone fired his gun, and that gave the alarm and spoiled our attack. Everyone started to shoot and there was much confusion. I tried to get to where the horses were, before they stampeded, but the Blackfoot yelled and charged. I ran. Ahead of me a man was walking, not running like everyone else, and I saw that it was my brother. 'I am sick,' he told me. I was afraid that we would be left behind and so I ran ahead to get my uncle to give us a horse, but all he could give us was a poor thing with a sway-back. We had to whip it all the time to make it run.

"About daybreak, we overtook some of our party, and as we came up to them, there was a great noise behind us, and Wandering Spirit began shooting. Five Blackfoot appeared, and they were laughing at us. Wandering Spirit chased after them, but they out-raced him, and someone shouted that a big party of Blackfoot were coming. We watched as they came, in single file. They were out of range for our guns, but they had good rifles and some of their shots fell among us.

"We took our stand in a hollow, but we were fighting to get to the river. I had forgotten about my sick brother then, and all I was thinking about was to escape. A mounted Blackfoot came near us, and I shot at him, but my arrow fell short. Wandering Spirit shot and killed his horse. We had reached the bank of the river, and I wanted to be where I could run fast. I could see that my brother too had forgotten his sickness, but our uncle had been hit.

"Someone yelled. 'Turn and fight. If one of you tries to run, I'll shoot him in the head.' I was in a fix, afraid to go in any direction. We all began shooting, and the smoke of battle was thick around us. Then *Ki-no-sāo* began to sing. His leg had been broken. Wren shouted, 'Let us run,' and someone else said, 'No, don't run'; but we all ran, and some were taken by the Blackfoot.

"My brother and I ran together, not in a straight line, but zig-zagging; I told him not to cry out, just to run. Then other Crees came to meet us, and it was the Blackfoot who ran. I killed one of them and then I fell down and was almost stunned by my fall. I could run no more. I was winded."

6.

Thunderchild Takes
Part in a Dangerous Game

Sometimes we had to camp where there was water but no wood, and the women would go to find it. The men rode out to keep guard. One day I went out with them, and I was riding a fine horse. The women scattered to gather wood and dry leaves. I sat on a little hill, holding my horse, watching, and after a while I stretched out on the grass.

Suddenly I heard a yell from the north, and I knew that it could not be buffalo, that something else had been sighted. A rider was coming, too far away for me to see him clearly, but I could hear the shouting, and saw that he was being chased. He came racing towards us, lying low on his horse, and those who were chasing him turned their horses and raced away.

It was *Mis-ta-tim*'s father, and he was greatly excited. His partner, *Ka-mu-ni-to-wi-num* (He walks like a god), had been killed not far from where we were, near a big stone that had Indian markings on it. The two of them had thought that they had seen buffalo, and they moved in slowly, hiding as they went. But it was the Blackfoot, not buffalo; and those who went to chase, were chased themselves.

Mis-ta-tim's father was riding a fast horse and he had been able to escape, though the Blackfoot got so close that one of them raised his club to knock the Cree from his horse, while the others raced around pretending to shoot at him. Then they saw us on the hill and raced away.

One of our number rode fast to the camp to bring help, but the rest of us stayed where we were, riding back and forth. When the others came, we rode to find *Ka-mu-ni-to-wi-num*. He had been scalped, and there was a bullet in his back and a stab wound in his shoulder.

We were many now, and we said, "Let us chase the Blackfoot," but when we went to the top of the hill we could see no one. "Wait," someone said, "there may be many of them too." And we stopped where we were while two rode to see from the next hill. To and fro, they rode. "They can see," someone shouted, and we all rode forward.

From the top of that hill we could see many Blackfoot, some of them preparing to fight, and others farther away. I felt a fearful delight. We were all singing as we went forward, some keeping back those who were too eager. From the other side of a hill we could hear the voices of the Blackfoot, and one of our number called out, "Wait, wait."

Now one of the Crees, a noted Warrior though he was no longer young, was riding a fine grey horse that pranced as it went; he was wearing beaded clothes and carrying the bag that held the sacred symbols of his spirit power.[30] He was singing, but his voice was weak; when he rode his horse to the top of the hill, he sat sideways, not facing the Blackfoot. They missed him when they shot, and he came back to us at full speed. He had done all that to encourage the rest of us.

Then another, one who was later killed in the Rebellion, did the same, riding a short-tailed fine black horse, his red blanket flying, but riding sideways again, so that he made less of a target.

Ee-yi-nieu, a Swampy Cree, decided to try. He was riding a low, fairly swift horse, and he had a bit of dogskin for a robe. His face was painted and his hair tied in two knots on his forehead, like ears standing up. Away he went, low on his horse and heavy looking, singing a song out of tune. He clattered up the hill, and then his horse stumbled forward, its tail flying up into the air, while *Ee-yi-nieu* slid over its head. His legs gave under him and he fell in a heap. The Blackfoot yelled. They thought that he had broken his legs, and they rushed towards him, while the Crees came from the other side, to rescue him. But *Ee-yi-nieu* stood up. "*How!* My horse stumbled," he said, and he looked so grotesque that everyone laughed. Suddenly it was all a game.

Now the Blackfoot did as the Crees did, first one side and then the other riding to the hill-top, chasing up and down the hills, making targets of themselves for brief moments. No one was killed, but everyone was shooting. It was wild fun. One young Blackfoot rode up, his horse jumping from side to side. He yelled that his name was Black Arrow, and he acted like a crazy wolf. He was wearing a short white coat, and he had his hair pulled high up on his head and tied, all thick with mud.

We yelled, "Wait, wait, see how brave this one is. Don't shoot him." We were all excited by the game. One of the Crees who could speak Blackfoot raced his horse up to meet Black Arrow. He held his gun high in the air, and shouted in Blackfoot, "If you are a man, drop your gun and come for this one." Each rider let his gun drop and raced for the other's, snatched it from the ground, and raced away with the new gun.

At last the Blackfoot rode away. A few of the Crees chased after them, just to make sure that they were going. They had many women with them, and that was why they fled. We watched until they had crossed the river, and we went on to the Cypress Hills.

27

7.

Encounter With the
Blackfoot in the Eagle Hills

A party of Crees were on their way to the Blackfoot country to fight. *Mas-ko-ke-sa-yim* (Sweet Grass) was with them, and *Che-wa-ya-nis, Ah-pis-chi-na-pew* (Little Man), and *Wu-tu-nee*[31] (Tail Feathers), and there were some women too, who came with their men as far as a creek at the branching of the rivers, in the Eagle Hills country. There they camped.

Now a Blackfoot party had come to the Eagle Hills too. There were ten of them, and *Ka-ya-pe-may-ska-nāo*, who was young and good-looking, was their leader. In the night-time, something seemed to whisper to him, "*Ka-ya-pe-may-ska-nāo*, go home. You will be killed." But he was ashamed to go back. Four times he heard that warning, and the fourth time he said, "I will go," and he turned back with the nine who were with him. They were travelling fast towards their own country when they saw the Cree campfires.

Ka-ya-pe-may-ska-nāo said that he would find out whether these were Crees or other Blackfoot, and three of his men went with him along the creek. When they came near the camp, two of them waited, and two went on. Then *Ka-ya-pe-may-ska-nāo* told his companion to wait and he would go alone to the place where the others must come for water.

In the bright moonlight, a woman came to the creek, and she was beautiful. *Ka-ya-pe-may-ska-nāo* confronted her. She knew him at once, from a time of truce between Crees and Blackfoot, and she cried out. He fled across the creek to his men, and they made their way through the underbrush to where the other six waited; but they were surrounded in the narrow hills, and they dug pits for themselves that are there to this day.

The Crees followed them, and the firing began. One reckless young Blackfoot thought that he should leave his pit, and he was hit in the head. He groaned and *Ka-ya-pe-may-ska-nāo* scolded him. "That sounds like *Ka-ya-pe-may-ska-nāo*," one of the Crees shouted. "Is that you?" But the Blackfoot called, "No he is not here." The Cree shouted again, "You lie. It is you, and you will be recognized anyway in the morning." This angered the Blackfoot and he shouted back, "A number of the best of you, I will kill first. Do what you can. Once the sun rises, you will not kill me. I am *Ka-ya-pe-may-ska-nāo*." And he sang his song.[32]

It was nearly morning. Little Man sang, and Sweet Grass called to his men, "Get ready. Let us rush them." He had been crouching at the end of the line, his spear ready in his hand, and when he jumped, they all jumped, hurling themselves at the Blackfoot.

Some of the Crees were killed, and seven of the Blackfoot. The three who escaped made their way back to the Blackfoot camp to get help, but the Crees were gone when they came again, and though they followed them until their horses played out, they were not able to come up to them.

Among their six dead, they found *Ka-ya-pe-may-ska-nāo*, knowing him by the skunks that were painted on his arms; and they sang his song over him, but he did not come back to life.

8.

A Fight With the Sarcee

Sweet Grass and two others were hunting early one morning when they saw a man looking over the country from the top of a hill. They were certain that he must be a scout for the Sarcees, and two of the Crees went back to the camp to tell the others, while Sweet Grass stayed to watch. But the scout had seen them, and he warned the others of his party, who began to shoot at Sweet Grass and to dig pits for the attack that they knew must come.

It was not long before the Crees came, racing therir horses and firing their guns as they rode. Many of the Sarcees were killed in the first attack. Then *Pe-ya-pā-se-se-mo* said, "Let me go down to the creek.[33] I may see them from there." He found a big Sarcee creeping through the bush, and he jumped out and grabbed him; but to keep from being dragged away by the big man, he had to hold on to a tree, and he lost his knife. Still, he would not yell, for fear of ridicule. Then another of the Crees, *Cha-cha-mo-kan*, saw the struggle and threw his spear, killing the Sarcee; he and *Pe-ya-pā-se-se-mo* went back to the fight again, calling out, "Let us rush them before they kill too many."

Pay-chak, a short stocky man, very dark, sang what was in his thoughts, "Ready, ready. Trouble lasts for only a day." Waving his spear, he leaped forward and others followed him in hand-to-hand fighting until the Sarcees fled, leaving twenty-two of their number dead.

Many Crees died in that fight too; when the women were mourning for their dead, one of them cried out, "Whoever avenges my husband's death, I will live with him and be his woman." Redwing heard her. He was too old to have taken part in the fight but he went then and scalped one of the Sarcees, and he brought the scalp to her, and she became his woman. That was the grandmother of *Moo-so-min*.[34] The hair on the scalp that was given to her was four feet long, and the Sarcee was Cut Knife. That is how the creek got its name.

9.
A Story of Friendship

There was a young man, *O-chi-ko-mi-sis*, who had a friend from whom he was never parted, and they had sworn to stay together as long as they lived. They had both made their names known in fights against the Blackfoot, and they held that daring was not enough without planning and foresight, and that in reckless flight a man was usually overtaken and killed. But *O-chi-ko-mi-sis* also believed that no bullet could touch him and that he was protected by the spirits of small lice.[35]

The friend's two younger brothers were with them on the day that the Blackfoot surprised them. They dug pits for themselves and they fought with coolness and killed many of the Blackfoot; but the friend was wounded in the chest, and one of his brothers was killed.

As soon as it was dark, *O-chi-ko-mi-sis* supported his friend down to the river and made a raft, with the help of the other brother, *Ma-ni-to-kan*. All that night, they drifted down the river and, as the sun was rising, they saw that they were approaching some rapids. The wounded man began to sing of his grief for his dead brother, ending his song with the cry, ''*A-a-ah-aha*, I cannot go back without my brother.'' He threw himself suddenly into the water, and they could not find his body in the swirling rapids.

They left the raft then, and *O-chi-ko-mi-sis* was very sad. ''I did wrong to bring such trouble upon my friend, and I must avenge him.'' *Ma-ni-to-kan* said that he would go with him, back to where the Blackfoot were camped. When they came there, they watched and waited until it was night. Then *O-chi-ko-mi-sis* told *Ma-ni-to-kan* to wait for him, and he went into the camp and took the best horses, bringing them one by one to the boy, until they had six.

The night was short, and they had to ride away swiftly before it was daylight. When they came to their own encampment, *O-chi-ko-mi-sis* gave two horses to Painted Face, who was his friend's father. That was not to repay him for his loss, but as spoils of war for his two dead sons. ''Together we made many Blackfoot cry.'' Then Painted Face went around the camp singing a victory song, and naming his two dead sons, until he could bear no more and went into his tent to mourn alone.

10.

Truce Making and Truce Breaking

For more than fifty years before we signed the Treaty there were attempts to end the warfare between the Blackfoot and the Cree nations; there were short truces during the time when treaty with the Government was being considered. Before that there were battles all the time.

I took part in one truce-making, and we were all uneasy. The Blackfoot had sent tobacco as a sign of peace, but we could not trust them fully. Still it was agreed that we should meet them in the early spring, west of where Calgary is now.

There are always people who think that they can do what others have not been able to do, and so I said, ''I will go,'' when I heard that truce might be made. ''Let many go,'' the headmen decided.

When we came near the Blackfoot encampment, we were met by great numbers of riders, who came at full speed, racing around us. Some of their Chiefs used their whips to control these riders, shouting, ''Watch out. Be careful, young men.'' And our Chiefs told us to keep together, and warned us, ''Do not go into any tent alone.''

The Blackfoot told us that the Bloods did not want a truce, and they advised the Crees to return quickly to their own country or the Bloods might attack; but first they arranged a dance. The Blackfoot were many, but I was not scared and I had a reckless partner. He said, ''Let us go to the Blood camp, and make a name for ourselves that our people will remember if we are killed.'' I agreed, and so we hid ourselves when the Crees returned to our own country, and the Blackfoot went the other way.

When all had gone, we travelled towards High Bluff, where the Bloods were camped, keeping ourselves hidden as we were. Soon we noticed that someone else was moving in the same careful way and we went stealthily down to a little hollow in which we had seen this movement. We found seven men and a woman, all of them Crees who had hidden themselves the night before just as we had, having also decided to go to the Bloods. We made ourselves known to them, and we decided to go on all together.

After that we saw a rider coming from the west, very tall because of the mirage. We recognized the brother of *Se-po-mu-ke-se-kow* (Crowfoot),[36] and when he came up we shook hands. He told us that *Se-po-mu-ke-se-kow* was near, with fifty tents, and that he was angry with the Bloods because they would not have a truce with the Crees. He himself loved the Crees. He had taken the pipe of peace to the Bloods and they had refused it. Now, his brother assured us, *Se-po-mu-ke-se-kow* would send men to protect us as soon as he learned of our expedition.

He rode back to his brother's camp, and soon ten Blackfoot came swiftly. They shook hands with us and said the same as he had of their Chief — that he was the friend of the Crees. But we were near the Blood camp, and they had seen the Blackfoot ride out to meet us, and were suspicious. One of them came to where we were, riding a fine horse. The Blackfoot recognized him, and the Chief's brother took the peace-pipe and went to meet him.

The Blood avoided him, and rode in a wide circle around us. We were sitting with our backs to him when he rode towards us, and not one of us moved. Then he took the best gun that we had, and still we sat. I watched him without turning my head. The Chief's brother said, ''That will be all. Pay no attention.'' The Blood rode away. Then we stood.

We could see where the Blackfoot were pitching their tents, and we went in that direction, half expecting that the Bloods would attack us. Our leader said, ''Hold on to your guns.'' The ten Blackfoot riders kept close beside us. When we came to the encampment, the Chief's tent was almost up, and robes were spread outside.

Crowfoot came to meet us in friendship. He thanked us for coming in peace, and we sat with him, the greatest of the Blackfoot Chiefs. When his tent was ready, he fed us. Then he turned to the Old Man who was his father, and he gave him a peace-pipe and some garments. The Old Man carried these out of the tent, but soon returned with them again. Then Crowfoot added a fine knife, and his father came back with everything as before.

Now, Crowfoot was angry. He said, ''The Chief of the Bloods is great, but not as great as I.'' He took only the knife himself, and his two sons followed him as he left the tent. ''Watch out,'' our leader said, and we sat still while the Chief and his sons were gone.

Crowfoot had gone to the Blood Chief's tent, and there he saw our gun. He picked it up and fired it as he came out of the tent. That startled us, but the Blackfoot standing at the flap of our tent said, ''It is nothing.'' We waited for the Chief to come back. He gave the gun to the man to whom it belonged. ''There will be no dance tonight,'' he said. ''I do not trust the Bloods. Some of my young men will stay on guard.''

I could not sleep. Just before daybreak, when my friend wakened, we left the tent together. He said, ''Let us visit the Blood Chief, grandfather.'' (We called each other ''grandfather'' in fun.) We went to the Blood camp, where there were about one hundred horses, and many tents. We walked boldly to the Chief's tent. When we entered, he was sitting naked, an Old Man with only a robe about him, beside the fire where a pot was boiling.

He looked up and greeted us, knowing that we were Crees. Then he took his knife and began to cut tobacco on a board. He filled his pipe before he spoke to the old woman who was stirring the food in the pot, and she left the tent. When she came back she brought another woman with her, one who spoke Cree and could interpret for the Old Man.

He said, ''These two young men have killed the anger in me by coming to my tent like this, in the early morning. If they are willing, I will take them as my relatives. I thought that I could never be friendly to Crees, for they took the lives of two of my sons. But these have killed the anger in me. They will be my sons.''

We thanked him, the woman translating for us, and said that we would be as sons to him. He told us, ''My band, the Bloods, will know that these two are my sons, and they need not fear. I am a Chief. When they are ready to go back to their people, I will give them two racers, but I want them to live with me here, and when we move camp they can ride my horses.''

He opened a case and gave us his sons' best clothing and ornaments. He gave many things to us, among them a six-shooter for me. We smoked together, and then we said, ''We must return to the Blackfoot camp, but we will be back.''

At Crowfoot's tent, our friends had been feeling ashamed of us. They thought that we had run away, and they were happy to see us again. They asked us where we had gone, and I told them, "I went with my grandfather to visit the Bloods." They would not believe me. "The old Chief wants us to live with him," we said, and we told them all that had happened. Crowfoot clapped his hands to his mouth in surprise. "Your hearts are stout," he said, "but do not go back. He is a great Chief, but there are greater, and they are angry. Do not go." But we did go to the Blood Chief's tent, and we stayed until the camp moved. Then we came back to our own people. It was not easy to do that.

In the spring of 1869, *Ma-ski-pi-ton* (Broken Arm) tried to make a truce with the Blackfoot. He was a noted Cree Chief, but there were many who did not want a truce, and only six men would go with him to meet the Blackfoot. Of these six men, two were his own sons, another his son-in-law and one was Ahenakew's cousin. Broken Arm could talk the Blackfoot language and was known to their Chiefs. When he neared their encampment they came to meet him; but a reckless young Blackfoot, Running Calf, reached the truce party before the Chiefs arrived. He shot and killed Broken Arm and all the men who were with him.

Sometimes it was the Crees who broke the truce. One winter, five Blackfoot came to visit Sweet Grass and his band. Now, the summer before, the Blackfoot had killed a woman of that band — *Pai-chuck*'s wife — and *Pai-chuck* had sworn revenge. "Any time that I see a Blackfoot, even in truce, I will kill him." Chief Sweet Grass had been warned, but he did not believe that *Pai-chuck* would carry out his threat.

The Blackfoot were in Sweet Grass's tent when *Pai-chuck* came with his gun. He watched from a distance, and called out, "I come to invite the Blackfoot Chief." Sweet Grass didn't know that *Pai-chuck* had come. Someone else told the Blackfoot Chief. He stepped out of the tent and *Pai-chuck* shot him dead. "I am *Pai-chuck*," he yelled. "I told you, Sweet Grass, that I would kill your Blackfoot. Blood for blood."

There was great noise and confusion, and the other Blackfoot jumped to their feet, but Sweet Grass called to them to wait. He got the four of them safely out of the camp, and he took the body of the dead Chief into his own tent. He was very sad. He had hoped there would be peace between the Blackfoot and the Cree.

Even after the treaty was signed with the Government, there was trouble. Once, eleven Crees were killed. They were reckless young men who went out to make trouble, and to steal horses. The Blackfoot tried to take their guns away from them, and a Cree woman who had married a Blood Indian interpreted for the Blackfoot. "Tell them," she was asked, "to give up their guns and not to be afraid. We will have a feast." The Crees consented. Then one of the Blackfoot, a foolish coward, rode around them, shooting to kill. It excited the others, and they killed all the Crees.

Neighbouring camps of Crees and Blackfoot could be brought close to warfare by such reckless actions. Chief Crowfoot tried to stop the horse-stealing. When they would not listen to him, he said to his young men, "Then I will be a Cree," and he took his tent and came to live with the Crees. There was no more trouble then. He made Poundmaker[37] his son. After Poundmaker was released from the white men's prison, he went to visit Crowfoot, and he died there, in the country of the Blackfoot.

Crowfoot ordered that Poundmaker's body should lie in state. "First, all the Bloods will see my son before his burial." Many great men, Indian and white, came to see Poundmaker, but his death had broken Crowfoot's heart. "I will not be far behind him," he said, and he died a broken-hearted and a great-hearted man. ...

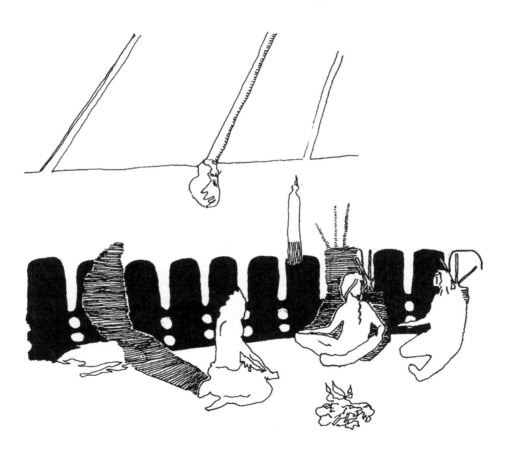

11.

Buffalo Pounds

In the days when the buffalo were many, there were Old Men who had the gift of "making pounds." Poundmaker's father was such a one, and he gave the name to his son. Another was *Eyi-pā-chi-nas*, and when it was known that he was "sitting at pound" — that he was seeking the supernatural power to bring the buffalo — hunters would gather.

One winter there were ten teepees, just for these hunters. Working all together, they cut trees to make a circular pound about seventy yards across. The trees were big, and they braced them on the outside for extra strength. They set heavy gate-posts, with a cross-bar above, and they hung an old buffalo skull there, that rattled in the wind. The gate was fourteen feet wide, and out from it they laid two long lines of tufted willows that spread farther and farther apart, to channel the buffalo into the pound. In the centre they set a great lobbed tree.

When everything was ready, other Old Men joined *Eyi-pā-chi-nas* and sang the buffalo song. Far on the plain, a herd of buffalo was sighted, and two young men rode out to watch. They were to blow their whistles as soon as the buffalo started to move in the early morning. Other men went out to hide behind drifts of snow, and when the sun was high we heard yells that the buffalo were coming. Scab Child went out on horseback,[38] yelling "*Yei! Yei! Yei!*" and others hid themselves along the way.

The buffalo were spread out in a long line, and the noise of their coming was like thunder. Whenever they swung too far one way or the other, the men who were hidden on that side would jump up and yell, "*O-oh-whi!*" and fire their guns. The buffalo came on between the lines of willow and through the gate, and they circled round and round the lobbed tree at the centre until the pound was filled. Then the hunters closed in, and stopped the gateway with poles and buffalo robes.

Sometimes it was evening before the pound was filled, and no one was permitted to shoot a gun or arrows until it was daylight once more and the slaughter could begin. Then it was all the same — yell and shoot ... shoot ... snatch arrows from the dead and dying buffalo ... shoot again ... all wild ... terror of animals ... lust of killing. ...

We would cut up the meat till late at night, and haul it with dogs to the encampment. It was fat and good, but there was more, much more than we could use. Young animals we cached, to freeze. Other bands came to join us and to feast. Their hunters wanted to make a larger pound for greater slaughter, but *Eyi-pā-chi-nas* would say nothing, just sit and drink the berry soup that the women made for him from the bones.

Towards spring, we took the hides to Fort Pitt, and the skins of many wolves that followed the herds. For twelve wolf-skins or three good buffalo-hides we got one blanket in trade. Chiefs who were chosen by the Hudson's Bay Company were given more than that, and their men brought them their furs to trade. Traders came to our encampments too, and it was always buffalo hides and pemmican they wanted. Hides. Hides. Shoot. Shoot. See who can shoot most. A curse upon man's greed and on the Crees for that inordinate slaughter.

12.

The Buffalo Chase

Buffalo would attack people only during the mating season. When we chased them, we always let the horses have their heads free, or there could be accidents. The closer one raced to the buffalo, the better it was, because of the dust. Some men were afraid to go close up to a buffalo, but I — we all boast when we talk of the chase — I raced close up and my pony was well trained.

The bulls had great agility in turning to fight. Up would go the tail first. I saw one hunter chasing a bull when it turned on him like that. The horse swerved aside, but the bull's horn caught the man's belt just enough to pull him off. Then it was like a ball — toss, catch, toss, catch — twice before he fell to the ground. The second time, the horn caught him back of the thigh, and it was as if a knife had cut him. I was ahead and I had to go on, but the riders behind me stopped to help him, and they killed the bull.

Our powder horns were small, holding just enough for one shot. We kept the bullets in our mouths, so that they were wet with saliva and needed no wadding when we dropped them into the muzzles of our guns after powder was poured in.

Once when we had finished chasing buffalo near a coulee (not far from the place that is now called Wilkie), some of the men decided to go back to the hunt. Lightfoot's father was one of them, and he was a good man in the chase. That time he did not return to the camp when it was night, but in the morning his horse was there, and the saddle was twisted under its belly. We went to look for him. Many of us looked. He was never found. Much later, hunters came on a wounded bull, and the buckle of his belt was round the bull's horn.

38

13.

The Grizzly Bear

I came once where there had been a fight between a bear and a buffalo cow.

We had been hunting, and were returning by Red Deer River, eleven of us. It was autumn, but the ground was frozen, and there had been a light snow. We saw something dark and big on the ground, with wolves circling around it. They ran when we came towards them, and we saw that they had been trying to take a buffalo kill from a bear that lay across it, almost covering it.

The bear rose up and we saw that it was a grizzly. We had six guns as well as arrows, but we stood still until it dropped to all four feet, and began to move away slowly, limping badly on one foot. It went as far as the river, about one hundred yards, and then lay down again, facing us, watching.

The buffalo was not stiff yet, and the meat was in good condition. We dressed it and took the fat. The neck had been completely broken, the head hanging only by the muscles and skin. Eight inches of horn were bloody, and the head was badly torn. ''That grizzly is strong. Let us kill him. He must be wounded.''

Our leader tried to stop us, but we were eager. As we moved towards the bear, the hair rose along its spine, and its ears went back. We shot, and saw it tremble, but its head was smashed with seven shots before it died. Its meat was fat, fat and good.

14.

Walking Wind
Tells His Story of the Grizzly

Pay-mo-ta-ya-siu (Walking Wind) was young the summer that he went with his uncles into a big patch of saskatoons, and found a grizzly there.

"We saw signs of bear, and I wouldn't go into the bush, but stayed near the edge. One of my uncles went around to the other side. A sound came to us on the wind, but my uncle made no noise, and I followed to see what it was. I came face to face with a grizzly, standing over my uncle, his feet on either side; and my uncle was killed. ... The bear looked at me, and I saw the blood dripping from its jaws. I turned and ran, and it chased me. I thought that I could jump over the creek, but it knocked me down. I lay without moving, my eyes closed tight, but it bit me through the shoulder and the chest, and blood dripped over me. Then the bear moved aside and cuffed my head with its paw. Blood flowed into my eyes, but still I dared not move, though I knew that the bear had gone back into the bush.

"Then I heard my other uncle's voice, '*A-a-a-a-ah!* A bear has killed my brother.' A rider saw me. He seemed far, far away, but he came nearer and heard my breath whistling through the hole where the bear had bitten. I tried to speak. 'My uncle?' He would not tell me that my uncle was dead, and that the bear had partly eaten him.

"Other men came. They wanted revenge, and they followed the tracks and killed the bear, but they would not eat the flesh, for the bear had killed a man.

"They said that I could not live, but I did. Since then I have been named for the sound of my breathing."

15.

Thunderchild's
Adventure With the Bears

In the springtime, four of us were following the river, looking for buffalo. We had only one gun, one quiver of arrows, and our knives. It was evening, just darkening, and we decided to camp across the river, at an old Blackfoot camp. We gathered wood as we went along, and then crossed the river to the rough, sandy camping place.

I saw shapes that were like big stones. *We-che-sees*, who was just behind me, said, "We are coming to strangers." He used the word "*O-ma-ni-ta-wuk*," and that was the meaning he wanted me to take — strangers — not the other — gut of bear — which made no sense. He was always joking, and I paid no attention. Then he laughed. "Can't you see them? Bears!"

It was true. They stood up and there were five of them. In the half-dark, they looked big, though some of them were year-old cubs that barked "*Ach! Ach!*" *We-che-sees* was carrying the gun and he said, "I think they are going to chase us," and made ready to shoot.

The rest of us stood still. One said, "Let us go, and if they follow, yell, yell!" And another said, "Don't run. Don't run!" but *We-che-sees*, holding his gun ready, could only laugh.

Ten yards away, the bears faced us, and then the foremost turned to run. Only then did *We-che-sees* shoot. He missed, but he yelled, and we all yelled fiercely. *We-che-sees* jumped towards them, and the young bears turned tail, whimpering as they ran. *Yah*, they had scared us too.

There was an older man with us, and he was angry. "You fool," he shouted at *We-che-sees*. We all knew that these were young grizzlies, and there could be full-sized ones in the bushes; but when he shouted, that only made us yell more, and pretend to chase after the young ones, just to tease the old man.

16.
The Foot-Race

When I was young, I was a good runner; but, in his time, my father was the swiftest on the plains. He ran against many others and was never left behind; but anyone who is good at something always has those who think that they can beat him. This is the way my father told the story:

"There was a time when Stoneys and Crees were camping near one another, and we had games in the clear space between the two encampments. I was playing a game when *Ta-te-pa-wa-ty* came to me and said, '*Ne-se-say* (Uncle), the Stoneys want to race against the Crees, four runners to each side. You are chosen as one of our runners.'

"'Who are the other Crees?' I asked him, and he named two who always thought that they could leave me behind. 'Let them run,' I said, but he came back with a short pipe-stem for me. '*Nes-chas* (cousin), you are the one who is wanted and I have come for you. I will give you a new gun.'

"I sat with the other Cree runners, and a young Stoney came past us, dressed in strange clothes. It was said that no one in the country to the east could leave him behind in a race, and the Stoneys were excited and put up more bets. To help me run against him, my friends chose a good runner to stay beside me at the start of the race and sing a spirit song.

"There was a hill in the distance that was called the blue hill. We were to run to that, and then around it, and back to the starting place. I said that I would wait until the others had started, and I let the one who was to run with me go on, and then I caught up to him and we ran together.

"As we came near the hill, one of the Stoneys passed us, tall and straight and springy. I was good-looking too, and my hair was long. I had it tied on the top of my head in a tuft. Stoneys on horseback raced around us, calling their bets. My brother and *Ta-te-pa-wa-ty* came on horseback too, and my brother said, 'Is that all you can do, grandfather?' teasing me. I said, 'I'm waiting for those two Crees who always say that they can run faster than I can. Let them win for us.' Then O-ho-sis (Little Owl) rode up to one of them and pulled his hair and neighed four times to make him ran faster but it made no difference. First one of them and then the other said, '*A-a-hay*, I am left behind.'

"My brother rode close to me, and pulled the fringe from my waist-band. I ran faster, and I said, 'I know there is no man with two legs who can leave me behind — a bird told me that.' The Stoney was still ahead, and I lengthened my step. I felt free. I left my partner behind. The tall Stoney ahead seemed to be standing still. I overtook him; I passed him on the right; I called to him, 'Run, namesake. This is a race.'

"The Stoney they were betting on was close behind me then and we were nearing the end of the race. Stoneys who were riding ahead tried to block my way, and my brother was really fighting them off. He called to me, 'He's going to overtake you.' Then I ran my best — I ran so fast and got so excited that I didn't know until the race was over that I had dropped my breech-cloth.''

17.

A Faithless Woman

Some of the stories that my father told me were sad. People, he said, could not always choose the way their lives would go.

There was a woman, a Cree, who had a husband and two children, the older one a boy, the other a small girl. Now their mother loved another man, and though it was not easy to meet him she talked to him in secret and told him he plan.

"I shall fall sick," she said to him, "and pretend to die. When they have put me on the high place for the dead, they will leave me. Come to me then and I shall go with you, dressed as a man. Those who see us together will think that we are companions and friends."

She told her husband that she was sick and could not eat. He brought medicine-men to cure her, but still she would not eat, and she became thin and weak. Then she said to her husband, "I am going to die. Do not bury me. Build a place high above the ground and put my body there, in the old custom of our people."

When she made it seem that she was truly dead, he laid her on the high scaffold that he had built, and left her there. In the night, the young man came, and she answered his voice. He climbed to where she was and untied her. He had brought food with him, and man's clothing, and they left her own clothing tied to look the same as before. Then they went into the wilds until she was strong again.

They were both good-looking, but the woman had a scar on the side of her head, and she wore an otter-skin over it, and appeared as a handsome young man. They travelled from one encampment to another, until it happened that they came to one where her husband was. When she saw her son, she felt that she must speak to him, and she beckoned him to her. "Are you well, boy?" she asked him, but she was uneasy when he looked at her closely.

Now when the child came back to his father's tent, he stayed so quiet that his father asked him what was wrong. "It seemed to me that I saw my mother again. One of those two young men who are strangers in the camp has a scar like my mother had, and his voice is like hers."

"That cannot be," his father told him. "Your mother left us long ago. But look again."

The boy was too wise to go openly, but he waited near where the young men were playing, and he watched. The one whom he was watching seemed to avoid him too, and the boy felt certain that this must be his mother. Then the father went to where the boy had been. He walked with a long twist of *shagganappi* trailing from his hands, softening it as

43

he went, pretending to pay no attention to the young men, though he saw that one of them, who was shooting with a bow, turned away from him always.

He was greatly disturbed, and felt almost sure that his son was right, but he had to make certain. He stepped close to the stranger, on the side where he knew the scar should be, and suddenly knocked the otter cap from her head. Her companion fled at once, and she tried to run too, but her husband gripped her arm.

"Wait. I had to be certain. It is as the boy thought. You are alive, and I have almost broken my heart for your little children, left without a mother."

He tore off her ornaments. "You are not human. You have had no thought for your children, only for yourself. I am going to ask your parents what I should do with you."

"Let me live," she cried, but he answered, "I cannot promise that," and he took her to his camp, and sent for her people.

"No one of us has ever done the like," they told him. "Do with her as you will." And he killed her.

It is not only now that woman causes trouble. That has been since first man was.

This is what happened. My father told me.

18.

The First Man

"This is of great moment," my father said, and it was from him that I learned the story of Pointed Arrow, that has been told by our Old Men since ancient times.

Pointed Arrow was the earliest man, and it was he who gave to us the legends of the time when man was trying to prevail over the animals and could speak with them. Earth had been destroyed, and it was after that time that Pointed Arrow lived.

He was inventive, and his name was given to him because he made the bow and arrow. He made knives too, from the ribs of the buffalo, and hide-scrapers from the leg bones. He made pots from clay, and bowls and baskets from birch-bark, stitched with the pliable roots of the spruce. He made awls from the sharp strong tendons of moose, and he chipped and shaped stones for many uses.

Pointed Arrow spoke to men of the power of love, and of immortality; through dreams he told of another man who would come to teach them. The one spoken of by Pointed Arrow did come, and when he in turn was old, he said, "Do not be sad at my death. When I die, put my body on a high scaffold in the trees." It was wintertime, and they wrapped his body in buffalo robes, and did as he had asked. In the late spring, he came once more to his people in their camp. ("This is sacred," my father used to say.)

Now when this man came again, he told the people, "I am not coming to live with you. I am sent to tell you that the spirit of man lives always. Use love, and work out your own future. Do what is right."

All this he taught through the Sun Dance so that generations that came after might learn things that are good.

19.

The Sun Dance

The lodge for the Sun Dance must be built reverently,[39] and always at that time of the spring or early summer when the trees are coming into leaf and the first blossoms appear.

In all the activities of the tribe or the band, scouts had a real responsibility. They were chosen as loyal and truthful men, able to report what they observed. Their part in the building of the Sun Dance lodge represented this trust. Scouts who go to search for the tree that will be the centre pole of the lodge follow the rules of their training faithfully and reverently.

The lodge is built with its entrance to the south. At the north end, a buffalo skull is placed to show the trust of the people in the Great Spirit who provided the buffalo. The men who take part in the dance sit at the west side of the lodge, the women at the east.

The Sun Dance is a sacred institution. Through it, prayer is made for all people; and in the camp there is reverence, with fasting for two days and nights, and abstinence from sex, as proof that it is with pure hearts that the people dance, or watch the dancing. Many sit in the lodge without dancing, but they fast. They sing four times, and those who are sick or in trouble make a vow to dance later, to give thanks for the help they will receive. In the dance, those who have made their vows to the Great Spirit during the winter, in any of the four pipe ceremonies, fulfill their vows.

The lodge is open to all who come in reverence, not only to Chiefs and headmen. Each person may have his own reason for taking part. When there is sickness in the family, a father or a mother may pray, "Save my child, Giver of all things." A dancer may remember his own needs, or express his own thankfulness for personal blessing, but the dance itself is a prayer for all people.

Offerings of food and clothing are made, and these are distributed to the lame and the blind, to the widows and orphans, to the old. Those who receive these offerings go in their turn to the centre of the lodge and there pray for blessing, not only upon the givers, but for the whole band or tribe.

When a man gives of himself to those who are unfortunate, when his heart says, "I thank thee, Great Spirit," can one believe that nothing comes of it? White people have not understood and they condemn the dance. I see only blessing from it; and when it ends, when all that can be done is finished, there is everywhere a spirit of deep reverence and contentment that lasts for days. ...

Today, the dance is forbidden; those who have made their vows cannot fulfill them, and it is heart-rending. *Ka-mi-yo-ki-si-kwew* (Fine Day) is one who is not permitted to make the Sun Dance that he vowed,[40] and the shock has stunned his wife, as though she had been shot.

Can things go well in a land where freedom of worship is a lie, a hollow boast? To each nation is given the light by which it knows God, and each finds its own way to express the longing to serve Him. It is astounding to me that a man should be stopped from trying in his own way to express his need or his thankfulness to God. If a nation does not do what is right according to its own understanding, its power is worthless.

I have listened to the talk of the white men's clergy, and it is the same in principle as the talk of our Old Men, whose wisdom came not from books but from life and from God's earth. Why has the white man no respect for the religion that was given to us, when we respect the faith of other nations?

20.

The Thirst Dance

As in the Sun Dance, the same prayer for all people is offered in times of drought and heat, when rain is badly needed. Certain old Men, like *Pe-ya-siw* (Thunderbird) and *Wa-pa-ya*, who have taken part in many Sun Dances, would make a dance to pray for rain, praying not just for a few, but that all the land might have the blessing of rain, for without it there can be no life.

Before we left our first reserve near Battleford, in 1909, to come to this one, there was such a dance. *Ka-ma-ni-to-we-num* (Moving Spirit) made it. The Indian Agent came from Battleford and he invited me to eat with him. He said, "I want to ask you some questions. Is there anything to this dance? Can they really make it rain?" I told him that I could not say, that I was not making the dance, but that I had heard that it was so.

"Then, let me watch," he asked. "Many people say that it is impossible to bring rain. Do you pay these Old Men to make it rain?"

I said, "No. We do not pay. We give tobacco."

Then the Agent filled a pipe with tobacco for some of the dancers who were tired out from thirst, and he offered me more tobacco and a piece of blanket cloth to give to Moving Spirit who had begun to call for rain. I told him again that the tobacco was enough, and he said, "Ask them to make it rain *during* the dance."

I went into the lodge, and I gave the tobacco to Moving Spirit, and told him what the Agent wanted. He said, "*We* must not mock at the dance, but he does not believe. Perhaps for him what he asks is no mockery."

Pe-ya-siw and *Wa-pa-ya* were with him, and someone said, "You Old Men can do all kinds of things. We shall do whatever you ask us." And *Pe-ya-siw* laughed and said, "Let us show him that we can make rain come." He took his place beside *Wa-pa-ya*, and tobacco was put into two pipes for them.

First, *Pe-ya-siw* spoke to the spirits. "I have raised my children to do as I was taught to do, and I have never mocked the dance. I rely upon it. This lodge was given to us to make the dance." He pointed with his pipe in the four directions of the wind, towards the sun, and to the earth, and then to the nest on the centre pole, and he prayed, "Today, drop water."

Someone called out, "The Agent needs to have his head hit with hailstones," and everyone laughed, but they did not laugh at *Pe-ya-siw*. In a little while a cloud appeared in the west, and it came on swiftly. There was thunder and lightning. The rain poured down. My old wife was in the camp, and there were three priests who came with Fine Day. One of them was Father Delmas.[41] They would all say that I am speaking the truth.

When the rain started, I went to the big tent where the Agent and the priests were

48

waiting, and when the cloud suddenly passed, the Agent beckoned to me. "Did you tell them what I wanted?" I said that I had, and that I had given them the tobacco. He laughed, "That is good — marvellous."

But what made the rain come, I wonder? Did it just happen that way, or can the faith of many bring it about?

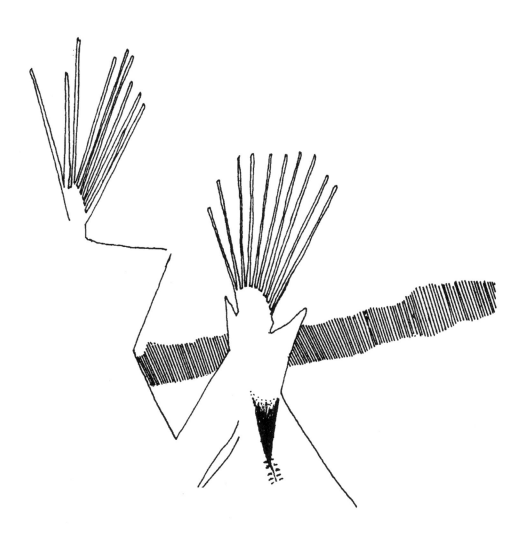

Thunderchild's Conclusion

It seems to me that since we have been fenced into reserves, the Cree nation has shrunk, that there are fewer of us. The white men have offered us two forms of their religion — the Roman Catholic and the Protestant — but we in our Indian lands had our own religion. Why is that not accepted too? It is the worship of one God, and it was the strength of our people for centuries.

I do not want to fight the white man's religion. I believe in freedom of worship, and though I am not a Christian, I have never forgotten God. What is it that has helped me and will help my grandchildren but belief in God?

He looks upon the wrong that is done on earth, and knows what would correct it. But we ourselves must find the way and do it.

I remember old Indians who were afraid of guns, even of metal knives.

In the days before my father, the Hudson's Bay Company had a wintering post at Battleford, but there was too much fighting there between the Crees and the Blackfoot, and so the Company went down the river and built Fort Carlton. They gave the Indians one boatload of goods for the use of the Saskatchewan River. That was soon past and forgotten.

This country lasted long with only Indians here, and then the white man came, and they came with might. That was permitted by God. Yet see how they treat the nation that is weaker. Surely our nation is not to be wiped out. In the days that I remember, an Indian would prepare himself to go on a long and difficult journey. So must all be ready for this road of life.

Introduction to Part II

Chief Thunderchild told of times that are past. He spoke as an Old Man to his people, but he was also their Chief, and they respected his counsel. Today the influence of most Old Men is practically gone.

Perhaps it is well for our race in the new way of life, and yet an Old Man may feel keenly the passing of his influence. He cannot be expected to understand that his own inability to adapt to changing circumstances has made him an ineffectual advisor to others; that his words, in fact, may be detrimental, his eloquence responsible for the tendency of the average Indian to dwell too much upon the stories of the past, to judge himself by those standards, to forget that what really matters is what he is now, not what his forefathers were.

As Indians, we must reject that tendency to look only to the past. In their day, our fathers faced the challenge that was before them. Using those same qualities to learn new skills, we must face the challenge of our day, not as white men, but as good Indians. We most truly honour what is past, when we seek in our changed conditions to attain the same proficiency that our fathers showed in their day and in their lives.

In the chapters that follow, I have chosen a representative character to interpret the feelings and outlook of Indians who have reached a certain stage in acquiring "Canadian civilization"; and I have named him *Old Keyam* — "old," not so much in years as in the sense of tradition because in this relationship to our past he is the successor to those Old Men whose role was a responsible one in the life of the tribe or band — and "Keyam" because that word in Cree means "What does it matter?" or simply "I do not care!" and so expresses the attitude of many Indians who stand bewildered in the maze of things, not knowing exactly what to do, and hiding their keen sense of defeat under the assumed demeanour of "keyam!" — while in fact they do care greatly.

Old Keyam is not a Chief, and he was born too late to make a name for himself as a warrior or buffalo-hunter. He is poor, inoffensive, and genial. His boyhood on the reserve was promising, and missionaries sent him away to school. It is said that as a young man he knew success, and then suddenly slackened all effort. He would work no more, and everything that he had won vanished into nothing. Some who are romantic say that it was because of a disappointment in love; some, with more cynicism, that he was naturally indolent; and others declare that he had a dispute with the Indian Agent.

Whatever the cause, he ceased to work or to care. He reverted to the old Indian way of life, he allowed his hair to grow long, and he chose to wander from house to house, reciting old legends, winning a reputation for himself as a story-teller. The children love him and call him *Ne-moo-soom* (Grandfather); their families welcome him, and even seek his advice at times, for he can read and write with ease, and he speaks English well. When he can afford it, he subscribes to a newspaper, collecting his copies once or twice a week at the post-office, and reading them all with careful attention. Material from this reading

51

lends authority to his opinion whenever he is given the chance to discuss problems that concern the people.

The reserve where life drifts past for him is in the beautiful parklands of the north-west, centred about a lake where ducks nest and the weird cry of the loon echoes in the summer evenings. Spruce and birch grow about the lake, poplars in the hollows and ravines of the hills that command a view from the north over all the gently rolling, sparsely wooded country that stretches south to the Saskatchewan. The members of the band built their first log-houses near the lake shore and from the beginning had their mission school and their church on rising ground that overlooks the lake, so that the tower is visible from all around.

In Old Keyam, it is true, much of the past lingers deliberately, though he is an inferior and garrulous successor to the Old Men. Still, he makes the effort to look also to the future. In his youth he had tried to fit himself to the new ways; he had thought that he would conquer; and he was defeated instead. If we listen to what he has to say, perhaps we may understand those like him who know not what to do and, in disguising their bewilderment and their hurt, seem not to care.

Edward Ahenakew

PART II

OLD KEYAM

1.

Wherever there was a gathering on the reserve, Keyam was almost certain to appear, sometimes only to listen. He knew the importance of the choice of the right time to speak, and the subject. Experience had shown him how to judge that time; and, when he chose, his own skill could direct the talk so that it seemed to flow of its own accord to the point where he could assume his role of Old Man.

If that moment should be delayed for weeks, he still enjoyed each opportunity to be with others, whether young or old; and he could usually count on being fed too. In the meantime, he had that much more time to rehearse his arguments, marshall his facts, and consider which stories might best serve his purpose.

On this occasion, his chance came early in the evening, in a side comment that he was prepared to relate immediately to previous disparaging remarks about the Woods Cree.

"Whether of the Woods or of the Plains, we are all Crees," he said firmly. "True, our forefathers ventured long ago from the forest, secured horses, and so were able to chase the buffalo and to wage war against the Blackfoot. Then, because they were free and far-ranging as the prairies, and proud of their skill in the chase and in warfare, they came to look down upon their more timid kinsmen who continued to cling to the safety and shelter of the forest. We need to understand the Woods Cree better, to realize the effects that hardship and isolation have had upon them.

"I have visited them in their remote and primitive dwellings. Once it was with a group of government officials arranging fresh terms of treaty. I was interpreter. We found them a friendly and hospitable people. The headman was a cheerful person, well past middle age, but full of vigour yet. He invited us into his shanty, talking pleasantly to us about things in general; and he placed another dwelling at our disposal, saying that he had built it specially for such wayfarers as ourselves. He offered us splendid whitefish and some moose-meat, both of which we were glad to accept.

"You call me 'Old Keyam.' I know that as the story-teller of this band, I tread but humbly and falteringly in the steps of those abler men of old who had great influence in the encampments. Their eloquence is not mine, for the song of the bird in the open tree is the one that brings true music to the ear, while that of the one in the cage is but a sad imitation. The one brings to its song something of the wide expanse of the sky, the voice of the wind, the sound of waters; the other's song can be only the song of captivity, of the bars that limit freedom, and the pain that is in the heart. So it is with my spirit, which may try to soar, but falls again to the dullness of common things, to the ordinary and the uncharitable.

"The imagination of the Indian can become so strong that it can create a world quite of its own, giving to scenes and events life that is not as others see it. Such imagination can

54

be a blessing; we can create a wondrous place of our own out of this intensely real and sordid earth. But we must remember that there are laws, man-made or natural, that demand conformity; that we live in a world of actuality, where most people look at things in a practical way; and we must act accordingly.

"For all our imagination, we too place a high value upon the practical. That is partly why, as Plains Cree, we look down upon the Bush Cree, believing that we are better equipped than they are to meet the changing demands of life. I do not say that we are wholly justified in this view. That is neither here nor there. I expect it is simply part of human nature that as a group we must believe that we are superior to certain other groups; but my visits to the Bush Cree have given me more understanding and more pity for their lot.

"Even to travel in their country is difficult. To the prairie Indian, used to open country, that road is one of the worst of all trails. It twists through heavy undergrowth, and is barely wide enough for a wagon to pass, scraping always against trees, bumping over fallen logs and stumps and roots, or crawling along side hills, over stones, deep ruts and mudholes — and all the while, clouds of mosquitoes or that fierce lean fly, the 'bull-dog,' driving the horses wild. It is said that because of those flies, the moose will spend most of the day low in the waters of lake or river.

"On the reserve to which that road led us, we found the most primitive of log shelters, poorly constructed, over-crowded, without ventilation or sanitation. The people live by hunting and fishing, and they often go hungry; squalor and poverty seem to be their lot; their talk lacks spirit and reveals much ignorance and superstition; degenerating factors of disease and inbreeding are at work amongst them, without any counteracting forces to build or repair. Even if good land were available to them, it is doubtful if they could be persuaded to move from their present reserve, which is all that they have ever known. Isolated as they are, disheartened to a state of unhealthy resignation, defeated by their hard life, they have no spirit to begin anything. Improvement seems impossible.

"Sometimes, one of them stands out as industrious or a good hunter, but he has no chance to better himself. Their idea of brotherhood implies common ownership. Such a man will not eat alone while the rest have no food; it is accepted among them that each shares with the others all his goods; and this has proved one the greatest drawbacks to any material advance among these kind-hearted people.

"Their viewpoint is completely different from the white man's, so that it is one of the hardest things to reason with them. We who are Plains Cree have come, in some ways at least, to see as the white man does; the Bush Cree have never had that same chance. Their lives would seem as remote, as harsh, as desolate as that rough trail we travelled to reach them — and yet I remember how the way opened suddenly upon a lake, a beautiful winding lake, set with islands thickly wooded with spruce and pine.

"The people called it Blackfoot Lake, and we wondered at the name, for the Blackfoot were mortal enemies to all the Crees, Woods or Plains, as far back as our fathers and our fathers' fathers could remember. It was the Plains Cree who met them more often in battle, but the Blackfoot often penetrated into the country north of the Saskatchewan River; and though great Chiefs sometimes made truces, they would be broken almost as soon as made, by reckless and irresponsible persons on either side.

"One of the Old Men of the band of Woods Cree at Blackfoot Lake, told us the story of that name. In the days of warfare, a party of Blackfoot had made an expedition into the country north of Fort Pitt, and they had captured a boy, one of the Bush Cree, taking him back with them to their own land near the mountains. Now, one of their Chiefs, a great warrior and a wise man, had lost his only son, a boy who died just as he was coming to the age when he might have taken his part in manly ventures. The Chief could not overcome his grief, and every evening he and the boy's mother would go to the grave of their son to mourn aloud. The whole camp was saddened, for the Chief who would have accepted with calmness the most severe wound inflicted upon his own body, wept without shame for his dead son.

"Then one day he saw the young captive, and his heart seemed to stop within him. It was not any marked physical resemblance, but something in the captive's bearing, in his quiet and unassuming manner, that made the old Chief recall his son. He spoke to the boy, found the yearning of his heart appeased as they talked earnestly together, and took him to his tent, receiving him as though he were his own son.

"The boy told him that in the northern forests there were Crees who were not like their brothers of the Plains, but peaceable, and kind, and brotherly; who welcomed all who came to their dwellings; who worshipped truly the *Ma-ni-to* of the vastnesses of the forest. He spoke from his own loneliness of his people, giving to them all the finer and gentler qualities that he missed in captivity; and he touched the heart of the old warrior, whose own fighting instincts had been quenched in the death of his son. He too yearned for that which is balm to an aching heart, the sympathy and goodness of one's kind; he wanted to know these men who were different from any others he had ever seen or heard of, and who would recognize the need that he felt for peace and reconciliation; and he determined that he would go to find them.

"The young Cree and a few Blackfoot warriors went with him, and on the way to Fort Pitt, they avoided any Cree encampments. After they had crossed the river they came to the forest country, and the boy guided them for two days, until they reached a beautiful lake. It was a calm and peaceful evening, and they could see a teepee on an island in the distance, and two men paddling their canoe on the still waters, a father and a son.

"The Blackfoot Chief ordered his men to lie down at the edge of the forest, while he went alone to the shore. He signalled to the canoe, raising his arm in the sign of peace, and the Crees saw him and turned their canoe towards him. The older man paddled steadily, but the young man cautiously raised his gun. At that, the other Blackfoot jumped from their concealment, and the Cree shouted, 'Ambush,' and fired his gun, killing the old Chief; and the others fired back at once, killing both father and son.

"When the people of the band learned what had happened, they said, 'Let this be called Blackfoot Lake, to remember how one of us, out of fear, killed the man who had come to us with peace alone in his heart.'

"I came to that reserve again in the wintertime, when our road went easily by frozen river and lake. We crossed on the ice to one of the islands, and stopped to cut some tall reeds along its shore. The day was very mild, and the warmth of the sun raised a slight mist. I looked up and saw a most beautiful exhibition of colours above us — every shade of the rainbow, in a great circle around the sky, with pillars of the same light resting at regular intervals upon the circumference, and lesser lights within, fainter in colour; and then above, another pillar of coloured light, the centre of all the circles.

"I knew that there was a scientific explanation for this whole wonder of nature, and yet the Indian in me, in its imaginative or superstitious way, carried my thoughts to the Blackfoot Chief who had come from his land with friendship in his outstretched hand, and had died on the shore of that lake. The colours of the sky made such a canopy as might have honoured one who came to make peace where peace was not accepted.

"He was a Blackfoot, and so the foe of our people; but he was noble, and he meant what was right and good. The Crees who shot him would have welcomed him had they understood his mission. Their ignorance of his intentions was enough to bring death, where peace and friendship might have been.

"For us all, it is that want of understanding and of vision that is still our weakness. The Woods Cree, perhaps more than we, are in the grip of old things that in another setting and another time had their value. It is not easy to change a way of life when it is part of a past that to Indian eyes appears a golden age. This applies to us, as to the Bush Cree. Patience must keep in mind their ignorance; kindliness heed their reluctance. A Blackfoot Lake must not forever stand between them and all that would benefit them."

2.

The chief had killed a moose, and those who gathered at his house were satisfied and at peace, for they had eaten well. Old Keyam sat in half-drowsed contentment, letting the talk rise and fall without a word from him.

One of the young men noticed this. "Last time we met, Keyam was almost a Bush Cree himself, so well did he argue that we should be as brothers to them. Tonight — full of moose-meat — he has forgotten the fish-eaters."

And another added, "I have heard that what they do not know about fish cannot be known. They eat boiled fish without stopping, letting the bones drop from one side of the mouth while they put fish in the other. No, Keyam cannot be one of the fish-eaters. Last week, at my house, he almost choked to death on one small bone."

It was just as they had hoped. Old Keyam was wide awake at once, and ready to argue. "Fish-eaters!" he stormed. "That is how little you learn. Always mocking. I have told you that we who are Plains Cree are seldom fair to the Bush Indians. You forget that the moose you have been eating came from their country. We were hunters of the buffalo, we Plains Cree. Or some of us were. In the old days there were those who lived near the Hudson's Bay Company posts and hunted for the Company, both furs and moose. Still, when spring came, even these Fort Indians would pull down their teepees and travel south to the open prairie, to spend the summer hunting the buffalo, drying its meat, and making pemmican.

"I will always say that it is not so much in the man himself as in the place where he lives that the true difference lies. We are told by some thinkers that between the material and the spiritual parts of man there is a great division, that there is no shading of one into the other. I cannot believe that. One affects the other, and the place where a man lives can shape his character.

"I am a Plains Cree, and on the prairies I can believe that I am the centre of the world — my world. The land of the forest, with its lakes and waters broken by islands covered with spruce and tamarack, is a good land; and though I am naturally partial to the plains, I can admire it — but from a distance only. When I am in the midst of it, the silence of the forest presses upon me; I feel small and of no account; I walk as though under a spell. And yet, in that silence, a man can think more. The forest lends its eternal calm to the human soul; it develops in man a quieter, more peaceable, more tractable disposition.

"In the north, we find such people. They are more discreet, less given than we are to reckless daring and boastfulness. Where they have adopted Christianity, their naturally strong religious feelings have turned from objects of superstition, and they live the teachings with simple fervour. Because they are remote from white people, they have not been affected by the spirit of indifference to religion. Their isolation, while it has hindered progress, has kept them from contact with the vices of civilization, and has served as protection. They are as yet untried and inexperienced. We who are Prairie Cree have little enough immunity to disease and vice; the Bush Cree is helpless and terribly susceptible. I have seen the sorrowful effects when some of them have come to live on the outskirts of a settlement.

"Because we have always been a bolder people, we feel superior to them. The Plains Indian had horses, and with them endless quantities of buffalo robes and leather for his clothing and his dwelling, as well as abundant food. He was skilful in the chase and in warfare. The Bush Indian had only his canoe, and when he ventured onto the prairie, he seemed awkward to us, for he was quite unused to the horse. He was timid too, and that we could never accept. When he showed nervousness in time of danger, he brought ridicule upon himself; and no Indian can live that down. Yet I insist that we are brothers. It is the nature of one's country, its effect through many generations, that makes the difference in men.

"I claim that our life on the prairie has bred into the Plains Cree a freedom that borders closely upon licence. It has made us, on the whole, of a daring and reckless temperament. It was Plains Indians who had never been dependent upon the white man, and who had resisted Treaty as long as possible, who led in the Frog Lake massacre in 1885. That reservation belonged to three bands of Bush Cree who would never have committed the deed themselves, had they not been influenced and over-awed by the reckless ones from the southern plains. Indeed these divisions in the council, and the reluctance of many Indians to continue the fight made it possible to end the Rebellion in weeks.

"It was the prairie Indian who exulted in dangers. He was a free and daring man, continually in contact with danger on the open prairie. The Blood, the Blackfoot, the Sarcee, the Piegan and the Sioux had been for generations his deadly enemies. Between any of these tribes and the Cree only brief truces were ever made, and there was never safety from the attack of an enemy who might be concealed in ambush anywhere. This tended to make the Plains Cree contemptuous of danger, for it was everywhere around him.

"Possession of the horse had made it possible to live on the prairie; it was the horse that helped to develop the reckless and often wild character of the prairie Indian. You may think that far-fetched, but I have not forgotten how in my youth I would ride with others like myself, racing at break-neck speed; how a feeling almost inhuman, wild and uncontrollable, would rise within me. I remember how a group of us were scolded one day by an old missionary who had enough of our blood in him to understand us well. Such riding, he told us, turned us into young savages, undoing all he was trying to achieve in us.

"There is still another way in which life on the plains has shaped us. The prairie Indian lacks one thing sadly. It is what I would call 'stick-to-it-iveness.' He dislikes to work at anything that requires sustained effort, that has in it the element of plodding. He wants quick returns. He will put forth great effort when the object to be attained is within view, but when the work has only remote reward, and to get it means the exercising of much patience, he either gives in altogether, or continues in a most apathetic way.

"This is the teaching of the prairie. There, whatever engaged him called forth the instant and sharp application of all his powers, both of mind and body. In the buffalo chase, he needed courage and skill, the best of everything that was in him; the chase ended, he would be finished, tired out, his horse panting in exhaustion. Then would come complete relaxation, and he might have nothing to do until there was another chase.

"It was the same on a raid into enemy country. He might have to go hundreds of miles on foot or on horseback to reach the Blackfoot encampment, watchful and cautious all the way. He would creep into the camp, steal horses from under the very nose of the vigilant enemy, and then ride the horses back to his own country, at top speed, stopping only when necessary to rest and feed them, in the almost certain assurance of pursuit until he had reached the safety of his own encampment. It was always so on the prairie — that intense application of all human power to almost superhuman effort, and then relaxation. But the qualities so developed in us are not now suited to our own advancement.

"I think that one of the finest qualities that prairie life bred into Indian character was the spirit of loyalty to the tribe. Only two relationships were possible — to be a friend or to be an enemy; and the Indian was true to his friends and bitter to his enemies. His loyalty to his tribe was intensified by his hatred of his foes. If the spirit of loyalty should die out amongst us, Indian national life would have no meaning; we would be only small and separate bands of people."

3.

The next time there was a meeting, Old Keyam needed no prompting to speak. His subject had been much on his mind, and he wanted only to be certain of an audience. With the first opportunity, he was ready.

"Last time I did my best to speak for the Bush Indians. Now I shall speak about ourselves, about the people of one reserve in particular, a true Plains Cree reserve. I do not say that the one I shall describe is typical of all reservations. I think it is more progressive than most, and I have visited many.

"You young men, of course, may think you know as much about reserve life as I do, but you do not take the care to gather your facts and to prepare what you have to say. I like to think that I can look at things from a disinterested and unprejudiced point of view, but you are not able to do that.

"Now, I shall not name the reserve that I describe, except to say that it is about forty miles or so north of Redberry Lake. The setting is of such a nature, that when I first saw it I was moved to write my thoughts in Cree, more expressive it seems to me than the English verse I sometimes frame:

> In beauty unsurpassed,
> Nature has gathered here
> All that is pleasing to the eye,
> In prairie, hill, and evening sky.
> The Indian still is Nature's child;
> She nourished him, and has instilled
> Deep in his unconscious self
> A love of beauty he may not express,
> That yet has led him always to retain
> The loveliest of woods and plain.

"Fifty years ago, there were five brothers who were noted among all the tribes in the West for their manly qualities. Leaders in every field of Indian endeavour, they came to own many horses, carts, and teepees — everything that was of value in those days. They were peaceable and not easily aroused to anger, and they preferred to hunt quietly rather than make expeditions into enemy country; yet no one questioned their manliness, for when they were forced to fight no one was braver or more terrible than they, and their names were feared, their encampment seldom attacked.

"They were respected and liked by the Hudson's Bay Company factor, who chose the eldest of the brothers as Chief of those who hunted for that fort. It was a wise decision, and he was only confirming what was in the minds of the Crees in that area. The younger brothers were well pleased, for does not the eldest in a family take the place of father in Indian life?

"There was no finer physique than the Chief's, no greater nobility of features. The stamp of leadership was upon him, the calm consciousness of strength in every movement. His eye was clear and true, yet dangerous when it glowed in anger. Avoiding no fights, he looked for none either, and he led his band to a life of peace and prosperity.

"Then the time came when the British Crown decided to make Treaty with the Indians of the West. The Chief recognized that change had to come, though he loved the freedom of the plains, and it pained his heart to give his name to the Treaty. He held many council meetings with other powerful Chiefs, and though what they had to decide seemed to them to be against all that they held right, they recognized the inevitable, and they placed their names on the document that is known as Treaty Number Six.

"The brothers chose for their reserve the site that I have described. They knew it well from their hunts; but those days were ended, and they counted it fortunate for their people that the young missionary[42] who was sent to them had a thorough training in agriculture. He and his wife began at once to teach the people the ways of settlement; a school was soon in operation; a church was built; and from this good beginning, the reserve benefited.

"They have long since gone, the missionary, the Chief, and his brothers; but their influence continues. About five years ago, I visited the reserve just before the spring break-up, and I watched thirty-one loads of logs, all in a line, crossing on the ice of the lake. I was told that the logs were to be sawn into lumber to build a new church, and that the Indians themselves were paying the cost of the building.

"I drove across a river on the reserve, a river not more than forty feet wide, but with banks one hundred and fifty feet apart; and the Indians had built a good bridge, a high graded road. I saw houses that were well built, and farms, large and small, with good horses to do the work.

"The school continues, and the young people mix freely with the white settlers. It is true that many of the older people still do not speak or read English, but they can all write in the Cree syllabics. Of the sons and grandsons of the first Chief and his brothers, one is now the Chief himself, others are teachers, one is in charge of a fur-trading post for Revillon Frères in the north. Some went away to school and college, where they distinguished themselves as athletes and students; one is a clergyman; another has begun the study of medicine; some are farming and making good livings for themselves.

"Indian dances, they tell me, are a thing of the past, and they have adopted the white man's way of dancing instead. No conjurer visits the sick, but the white man's doctor is called to give his medicine to the ailing. Why, it seemed to me, the last time I went to that reserve, that the Indians had even become a shade fairer in complexion. They have a fearless, and yet not an insolent look; a manner more usual to Indians long ago, in the freedom of the plains. Is it that the Department has a wiser policy with that reserve than with others? Or is it that the band has been more fortunate from the beginning? They are a contradiction certainly to much that I have known.

"I feel that I am an Old Man now. Most of my life, by my own choice, belongs to and rests with things that were. I would not have Indians become white men in mind and feeling, yet you must change your outlook, you must learn to depend upon yourselves. You who are young men should not look to the past, in order to boast. The future is yours. Take it and hold it, with faith in your manhood, as Indians.''

His own words, his own account of a progressive reserve, had worked Old Keyam to great excitement — or else it was the remembrance of his own lost days and opportunity. When he ended, his voice fell into silence, and that seemed to him some evidence that his words were not without effect, if only for the moment. They had listened at least without interruption, though he sometimes wondered whether it was with true respect on the part of some of the younger men. As soon as the door was opened, he watched them crowding their way out, pushing and laughing in youthful high spirits.

He decided that he must leave too, for the close air of the crowded room made him yawn suddenly. He was overwhelmed with drowsiness for the moment, though as soon as he stepped into the cool night air, he felt revived. *Ah-hai!* Spring would be coming soon, the snow would melt, the ice go out on the lake. He could pitch his tent again, watch the wild geese on their way to northern nesting grounds, honking as they swept in wedge formation low against the sky, see the ducks returning in their hundreds, hear the strange, haunting cry of the loon, glimpse in the wood-smoke of this camp-fire a vision of days long past.

The air felt good, and the stars were bright above, though the moon just over the crest of the hill was half-obscured by clouds. He had only a short distance to go to his one-room log dwelling, and the road was smooth, hard-packed by the runners of many sleighs. That it led past the graveyard was another matter. It was well, he thought, that he was not superstitious; and better still that he could walk briskly, for the way was shadowed by trees.

It was just as he reached the corner of the graveyard that the sounds began — moans, and a wailing cry that seemed to rattle in the throat. Without volition, Old Keyam started to run, stumbling forwards, falling at last to his knees. It seemed then that he heard laughter, full-bodied and clear — loud young laughter.

"*Nnnnnnnch,*" he muttered, and felt a surge of humiliating shame; but when he rose to his feet, it was with dignity that would not permit even a backward glance. Stiffly erect, he walked slowly on, his feet moving precisely, one before the other in an even track, the toes turned slightly in, as he had learned from earliest childhood. His eyes glinted fiercely. "I'll show them," he was muttering to himself. "I'll teach them to respect the superstitions of their own people — and the Old Man of the band."

Only once did he stop, to listen intently; but the silence was quite unbroken, until with a rustling of great white wings an owl swooped past him, and its prey screamed in terror. Then far in the distance, a coyote howled, and every dog on the reserve seemed to respond. Keyam shook his head. Only the sounds of a winter night? Just his imagination? Whatever it had been — "I'll teach them," he repeated under his breath.

4.

When his opportunity came, only a few nights later, he introduced his subject with commendable restraint. ''After our last talk, it was close to midnight when I went past the graveyard, and there was something in the air, something strange. It was not that I expected to see or hear anything unusual. I have long since outgrown such foolish ideas. Still, I did feel strange, for the superstitions of our forefathers have left something of themselves in me. Some beliefs persist. The spirit may be enlightened, but the flesh is primeval.

''Every nation has its superstitions, born in times when ignorance was general, when people saw the world as through the eyes of childhood, when anything could have an air of unreality. Superstitions continue, and many believe in them even in these matter-of-fact days of more enlightenment.

''Our own early environment encouraged superstition, for the Indian lived in the unchanging stillness of centuries, small in the vastness of land and sky. It was awe, born of his own helplessness and his vision of the vastness of his world, that excited his deep religious feelings; that, in its effect upon his highly imaginative and untrained intellect, led him to believe in many supernatural beings. I am going to remind you tonight of some of these.

''First of all, there is the belief in the *We-ti-ko*. On this reserve, where nearly everyone has had some schooling, we do not disturb ourselves too much with thoughts of him, though mothers may sometimes use that old fear to make a mischievous child behave. Where the teachings of Christianity and the white man's education have not affected Indian life, the *We-ti-ko* is still believed to be a reality, and — usually in the early springtime — he is almost certain to be sighted by some Indian, who then carries the terrorizing report that *We-ti-ko* is prowling to find someone to eat.

''*We-ti-ko* is not a devil nor a demon, nor a disembodied spirit of any sort, nor of prodigious size. Those who claim to have seen him say that he is clothed in rags and very dirty; that his hair is long and matted with filth; that his face repels with horror anyone who glimpses it. He began life as a human being, born of human parentage, and may have appeared normal for years. Only when signs of abnormality became evident would he leave his people and wander alone in the wilds, hunting his own kind, becoming a cannibal.

''There seems little doubt that *We-ti-kos*, or cannibals, have existed — especially in the forest areas where people live in small groups. There would be seasons when game became scarce, when rabbits would disappear, when larger animals left no tracks — when, as the people believed, someone who hated them had enough spirit power to bring a curse upon them, and they would starve. Then one of the group could be tempted to kill and eat a weaker one.

''Some say that once a person had tasted human flesh, he lost all human feeling, became a fierce carnivorous beast, with supernatural power. It is that element of the supernatural in all stories of *We-ti-ko* that proves, to my mind, how rare cannibalism must have been among Indians. In these stories, the supernatural power of the *We-ti-ko* is an evil development, wholly malignant, resulting from the individual's criminal action, and destructive to all humanity in him.

"Now the spirit power[43] (*pu-wa-mi-win*) that is secured through dreams, according to our belief, enhances and strengthens a person. We have all heard of those who in dreams have been adopted by a spirit that dwells in nature, or by many spirits, some more powerful than others. This is one of the oldest and most prevalent of Indian beliefs. A person so endowed — a man, a woman, even a child — does not depend upon any physical strength, but upon the spirit power given through dreams, and will not only sense the approach of danger, but is willing to meet and kill the *We-ti-ko*.

"Preparations for defence begin as soon as it is known that a *We-ti-ko* is near. All await the monster in great fear, no one daring to leave the camp after dark, few having the courage even to sleep. When the *We-ti-ko* does appear, the one who will challenge him goes out to meet him. The *We-ti-ko* gives a terrible yell, so loud that it resounds through the forest, paralyzing with fear all who hear it; but the challenger yells too, and if he can yell louder than *We-ti-ko*, the chances of winning are good. The two grapple, and the force of their impact hurtles their bodies into the air, where they struggle until the *We-ti-ko* knows that he is defeated. Then they fall to earth; the monster, unresisting now, is beaten to death; his body is burned to ashes. This is not easy, for it is said that his veins are filled with ice, that his body is invulnerable to bullet, arrow or the blow of an axe dealt by any ordinary man.

"I had an experience when I was young, of how real the dread of *We-ti-ko* can be. I had gone to one of the reserves in the bush that winter, to teach school — for Old Keyam has been many things in his day. Now, as I reminded you, it is in the spring that *We-ti-ko* generally appears to terrify people, and these were pagans who were ready to believe that *Ka-pā-ya-koot* (He who is alone, the *We-ti-ko*) was lurking near. When spring came that year, the children were particularly frightened, and the only way that I could get them to school was to go for them, and then take them home again as well.

"There had been times when everyone on that reserve lived in fear. ... *Mey-wa-chi-mo-we-yi-new* (Good News) told me a story about that. He was the Chief's brother, the only Christian Indian on the reserve. He had tuberculosis and was not strong enough for any manual labour, but he ran a small store to earn a living. This is the story, as *Mey-wa-chi-mo-we-yi-new* told it to me:

Some years ago, everyone was afraid. Even my brother, the Chief, was so afraid that he carried a rifle slung on his back when he was plowing the field near his house. People barred their windows; many of them came to my house because they thought I might have the power to resist *We-ti-ko* since I was not afraid. And they slept on my floor at night, with the lamps lit until it was morning. If one of them had to go outside while it was dark, they would all go with him; and once, just before it was light, they came racing back into the house, crying that they had seen the *We-ti-ko* standing on a big pile of manure near the stable door.

Now *Nā-cha-wi-ka-po* (Good-stander) was one of them, and he began to sing a song that had been given to him by some spirit, calling upon the wind to blow *We-ti-ko* up to the skies. While he was singing, the dawn came, and I decided to see the fearful monster for myself. I saw it, and there was light enough to recognize it. It was a calf. I called to the others to come out and see what I saw. Then *Nā-cha-wi-ka-po* stopped singing. I told him that I did not want my calf blown away.

The next night they stayed in their houses, and we all slept more peacefully. I admit they had me scared too. Christian belief hasn't entirely freed me from superstition.

"*Mey-wa-chi-mo-we-yi-new*'s story happened years ago, but all of you heard the story just last spring from the same reserve that old Mink's wife was becoming a *We-ti-ko*. There had been suspicions about her before, and the people were frightened. This time they sent for the missionary, thinking that he might be able to call upon spirit help. He recognized that her mind was failing. She had a naturally scowling appearance that was enough in itself to give people ideas. Forty or fifty years ago, she would probably have been killed.

"Some of you have heard about *Wu-wā-si-hoo-we-yin* (Dressyman) and the *We-ti-ko*. That happened in 1885, when Big Bear's band were camped near Tullibee Creek on their way from Frog Lake to Fort Pitt. An old woman kept pleading to be killed, for she was afraid of what was happening to her. 'Every time that I hear a baby cry,' she told them, 'I think it is a buffalo calf, and I have a strong urge to kill and eat it. I am turning into a *We-ti-ko*! I do not want to hurt anyone. Kill me now!'

"She came with her pleading to the headmen, and they held a council. It was decided that she was right, and must be put to death. *Wu-wā-si-hoo-we-yin* agreed to it. He was one of the best Indians in the camp, and he only believed that he was helping everyone when he killed her. All that night, they burned the body of the old woman, until nothing but ashes remained.

"Now, when the Rebellion ended, the Indians accused of crimes were brought to trial,[44] and *Wu-wā-si-hoo-we-yin* was one of them. Fortunately for him, there were white men at those trials who understood the Indian mind and beliefs, and who had influence. They explained that Dressyman believed that he was doing what had to be done, and murder was not in his heart. He was sentenced to ten years at Stoney Mountain Penitentiary, but was released after two or three years' imprisonment."

"Not all our superstitions are as terrifying as that of the *We-ti-ko*. Speaking of the Rebellion brings to my mind a superstition that I would rather call an Indian belief, because it will always have meaning for me whenever I see the strange wondrous beauty of the northern lights. I have been told how in the last days of March in 1885, *Ah-tah-ka-koop* (Starblanket) called to his people from the door of the Chief's teepee, late at night, 'Come my children, come from your teepees. See how the spirits of the departed dance. Lo! the lights are red. Prepare to learn of pestilence and trouble in our land, or of the shedding of blood. When the ghost dance is red, calamity is at hand. So it has been taught by our Old Men.' That was just before the fighting at Duck Lake, before the Rebellion had broken out.

"As for myself, I often remember something of the same kind that I experienced. I was travelling that summer for about two weeks, going from one reserve to another. I had a little white boy with me, a missionary's son, but we had been meeting only Indians, talking only of what concerned them, and always in Cree. I had said that if the boy wanted

INDIAN CHIEF PA SIC WA SIS.

Chief Thunderchild (Peyasiw-awasis) wearing the Queen Victoria medal given to him for his loyalty during the 1885 Rebellion, and dressed in full ceremonial regalia, about 1890. Courtesy the RCMP Museum, Regina, Saskatchewan.

Harry Nash and Thunderchild, Battleford, 1890. Courtesy Fort Battleford National Historic Park Library.

Chief Poundmaker (son of the famous Chief Poundmaker) with his wife, after their wedding at Little Pine's Reserve in 1924. The clergyman is the Reverend Edward Ahenakew. Courtesy Saskatchewan Archives Board, R-A8788-1.

We all have learnt a lesson after losing
our day school. We see too late the value of it.
There are difficulties in the way re the attendance.
We have our winter quarters in Turtle Lake where
we winter our cattle: I pointed out to them
the difficulties, told them to act slowly and
not to promise what they cannot perform.
We talked ways and means by which the
attendance could be maintained high enough
to warrant the opening of a school - We counted
the children of school age here and there were
36. We thought the fair average should
be 25. We are willing to talk to a man
to go back to what we used to do when we
had more cattle, make hay and then send
a number of men to go and attend to them
during winter, the rest of us keeping to the one
home instead of two homes - We are willing
to meet half way any arrangements that may
be made if you and your officials
   If you would prepare accommodation
at the school for a child or two in some diff...
cases when father & mother have to be both away it
would be better still - One suggested this but
we are all of one heart in asking for the school.
   Judge us not regarding this from the past
fate of our school at the old Reserve or from other
schools, but believe when I say that a new
spirit is born in most Indians of the West
with regard to the Education of their young.
   This is as near to a prayer as any
thing can be that is from man to man. I ask
in all good faith -
            Your
                          his
         Chief Thunderchild
            mark.

99

Page 99 of the ledger-book in which Edward Ahenakew transcribed in English the draft of
a long letter to Bishop Lloyd, that Thunderchild dictated in Cree. In December 1923,
Bishop Lloyd replied that the Department of Indian Affairs had agreed to pay the
teacher's salary but would not build a school on the reserve. Ahenakew and members of
the band built the school themselves. It was opened on 15 May 1924. Courtesy
Saskatchewan Archives Board.

Pound

One old man 'sitting at pound" — to tents ᐃᔥᐧᕆᔑᐞ
Wonder if he will succeed — Sent for men out — Cutting
big trees . Pound about 70 yards diameter. Big big trees
Braces from outside . Big gate posts . Gate 14 feet wide
In centre is lobbed tree . Old buffalo head put in door
ᑭᐟᐸᐣᐨ ᐃᐧᐁ ᐃ᙮ ᐯᐃ᙮ᐨᐤᐁ᙮ᐟ . Tufts of willows in 2 lines
Old men sing to help leader . Sing buffalo song..
Many buffalo . Two young men to go & Buffalo.
" When about to start blew whistles ." Soon sun getting
high — yells that buffalo were coming . All ᔅᐠᐅᐨᐠ
Scab Child & Onimkate on horseback went to meet buffalo
" Yei Yei Yei " Coming — Buffalo came in a line.
noise as of thunder . Men hide behind snow hills .
when buffalo opposite they arise O-oh-whi !
Shoot. Shoot! See who can shoot through — Cut up beef
till late at night . Haul meat with dogs. Fat .
Unable to use all meat Young frozen . Other bands
Come . — " Make pound larger ." Great slaughter
Old man keeps drinking berry soup . Towards spring
all the hides given to Fort Pitt . Traders came on'.
Hides - Pemmican + wolves . Curse' on the Cree for
inordinate slaughter .

 One evening buffalo full . Dont shoot
with gun size arrows till day after . Shut up door
with robes . Morning — dress up ! dress up . ! horror of animal.
Yell & charge ~ Take arrows away from each other is
those in the animals. ————

 One Blanket - 3 buffalo hides (good ones) 12 big
wolf skins = 1 blanket .

 Some H. B. Chiefs : — much given them . fur given them
by their men .

Page 113 of the ledger-book in which Edward Ahenakew made his notes of Chief Thunderchild's stories. Note the Cree syllabics. Courtesy Saskatchewan Archives Board.

Seeskaskoatch Indian Reserve (Onion Lake), 1914. Courtesy Saskatchewan Archives Board, R-A4046.

Signing of Treaty No. 6 at Fort Carlton, August 1876 (see Appendix). From a sketch by M. Bastien in *Canada Illustrated News*, 16 December 1876. Courtesy Saskatchewan Archives Board, R-B3404.

Big Bear in 1886, during his imprisonment at Stoney Mountain Penitentiary. "My heart is broken. ... A little mistake, and I had to answer for it. I will not last much longer." (Big Bear to Thunderchild.) That winter he died at Little Pine's. Courtesy Saskatchewan Archives Board, R-A6276.

Chief Poundmaker in 1886. Poundmaker was released after several months imprisonment at Stoney Mountain Penitentiary in Manitoba, but died that summer. His prison garb in this picture is like Big Bear's, but Poundmaker was permitted to keep his long hair. Courtesy Saskatchewan Archives Board, R-A2872-1.

Typical Cree camp, ca. 1905, near Saskatoon. Notice the Red River cart in the foreground. Courtesy Saskatchewan Archives Board, R-A2339.

Kopiassiswean ("Bird Skin"), Cree Indian, 1884(?). Courtesy of the Notman Photographic Archives, No. 1455 View, McCord Museum of McGill University.

Photograph of four Indian Chiefs from Western Canada, October 1886, on the occasion of the unveiling of the Brant Memorial. From left to right, seated: Ah-tah-ka-koop, Flying-in-a-circle, Mis-ta-wa-sis. Standing: Ousoup (Chippewa Chief), Peter Hourie (interpreter). Courtesy Saskatchewan Archives Board, R-B2837.

Fine Day of Sweetgrass Reserve (c. 1847-1941). Photograph taken at Battleford in 1935 or 1936. Courtesy Saskatchewan Archives Board, R-A7193-4.

Crowfoot, Chief of the Blackfoot (c. 1826-1890). Courtesy of the Glenbow Archives, Calgary, Alberta, NA-29-1.

The Sun Dance lodge, ca. 1890. Courtesy Saskatchewan Archives Board, R-B642.

The Sun Dance. "Praying at centre pole" (1887). Courtesy of the Glenbow Archives, Calgary, Alberta, NA 261-1.

to travel with me, it had to be as one of us, in our way. On our last night, however, we camped near a homesteader's shack, and we had supper there and talked English. After we had gone to our tent, we heard the settler's wife calling to us to come out and see the northern lights. They were red! I have never seen a more magnificent display.

"Now usually when I am with white people, I try to do as they do, even to think as they do. I told those people the story of Chief Starblanket, and his words; I joked about it a little, saying that if the Old Man had still been alive that sky would most surely have brought all his prophetic powers into play. I wanted those white people to think that I was an Indian who had grown beyond such notions. The boy was not deceived. He watched those lights with the same awe that I felt.

"We returned to his home at the mission, and we heard the news that had just come from the telegraph station on the hill. War had been declared. It was August 1914, and many of our own young men were to fight and die in that Great War. I thought of our ancient belief that the northern lights are the spirits of the brave departed, who dance, sometimes in joy, sometimes in forewarning — and that if we whistle to them, they will increase in magnitude, will come nearer to the earth that they have left.''

"It is hard to shake the beliefs or the superstitions that one learned in childhood. Let me tell you my grandmother's story about *Mā-mā-kwā-se-suk*. She said they were *U-pes-chi-yi-ne-suk* (little people or pygmies). Now my grandmother was not a foolish woman. She was *No-tō-kwā-wi-ku-mik* (Old Woman's Lodge), the sister of Chief Poundmaker; and she said that she had known people who had seen the little people.

"It seems that these *Mā-mā-kwā-se-suk* live beneath the ground in the sand hills or on river banks. They are very small, no taller that a two-year-old child. The people who saw them, my grandmother said, were startled. So were the little people, for they are sensitive and very shy. With their arms bent, they tried to hide their faces, strange little faces, with protruding foreheads and sharply tilted chins that enclosed the other features as in a hollow.

"'You speak to the strangers,' they said to one of their number, whose face was less buckled together. 'You look more human than the rest of us do.' But the little one was too shy to speak, and yet it was the Cree language that they used. The women noticed how nervous the little things were, and so they moved a short distance away, and when they looked again the creatures had vanished. There were tracks, but they led nowhere; then on the side of a little hill, where the sand was disturbed, the women found a flint arrow-head. They had been told of the sounds that came from underground where the little people worked to shape these flints; they did not want to look further, or trouble the little ones. When they told their experience to the Old Men, they found that it agreed with stories of former times about these harmless, shy beings.''

"We have all heard of another small creature, and he is not harmless, for he is *Pah-ka-kōs*, the hard-luck spirit. I was travelling once in the northern bush with Sam Cook, of the Sekaskooch band. The 'bull-dog' flies were so bad that our horses stayed near the smoke of our smudge-fires all day, and we drove at night. We left *Mi-ni-sti-kwan* (Island Lake) one evening, and stopped to rest our horses beside a creek flowing out of Blackfoot Lake. I am used to the open country, and at night that forest seemed to close in upon us, primeval, almost unearthly. Then Sam told me his experience with *Pah-ka-kōs*, and in that setting it was impossible for me to doubt him.

"We were standing by our camp-fire, waiting for the water to boil in our tea-pail, and he pointed to a tall spruce on the other bank of the creek, black in the moonlight. 'That is where François Ladouceur[45] and I saw *Pah-ka-kōs*,' he told me. 'We had been busy making camp, just like now, and we hadn't noticed him, until suddenly we heard his cackling laugh and looked up. We saw him, right there, on a branch of that tree — a small creature, like a man in build, but so thin that he seemed all skin and bone. He had a dry stick in his hand, birch, about three feet long, and his queer little face was so full of malice that it angered me, though I felt fear too, and a kind of foreboding. I ran to the wagon for my rifle, but before I could reach it, that shrill cackling laugh came again, and when I looked I saw *Pah-ka-kōs* flying away, without wings. But first he had hurled that stick of birch, and it exploded with a sound like the report of a gun. And the *Pah-ka-kōs* was gone.

"'I had not wanted to camp there. That was Ladouceur's idea, and now he wanted me to hitch the horses and go on. I would not, and he was too scared to go on alone. I put on a bold front but I can say now that I didn't sleep any more than he did that night.'

"That was Sam Cook's story, and it was not the first time that I had heard of *Pah-ka-kōs*. My father's cousin, *Mā-su-skā-pew*, had a story too.

"He had been hunting for days in the bush country, looking for moose but finding none, and he was very tired. He decided to sleep just where he was, under one of those great spruce trees. 'Then suddenly I woke up,' he told my father. 'I felt that all was not well, not as it should be. There was a weight on my chest, something that moved, that was alive. I was afraid, but not crazed with fear. I opened my eyes just enough to see, and there was this small creature. I knew it was *Pah-ka-kōs* by that crafty smile on his bony little face. Nerving myself under my blanket, I suddenly grabbed his legs, and held them firmly. He struggled, but I was too strong for him. Then I said, "I am going to hold you here until dawn, and then take you with me to the camp."

"'At last he gave in and began to plead with me to let him go. "Over there," he told me, and pointed in the direction of the camp, the way that I would have to go, "I give you two moose." When he said that, I let him go, for I know that *Pah-ka-kōs* has such power. He shot up into the air and disappeared.

"'In the morning, I started back to camp, and as I went, I came on three moose. I killed two easily, but I did not shoot at the third. *Pah-ka-kōs* had said, "Two." Now tell me, did I really see *Pah-ka-kōs*? Did I hold him by the legs? Did he promise me two moose? And did I kill two moose?'

My father could not answer all those questions, for he had never seen *Pah-ka-kōs*. Nor have I, but once I had to take part in the dance that is his, the dance that is called *Mah-tah-e-to-win* (the give-away dance).

"It happened when I was travelling again to *Mi-ni-sti-kwan* (Island Lake). I heard the sound of drums first, and saw the tracks of many wagons and carts, making a trail that turned off the road that I was travelling. I decided to follow it, and came upon the camp, right in the heart of the bush — a camp filled with excitement, everyone moving about in a kind of frenzy; men, women, children, even the dogs so it seemed, all of them dancing as they moved, and handing things to one another.

"I was invited to the Chief's tent. I had not been there long when a young man came in with a pair of worn moccasins. He gave them to a woman, saying 'These are a pair of *new* moccasins.' That is what they must say each time, that the gift is new, *o-ska-yi*. The woman took the moccasins from him, and she danced a few steps with him while one of the men sang and beat a drum.

"Then a man whom I knew came in, and he handed me a pipe. '*O-ska-yi*,' he told me, and he waited for me to dance, but I was embarrassed, not knowing what to do. I am no dancer, nor the son of a dancer, and I could not bring myself to try even the little jig that seemed to be required of me. A young woman noticed, and she jumped up to dance for me. I am certain that her performance was much more pleasing to *Pah-ka-kōs* than mine would have been. Twice again, men came to offer me presents, but I declined with courtesy and they skipped out good-naturedly, to offer them to someone more receptive. We had just started our supper, when a gun was fired outside the teepee. No one seemed surprised. Then a man came in with an ancient firearm and handed it to the Chief, saying '*O-ska-yi*,' and the Chief stood up and solemnly danced, chewing all the while on a large piece of moose meat.

"It was all strange to me, and when we had finished our meal, the Chief took me to a place just outside the camp where I saw *Mah-kā-sēs* (The Fox), an Athasbascan Indian, the Old Man who was 'making the dance.' At each corner of a cleared square, there was a tall lobbed spruce, and in the centre a fire that the Old Man had to watch day and night, to keep it burning as long as the dancing continued. The lobbed trees were there for *Pah-ka-kōs*, of course, should he decide to watch the dance that was being given in his honour; the fire would draw him to the place. 'This bad-luck spirit must be propitiated,' the Chief explained to me.

"I remembered that in old days an encampment sometimes found itself suffering misfortune and bad luck. The best of the hunters could kill nothing, and the people starved. It was all due to *Pah-ka-kōs*, they believed. Perhaps someone in the camp had offended him directly, or had angered a person in another camp who was under his protection; for *Pah-ka-kōs* does not bring bad luck indiscriminately upon people, though he may turn even upon his favoured one should that person fail to carry out a promise made to him. There is always that element of human vindictiveness in him; and since he has control over game, it could be fool-hardy to anger him or to give offence to one he favoured.

"It is because *Pah-ka-kōs* can be so lavish in his favours, that those who take part in the dance which honours him give away their horses, harness, clothing, bedding — anything that is theirs. One such man came towards us while the Chief and I were watching the dance, a man whom I recognized. I think that was why he looked at me with such hatred, because I witnessed his humiliation and shame. He had given away his team, his wagon, his clothing, everything that he possessed — and he had given all this to people who were too improvident to give him anything of value in return.[46] This all happened years ago, and yet I can never forget the fierce anger that flashed suddenly across his face when he saw me, and the equally strong resentment I felt that he could hold anyone but himself responsible. I knew then why the dance is prohibited by Canadian law, for it is like a drunken orgy, releasing all that is most reckless in Indians.

"For myself, I cannot believe in *Pah-ka-kōs*, nor, for that matter, in *Mā-mā-kwā-se-suk*, those shy and gentle little people. Yet I would not have all remembrance of them fade from the Indian mind, and the land through which they were supposed to have moved recall no memory.

"It is the same with the legends of *We-sa-kā-cha'k*. Grandparents still tell these to children, but never in summertime, for it is said that to tell them can entice snakes to crawl into the teepee.

"*We-sa-kā-cha'k* was a strangely likeable fellow for one so unscrupulous, deceitful and ungrateful. He was always into scrapes with people and animals, yet his agility and quick thinking usually saw him through his troubles, though never with that personal courage and dignity that is the pride of the true Indian.

"Stories drift about that he is somewhere on an island in the sea. It is admitted that he must be getting on in years. What is most surprising is that for some Indian children, *We-sa-kā-cha'k* has come to be just another name for Santa Claus, that genial Christmas visitor.

"Perhaps, now that I am growing old, I am becoming more like those children — not willing to give up my past beliefs entirely, until I have better ones to put in their place.

"That is how I feel about the legend of *Pe-ya-siw* (Thunderbird), the name we give to the Great Birds that are usually invisible, enormous in size, the rulers of the universe, from whose eyes come the flashes of lightning, and from whose throats the thunder that rumbles or tears the firmament. The deep-toned ones are the old birds; those with piercing peals, the young. Sometimes in their anger with a mortal, they slay him with the fire of their eyes; but that is only in the summer, for they migrate south in wintertime, like birds of lesser worth.

"Long ago, I was told the story of a great struggle between *Pe-ya-siw* and a huge serpent. A band of Indians witnessed it as they travelled on the prairies to the south. At first they saw what seemed to be only a small cloud above a lake, but then a flash of lightning came from the cloud down into the water, and they saw a wriggling giant serpent being lifted towards the sky. It went up and then down again while they watched, and they knew that they were witnessing a struggle between a snake and *Pe-ya-siw*.

"The bird's thunder-cry was piercing, not deep-toned, and they realized that *Pe-ya-siw* was young and was beginning to tire. The struggle went on, but it was lower and lower to the water, until the snake was returned partly to its own element. Then the water was hurled in a great spout upwards, and both combatants were submerged. The snake had pulled *Pe-ya-siw* quite below the surface. Ever since then, the waters of that lake have rumbled, for the struggle still goes on; that is why the lake is called 'the waters that rumble.'

"My great-grandmother once saw *Pe-ya-siw*. 'It was beautiful,' she told her children. 'Its eyes flashed, and the low rumbling of thunder came from its throat; its plumage was like the rainbow, the colours so bright that they cast their reflection on all the land about.'

"I do not mind telling these old stories. They cast poetic imagery over the harsh substance of our Indian life. Superstition will vanish in education. There are worse things than superstition assailing Indians. We need our strength to combat these, without wasting effort trying to wipe out fancies that are harmless upon the whole, and that do not always lack beauty."

Keyam looked about the room. Some of the oldest and some of the youngest present had fallen asleep.

"*Wah!*" he exclaimed, "It grows late. But if I had stopped after telling you about the *We-ti-ko* and *Pah-ka-kōs*, there would have been none of you brave enough to go home alone. Well, tonight no one will loiter for foolish games. Go now. For myself, I'll sleep here. When I go home, the sun will be up, and no *We-ti-ko* or *Pah-ka-kōs* can waylay me."

5.

After such a night of story-telling, Old Keyam was assured an attentive audience when he spoke again, about a week later.

"When I last talked to you, I scared you," he began. "That was my intent, for sometimes you deserve it, and you know that. I talked to you of our old superstitions, and of the terrors that wait in all primitive life. I showed you as well that the Indian responded to the majesty and wonder of nature. It is through knowing our past, that we can come to know ourselves; if a man understands himself, his heart is strong to meet the difficulties of life.

"I was born just before the Plains Cree began their life on reservations, and I was still a child when the Rebellion broke out. Our band took no part in that. When it was over, I went away to school; I tried to fit myself to the white man's way of life — and I failed. In my failure, however, I still kept to what I believed was the best in Indian life; I have seen the degradation and shame of others who did not hold to that. You call me 'Old Keyam' because you think that I am both old and indifferent; I am neither. It is discouragement and failure that have aged me; it is heart-break, both for myself and for others, that has made me 'Old Keyam.'

"When I talk to you, it is to make you know yourselves and your people; and sometimes I hope that my words may reach out to others in this country. Indians have been too long without a voice in the affairs of Canada, sitting as silent as women in a council of headmen. Some of the fault has been our own lack of education, so that we sit as though we were dumb, permitting others to form opinions and to shape policies that concern us, and that are often wrong, quite wrong.

"Sometimes I feel that I must shout to make these others hear; words burst from me as though I were speaking directly to them, and not to you only. It may be that way tonight, and you will wonder to whom I am speaking, for I am going to try to present the Indians' side of the story of the Frog Lake massacre of 1885. That is long ago, I know, but its scars remain in our relationship with the white man; and sometimes, for us, the wounds bleed afresh, which only adds to our self-pity and the harm that that does to us.

"I am one who has tried to observe what affects our lives, and it makes me sad, my children, when I hear anything that reflects wrongly upon us. It is our responsibility to correct that, however limited we may be. White men's accounts of that fearful day at Frog Lake make it appear that it was our thirst for blood that brought about the massacre. I have been told of many private incidents in the days and months before that bloodshed, and I am not surprised that ill-feeling against some of the men who were killed should have come to a head with the news from Duck Lake.[47]

"The accounts of the massacre vary, and that is natural, for the events happened rapidly and not all at the same place. Excitement was intense. The story is becoming almost legendary, yet it is not yet so far removed in the past as to have made it impossible for me to have heard accounts from men who were eye-witnesses. Some of these men may have done more than simply look on, but that need not be pried into now, for the Government made a careful investigation, and all who had taken an active part were supposedly brought to justice.

"When I talked to men who were there, they said, 'It was the fault of Indians from the plains who had refused Treaty, and who came to our camp as desperate men.' But these desperate men, these last resisters of the white man's power, represented Indians who had lived and roamed over these great plains, who had breathed that freedom, whose will had never been called into question, and whose only restraint had been through the persuasion of the Old Men of the tribe. They knew the ways of their country, they had mastered its hard conditions, and from that life had drawn the manhood that surged within them. Their freedom was intense and vital to them; they could only resist whatever threatened to restrict it, as unnatural and wholly wrong.

"Now the first white men who came amongst us experienced all that too, and understood it and the Indians. Many of them took our women as their wives. There was mutual respect between them and the Indians, for they knew us as individuals, and they judged us as men, and not simply according to our race. It was undoubtedly to the interest of the fur-trading companies to maintain this respect and friendship. Even to this day, it is generally true of the Hudson's Bay Company, but it was most evident when the Company, through its charter, felt responsibility to maintain law and order in the land.

"Then the Government of Canada assumed that responsibility with all the others; and settlers, who had come at first only in small groups, came by the hundreds and thousands when the railroad was built. These people regarded the Indians, sometimes with fear, sometimes with derision. Only a few came to know us, or could possibly do so, for we were living then on reserves.

"We were to become farmers, it was decreed. That seemed logical and proper in a society where agriculture was the primary industry, and endless work was highly regarded. But the Indians had been nomadic through countless centuries, through all our history; to settle down as farmers meant the complete reversal of habits bred into us by our previous way of life.

"Farming in those first days of settlement was indeed hard labour, under conditions that could drive even the white settler to desperation. But it was possible for him to escape to another way of life. We were hobbled like horses, limited to our reserves, and quite unfitted for any life outside. It was natural for the Indian to become discontented, to look back to the days when everything that he needed came with more readiness to his hand; and that feeling of discontent and resentment waited only to be brought to a head by any provocative action.

"There were many who could not agree to the signing of the Treaty, though they were over-ruled in the decision. Some said that it was the liberal distribution of money and the easy purchase of many things in the Hudson's Bay Company posts at that time that made an impression on the people, so that even the dissenters wavered. I am not discussing the justice or the injustice of the Treaty. I am simply speaking of things as they appeared to the untrained mind of the Indians at that time. They could not realize what the signing over of their land meant.

"Only in this present age is it understood that abrupt change can bring serious shock, with harsh effects upon a human being. The Indian could not know that he was totally unfitted by previous training for settled agricultural life. He could not realize that it meant continuous application of mind and body to one end, if he was to succeed; nor that such steady application was the very reverse of his previous life. No more did he recognize that he would have to live within a definite code of laws that would fence his spirit utterly, and that this ever-tightening hold of the law would come to rouse his deepest resentment.

"Government agents were no wiser in their turn, for many of them were small men who owed their position to political patronage alone, who used the law to become despots in their own areas. It seemed to the Indian that the Government was pulling the reins of control even tighter, that the white man's customs were steadily asserted, the Indian ways shoved aside, and that finally he would be ignored altogether in the making of policy.

"The times were very hard, for the buffalo had disappeared from the plains, and the Indian quite rightly associated this with the advent of the white man. He recognized that he had taken his own part in that indiscriminate slaughter, but it had been encouraged in the Canadian west, and it had been a deliberate policy, he knew, south of the international border, to subdue other war-like tribes through starvation.

"What people, unless totally devoid of spirit, unless slavish for a thousand years, would not have felt bitter resentment, would not have blamed the white man for it all, for all the misery, and all the degradation?

"The Treaty had been made in due and proper form. There had been justice apparently, and kindliness too on the part of those who represented the Crown. Yet at the signing there were men, both white and Indian, who were sick at heart because they knew the almost certain outcome, yet could see no alternative.

"Looking back now, we can recognize that the massacre at Frog Lake was the last effort of the Indian to register in letters of blood his opposition to the ever-increasing and irresistible power of another race in the land that had been his."

Keyam had risen to his feet, his clenched fist emphasizing his words, his actual audience forgotten while his voice called to ears that would not hear: "You Anglo-Saxon people, who never called any man or nation master, who since the days of the Norman kings have never had the manners and the customs of others forced upon you — how can you understand?

"We too loved our ways, humble though they seemed; we too preferred to run our own affairs however poorly it may have been; we too loved our freedom. In all conscience, how can you blame the resentment of uneducated Indians, primitive and wild?

"If it has been for our ultimate benefit that you took over our land, and if in gratitude we should go down upon our knees to thank you for doing so, then might it not have been to your benefit that the Normans came to England? And did the Anglo-Saxon drop upon his knees in gratitude?

"You would not have been the race you are today, if you had been capable of that. It is right that you should be conscious of your worth, and of the greatness of your nation, but has that left you unable to see why other peoples do not readily forsake their own way of life in order to take yours, under coercion? The love of freedom that has flowered so splendidly in you national life can be found in the breasts of humbler people.

"'But the Indians have freedom!' perhaps you say. Then ask yourself: In 1885, was the Indian — or is he now — in a position to recognize a freedom based on a highly complex system of laws? Would that freedom, to ignorant eyes, not seem something quite the opposite?"

Keyam's own eyes fell upon his actual audience, intent, seeming to believe that all those others were listening too. With a shrug of his shoulders, he brought himself back to reality, denying the fantasy. "*Na-moitch!* Never mind!" His voice was calm and resigned. "They will not hear! But I've shown that I know some other history than our own. Let us talk about ours.

"In those days before the Rebellion, the reserve at Frog Lake seemed to be developing. The Indian Agency was there, and an outpost of the Hudson's Bay Company from Fort Pitt. There was a mill too, run by water-power. Everything is gone now, only the cellars remaining, and a heavy wheel from the mill.

"The Chief of the reserve was *Chas-cha-ki-s-kwās* (Head-upright), and he and his band were Bush Cree, a quiet and peaceable group. But there were five bands in all encamped at Frog Lake, each under its own Chief. The Plains Cree under Big Bear were long used to bloodshed, brought up from childhood to regard battle as the highest test of their manhood, ever at war with the Blackfoot and the Bloods in a feud that meant killing at sight, in the quickest and most practical manner. The other bands were Indians who had lived in closer proximity to the Hudson's Bay Company posts, somewhat in that protection, yet familiar with warfare, and living by the chase.

"The winter had been severe, and with so large an encampment the hunting was difficult. The presence of Big Bear's band fostered discontent and resentment, and envoys from Batoche did all they could to enlist Indian sympathy for a possible uprising, even before news came of the incident at Duck Lake. The immediate cause of the massacre, however, was the dislike that some of the Indians had for certain of the white men at Frog Lake.

"They had kept this to themselves, because a personal quarrel was always a dangerous thing in Indian life, usually meaning death to one or the other involved; and, with no evidence of open strife, the white men may have thought that all was well and that the Indians were friendly. I am not going to speak of the reasons for that bad feeling. They have existed always and are with us still today. What is past is past, and paid for in lives. The feeling did exist, however, and there were grounds for it, though nothing might have come of it all, had that spirit of unrest not prevailed throughout the North-West. Insults become unbearable in times of great stress and excitement.

"Immediately after word came of the fight at Duck Lake, the Indians held a council. Wandering Spirit was present, as one of Big Bear's headmen, and I have been told by those who knew him well that he was utterly wild and reckless, 'a no-good man' were the words used of him. The Indians listened with more confidence to those who, like *A-yi-mi-sēs*, Big Bear's son, urged a council meeting with the Chiefs of Onion Lake and Long Lake, who were moderate men.

"The day before the outbreak of violence was quiet except for the business of preparing for a feast and dance, yet a feeling of foreboding hung over the camps, even the dogs howling now and again as though they could sense trouble. Then the dancing began, and though it was not a war dance there was bound to be recklessness where so many young men were gathered. Everyone who has told me of the tragic happening has said how the excitement and restlessness mounted steadily, until by midnight it was truly alarming.

"The first real act of hostility came in the early morning when a young Indian took a horse that belonged to one of the white men. Then the young men began to race at full speed about the encampment, yelling as they rode, more and more out of control. The white men were gathered together, and the Agent was the first of nine to be killed.

"Big Bear is often blamed because he was Chief of the band to which the leaders in the massacre belonged. I believe that he was no more responsible than any of his headmen, and much less responsible than some who only incited the killing. That he was

Chief gave him no power to command without question. It was possible for any reckless spirits to go against his advice in a time of great excitement. When the first shot was fired, he yelled at his men to stop, but it was too late. They were past obeying any orders.

"The scars of that day are with us still, for the bitterness that led to the massacre infects the wound and must first be healed. That fatal day at Frog Lake is like a curse upon us all and upon our relationship with the white man."

His words lapsed into silence, and Keyam looked old and tired. His head drooped for a moment before he raised it to say simply, "I have spoken. Let my words be heard."

6.

The winter spent its last fury in days of storm, and Keyam kept to his own dwelling. When he reappeared he was rested and in good spirits.

"I spoke to you sadly last time," he reminded the gathering, "telling only of bitterness and tragedy. Let us talk of something quite different tonight. Those of you who are young men may have thought that I would talk again of warfare and bloodshed and daring. Well, I have decided to talk about women.

"You needn't grin at me. You may think that because I have never married, I am in no position to speak with authority on that subject. You are mistaken, at least in part. I have observed, I have used my judgment, I have lived more years than you have, and in my childhood and youth I had a mother whose care for me merited a much better result than my life has proved to be.

"In my travels about this north-west country of ours, I have seen Indian women of differing tribes and differing appearance. I have observed many white women too, of different nationalities. Some of these women were young, others in full maturity, and still others declining in looks and in ability. There has been opportunity for the talk to range from family and community, to politics and religion, and even to marriage. I have listened to them talk, laugh, sing, cry and scold. I have noticed their little tricks of speech and action and dress when they wanted to captivate a masculine heart. I have seen them in their own homes when they have captured the ones they stalked.

"And what is the result of all my painstaking and disinterested research of a life-time? One conclusion — that there is a certain fundamental similarity about them, regardless of colour, race, tongue, nationality, or age. Man acts according to the light of reason, and woman in the light of everything but reason — *Ches-qua!* Wait a minute! I am not saying that to be unkind, and you who are women need not take it to heart. In reality, I am offering a most delicate compliment when I imply that women live and have their being in realms that transcend the common and the rational."

Old Keyam was pleased with his own adroitness. He had caught offended glances from the few women present, and with long experience had managed to right himself, or so he believed. As a story-teller, he was always safe from random interruption, but he was good-natured, and he liked to leave the best impression with all his listeners.

"White women seem to know very little about the Indian woman," he went on, "who has always moved in the shadow of her husband. It is not that there is any marked difference in degree of status between the Indian and his wife, and the white man and his. That I know. The Indian woman in her own home has the same amount of authority in family matters as the white woman has in hers, and sometimes more. If she chooses, the Indian woman can make things just as uncomfortable for her so-called lord and master as can the most determined and shrewish of her sex among the whites. Or she can, with her charm, manipulate a strong and apparently dominant husband. In fact, it was my wariness of all this that has kept me from taking in holy wedlock any one of the many who showed by the winking of an eye, the dimpling of a cheek, the soft flushing of her face, that she was not averse to placing — shall I say her welfare? — in my keeping. But that is neither here nor there.

"In public, there is a certain difference between the attitude of the Indian woman and of the average white woman. With us, the warrior was always the protector and provider. His life belonged not to his family alone but to the band or tribe, to the people as a whole. His was the responsibility in matters that concerned them all, and consequently his was the decision too. In council, he was removed from all feminine influence. He spoke and acted with all the wisdom that he had, and his woman had no right to interfere. Her duty was to the family, his was to the tribe or band.

"White women think of the Indian woman as a drudge, doing all the work of the camp, gathering wood, carrying water, while her man loafs. They picture an Indian woman with her baby on her back, plodding behind her armed husband, often leading a pack-horse. Once this was a familiar sight, but it was still deceiving.

"First, consider that business of wood and water. It was no great hardship. The camp was always pitched with an eye to the water and wood supply, and to fetch them was not difficult. Remember that there was no constant housework for the Indian woman in any encampment, none of the cleaning, baking, laundry work of the modern housewife.

"As for the Indian wife walking behind her husband on the trail — that was to his credit in former days, when there was danger from man and beast, when an enemy might fire from a clump of bushes, from some hidden ambush. Was it not wise for the woman to be separated by that space from her husband, who would certainly be the target of attack? She and her children walked in comparative safety behind; he moved ahead, unencumbered, alert, and watchful for their protection. Believe me, the woman was well satisfied to take this less honourable but much safer position to the rear. Some Indian women still prefer this order of place, for habits die hard, and conditions for us have changed swiftly. Customs of other races may not be as easy to explain as that one of ours.

"Take as another example of hasty judgment the accusation that the Indian woman is a poor housekeeper. Can anyone really wonder at that? In the first place, what house has she to keep? Only an extraordinary being could manage to keep her family, herself, and her habitation clean, when that dwelling is a one-room shanty of falling logs, mud-chinked, that has to serve as bedroom, dining-room, play-room and sitting-room all in one. She might scrub every day, and sweep all the time, but it would still be impossible to keep that one room neat and clean. It discourages her, and she abandons the effort that had been hopeless from the beginning. It is these shanties that have killed all natural regard for cleanliness, the regard that any right-minded Indian woman had in the teepee life of long ago. Even I can remember how the women would cut fresh grass each morning to spread over the ground inside the teepee, and the encampments were moved frequently.

"In addition to that charge, however, our women are often accused of being bad-tempered. It is white women who make that statement, and I know the reason. These are women who hold some position on the reserve and often adopt an attitude of superiority. Now the Indian woman has her own views of feminine excellence in looks and deportment, and she resents what is an unwarranted attitude. She may say nothing for a long time, taking it all with what grace she can muster, until the day that her control gives way, and she makes such plain remarks as will brand her from then on as bad-tempered, surly, uncooperative.

"Yet amongst her own, she may be regarded as gentle, as helpful and peaceable. I have witnessed such incidents more than once, and have learned not to be too strongly disturbed by them. This world of ours would scarcely recognize itself if all misunderstandings ceased, I say to myself. But then, I am not a woman. Is it simply that like other men, I can dismiss as trivial what concerns the women?

"Well certainly like other men, I acknowledge the respect, even the reverence that I feel for motherhood. Look at me today, poor, useless, unwanted; yet I had a good mother, and she was an Indian woman. She accepted, and she lived by the Christian faith. I have watched her read her Cree Testament in times when she was deeply troubled, as when she let me go away to school so that I might have the advantages of education, though she was fearful that she might never see me again. I have never forgotten the words that she read aloud on my last night, at home: '*Ā-ka-we-ya kitta mi-koos-ku tā-yi-tu-mo-mu-ka-nwa ke tā he-wa-wa.*' ('Let not your hearts be troubled. Ye believe in God, believe also in me.')

"At first, I think that I was worthy of that love. I was a hard-working boy and when I became a man it seemed that I would earn a good living. Then it proved too hard for me, and I gave up. My name has been 'Keyam' for many years, and I have deserved it.

"O my children, never let things slide; keep a steady hold, each one of you upon yourself; do not throw away your life simply to spite another; take warning from the failure that I am."

Keyam stopped on that revealing note, and his listeners respected the Old Man's silence, saying nothing to him as he sat with bowed head. Then he left abruptly, taking his lonely road to the camp that he had pitched that same day. The last snowdrifts still lingered in the bush, but the ice had given way on the lake, and winter was ending.

When spring came, it was with a sudden rush, and everyone busied himself with his own affairs. Keyam still wandered about, visiting here and there, stopping often to inspect the planting of his neighbours' gardens and fields. He noted that the work in the teacher's garden was well advanced, then crossed the road and climbed a winding path to the mission garden. The new missionary was young, but he had known Indians all his life and spoke their language readily. Keyam had been a welcome visitor to his parents' home in earlier years and was an old friend with whom talk could flow from Cree to English, as the subject or their own inclination might prompt.

That day, the young man remarked, Keyam was not the first to visit him as he worked in his garden, and pointed to a small figure crouched farther away, beside the fence. He used her English name, Georgina, and Keyam was puzzled for a moment, until he realized this must be Chochena, widowed and alone, keeping to a quiet, shy existence all winter, sheltering in one or another of the homes of her relatives until she could escape to her own camp when spring came.

She had appeared at the mission only the day before, out of nowhere; like *Mā-mā-kwā-se-suk*, the young man said with a smile, or others more real, but almost as shy, whom he remembered from his childhood, and who dressed as she — that long full black skirt, the beaded moccasins, the shawl, the black kerchief knotted about her head. He had stopped his work to talk to her, to brew her a cup of strong tea, to offer tobacco for her pipe; when he returned to his digging, she had stayed there watching him, wrinkled hands cupped about her pipe, smoking contentedly, speaking only now and again. When morning came again, he had not been surprised to find her tent pitched close outside the fence at the far corner of the garden — and whether it was to escape her own loneliness, or to take him under her wing, he would leave to Keyam to determine.

After that first day, Keyam became a frequent visitor, and it was soon taken for granted that he should wander on to Chochena's camp, sometimes with a small gift from the mission pantry, sometimes with game or fish that he had brought with him. The young man would see the smoke of her camp-fire, hear Keyam's voice, and the occasional sound of laughter, and reflect that the Old Man was in good form, having found even this small audience.

Other matters in the organization of his summer's work took his attention more, and he finally called a meeting to discuss church business. It had had to be postponed until the spring work ended, but the response was encouraging, and the attendance good. After the first few moments, however, the talk became uncertain, with frequent silence, even the Chief reluctant to express any opinion for the band. This disturbed the young man. Was there some difficulty, some misunderstanding, or were they simply waiting for the right moment, for the right person to speak for them? Then the questions came. Where was Old Keyam? Why was he not present? Had anyone seen him that day?

The missionary's face relaxed, and he laughed, "So, that's it," he said in relief. "Then we'll have to call another meeting after a few days. Keyam went fishing up at one of the other lakes. I lent him my horse and rig. He and Chochena left right after their wedding."

The men sat in stunned silence. This was too much, even for their impassive natures, their boasted control. Then the Chief said, "You're joking, of course." "But I am not," he insisted. "Two of my friends were here, and they were the witnesses. You can see the register at the church. Just two old people who decided that life could be less lonely for them, together. That's all.[48] I supposed that everyone knew. There was nothing hidden or secret about it."

"Nothing secret!" the Chief exclaimed. "That old scalawag! Sure, we all saw him coming this way, day after day. What for? To give the new missionary a lot of advice, of course; to have someone else to listen to him."

And then the Chief laughed outright, and the others joined him until tears streamed from their eyes. "Telling us about women, and how he had escaped all their wiles. Why the Old Man talked himself right into this! And he'll talk the rest of us now into building a new house for him and Chochena."

7.

When the people met again the trees were in leaf, the air warm, and they sat outside the Chief's house. Keyam and Chochena came when all the rest were assembled, he walking with calm deliberation to take his place among the men, she with equal dignity to sit among the women.

Someone remarked that his face was rounded a bit, as though he had fed well on the good fish that Chochena had been cooking for him, and one of the young men said aloud, "Fish-eater!" The Chief asserted his authority then, and, in his "council voice," declared, "Tonight, a newly married couple are with us. Keyam, as a single man, proved more than once to be a match for any or all of us in a contest of wits. We may beware of him now, in this double capacity. But it seems that with both Keyam and Chochena orphans, as it were, it is up to us to endow their marriage. It has been decided that every man present will give his help to build a snug house for them before the winter comes again."

It was Keyam's turn to speak, and when he had thanked them with quiet sincerity, he began the talk that he had been preparing for days, his low deliberate voice gradually mounting in emphasis and pitch.

"My wife and I welcome your kindness. I have entered into marriage seriously, and am ready to accept my new responsibility. As a family man, I may say that my view has altered. I look forward now, instead of to the past. I think of the young of our nation, and though I may be too old to change, that does not keep me from trying to shape the course that must be trodden by my children."

At that, some of the young men could not restrain their mirth, and Chochena gave so heart-rending a sigh that everyone laughed, even the Chief and Old Keyam joining in, good-naturedly. Then Keyam recovered himself.

"I know," he went on, "that a new marriage always brings teasing, and that I can be no exception to that. But I repeat — my view has changed. I am much more concerned for the future of our nation, for the future of the Indians — and the Indians are my children.

"I think that we are the most vexing problem that the Government of Canada has to meet. The work amongst us has been slow and discouraging. It needs men — both in the Government and amongst ourselves — who can see the vision of what can be attained, and who can persevere in spite of every discouragement. There is tremendous work to be done before Indians can take their place amongst other people with full self-respect; we need leadership from men of character, men who are not merely routine friends of the Indians.

"In theory it may seem that every phase of Indian life is given attention — the Church concerned with the spiritual aspect, the Government with the practical matters that are a part of the promises made in Treaty. But our life is not so easily divided. It is one life.

"On some reserves, I have recognized that the work of the Government is well done.

Yet, as an Indian, and sensitive to such comments, I have been aware too often that the work is regarded as uninteresting and quite hopeless by certain officials who have been selected simply as supporters of the party in power. The same may be true in other departments of government, but the white man's Canada will in time overcome this hindrance, or progress in spite of such political abuses.

"It is when abuses eat into the work done to reclaim a weaker people like ourselves that it is a matter of much greater significance. To us, each slight advantage or disadvantage means all the difference between a successful struggle to safer ground from the morass of our lives, or that slipping back from where there may be no advance again. Every year spent now in the continuation of an indifferent educational system, for instance, means ten years of heart-breaking struggle for Indians in the future; every wasted dollar means a hundred to reclaim it later.

"The Indians can become a race of degenerates — a poison in the stream of Canadian life — or, through wise leadership, we can take our place beside the whites — Indians who are independent, self-respecting, productive citizens of a great state. I long for that.

"I cannot believe that the fault has been all ours, an inherent 'cussedness.' I believe that with the right conditions, the majority of us would work willingly to achieve such ends, and work in unity with others. We have not progressed as we ought. It is natural for such a one as myself, who has failed, to make an attempt at self-excuse, to blame others. Yet I am not blind to the Indian's failings and his weaknesses. We are a difficult people to help.

"There have been times when I have been greatly discouraged, have thought it all deceptive. Then from such black discouragement, I would turn to hope and, as now, urge you to be strong and brave, to take your part in this struggle, to do your work as men."

Old Keyam's voice had risen with the passion of his words; then it dropped to a calmer pitch, and he waved his arm towards the women, where Chochena sat, her wrinkled face warm with pride. Instantly, she dropped her head, covering her face with her shawl, in the gesture of shyness that she had known since girlhood.

"I have spoken about this with Chochena," he went on, "and she has advised me to talk to you about the part that the Indians took in the Great War less than ten years ago — when the young men of our nation took their places equally and proudly with soldiers who were white.

"It may surprise you that Chochena knows about warriors. Some might say that she has been a warrior herself, for that scar that she bears is the scar of battle. It happened in one of the last encounters with the Blackfoot, when she was very small, just learning to walk and run. That was why she lived — because she was small enough to hide — but that day was so terrifying that she can never forget, even if there were no scar to remind her.

"The encounter was in the country near Fort Pitt, not far from the river, when the Crees were expecting no danger from the Blackfoot. It was berry-picking time, and the people had separated into small groups. A Blackfoot raiding party surprised one of these camps, and though a runner escaped to bring help, when other Crees arrived they found only Chochena alive. She had been wounded, but she hid in the bushes, and from that hiding place she had seen all her family killed, and many scalped. When she was found by the Crees, a woman took her as her own child and nursed her back to health, but — as Chochena puts it — she 'wandered for three days and nights in the spirit world.' I am educated, and I know that means that she was delirious. I think it may have been the whole experience that bred into her a war-like disposition, though she appears mild; that is why she said to me, 'Tell them about our men who fought in the Great War.'"

Keyam took from under his arm a tattered copy of an official report, and adjusted steel-rimmed spectacles on his nose. "This is the report of 1919 of the Department of Indian Affairs. It is written by the Deputy-Superintendent- General, Duncan Campbell Scott, who is one of Canada's poets. These are his words:

> In this year of peace, the Indians of Canada can look with just pride upon the part played by them in the Great War, both at home and on the field of battle. They have well and nobly upheld the loyal traditions of their gallant ancestors who rendered invaluable service to the British cause in 1776 and 1812, and have added thereto a heritage of deathless honour which is an example and an inspiration for their descendants.

"Let us not forget these words, my children." Keyam pointed to the report, holding it up before his audience. "They are something that we can prize. You say that all that is part of our tradition as warriors. It is true that in the days of the Blackfoot wars, the idea of meeting sudden death was always in our minds; we never lay down to sleep with any feeling of security; any night our enemy might surprise and attack us viciously, and we had to be on the watch always.

"Old Men have told me that in the long distant past the Blackfoot had control over much of the country, even as far as Fort Pitt, until they were driven back by the Cree; but how the quarrel between us arose is hidden in the darkness of that past from which no light penetrates to the present. We only know that there was deadly hatred between our tribes until the signing of the Treaty with the Crown in 1876; that no quarter, no mercy was either asked or given, that each of us was bent upon extermination of the other, and in the constant struggle became imbued with a martial spirit, developing strategy that I have been told has been adopted in modern warfare.

"The news of the outbreak of the Great War, however, fell with a shock upon us, seeming more terrible to us, perhaps because of our ignorance, than it did to the white people. Their knowledge of geography at least helped them to realize the distance Canada was from immediate danger. The Indians lacked that knowledge. I remember an Indian from a northern reserve telling me that he had heard that the fighting was taking place in Saskatchewan somewhere east of Battleford; another of the peaceably inclined Indians from the bush fled still farther north to regions unknown. Whether he ever stopped in his flight, I do not know to this day.

"In time, however, the Indians did understand. Our Old Men, who remembered the days of warfare, were opposed to our people taking part and did what they could to discourage it — not from disloyalty, but because it seemed against nature to them that an Indian should go to fight in a distant land and perhaps lay his body to mingle with earth that was not ours. It did not seem even England's quarrel, and much less Canada's. As they understood, England was helping other nations, and not fighting for her own life. 'If our land were attacked,' they said, 'then it would be up to every man to fight; but not in this way.' Their talk went unheeded. Youth is youth the world over.

"The official report says that more than four thousand Indians enlisted for active service with the Canadian Expeditionary Force. That is more than a third of the Indian male population of military age in the nine provinces, and there were undoubtedly some cases that were not reported to the Department. They gave an excellent record of themselves too, their officers speaking highly of their courage, intelligence, efficiency, stamina, and discipline.

"And all this means even more when we remember that Indians were specially exempted from the operation of the Military Service Act, and that they were prepared to give their lives for their country without compulsion or even the fear of compulsion. ...

"More than that, a large part of the Indian population is located in remote and inaccessible places, is unacquainted with the English language, and could not understand the war, its cause or effect; yet the percentage of enlistment is equal to that in other sections of the community, and far above the average in a number of instances.

"That large enlistment, and the Indian share in the thick of the fighting, brought heavy casualties. In common with our countrymen of the white race, we mourn the loss of many of our most promising young men."

Keyam peered over his spectacles. "That's all right here, and based on hard dry facts. Let me take a few more points from the rest of the report:

"I think that the battalion that interests us most in the west is the 107th, which was commanded by Lieutenant-Colonel Glen Campbell of Winnipeg, who had formerly been chief-inspector of Indian Agencies. There were more than five hundred Indians on the roll of his battalion — Crees, Saulteaux, Sioux, Mohawks, Onandagas, Tuscaroras, Delawares, Chippewas, and Micmacs. The Indian Company distinguished itself under heavy fire during the terrific bombardment of Hill 70 near Lens.

"The fever of war took hold of Indians everywhere. John Campbell, a full-blooded Indian, who lived on the Arctic coast, travelled three thousand miles by trail, by canoe, and by river steamer, to enlist at Vancouver.

"It is not surprising that the Indians proved to be expert marksmen, and that they distinguished themselves as snipers. It is said that they did much towards demoralizing the entire enemy system of sniping, for they showed extraordinary patience and self-control, and would wait for hours for the appearance of an enemy sniper, locating whole nests of sharp-shooters sometimes and then losing their own lives. Johnny Ballantyne, of Battleford, and his brother were both snipers who recorded their individual prowess in the time-honoured way, notching their rifles for each recorded hit. Johnny injured his knee in a football game and was sent back to Canada, but re-enlisted. His brother carries a piece of German shrapnel in him near his heart.

"Deeds other than sniping are recorded too. Johnson Paudash of Ontario saved lives under heavy fire and brought back information that saved a strategic point. Sergeant Clearsky crawled to a wounded man in no-man's land, during a gas attack, and gave him his own mask, almost losing his life.

"Name almost any reserve, and its men were there. One small band that had only eight men, sent seven. The eighth was a man of over seventy, and the Army would not take him. At File Hills Reserve, there were thirty-eight men, and twenty-four enlisted. The Cote band at old Fort Pelly sent twenty-two out of forty-three.

"This was not all that the Indians did. They gave generously to the war effort in money too, making a total of more than forty-four thousand dollars; they would have given more but the Department ruled against it. Our Indians in Saskatchewan gave over seventeen thousand dollars, while our women formed Red Cross Societies and patriotic leagues, made bandages, knit sweaters and mufflers, raised money with the sale of basketwork and beadwork.

"Is more proof needed of what we can do when we are roused? This should make the white people realize that we have made progress, that some of us have grown almost to the stature of manhood, that we have that in our nation which can be of value to this country."

Keyam stopped for a moment to unfold another newspaper clipping, and when he spoke again the sharp edge had left his voice. There was calm assurance once more, a note almost of authority.

"Here is something more that you should know from this long report. Mr. Scott makes a recommendation that is disturbing to some of us. He says: 'I think that it would be to the interest of good administration if the provisions with regard to enfranchisement were further extended so as to enable the Department to enfranchise individual Indians or bands of Indians, without the necessity of obtaining their consent thereto, in cases where it is found upon investigation that the continuance of wardship is no longer in the interest of the public or of the Indian.'

"It is that phrase 'without the necessity of obtaining their consent' that is meeting with opposition among eastern Indians, though we have not been too concerned about it yet in the West. The Indians in the East believe that better educational facilities are more important than enfranchisement at this time; they also fear that it could mean the disintegration of the Indian nation. Without that compulsory element, however, enfranchisement would be much more acceptable.

"The Indian feels that he has proven that he can do a man's work. He will never again be content to stand aside like a child, with no voice whatsoever in matters that affect him. The spirit of unrest has taken hold of him, has stirred up in him desires that he never dared to express before. He chafes under the conditions that render him dumb before the public.

"From the Atlantic to the Pacific, there is a feeling of brotherhood among the Indians, a desire for union. Tribes far apart, once unknown to each other, now correspond or exchange opinions. A League has been formed,[49] and reserves all across Canada are joining. It is the first such organization of Indians in Canada; it is a sign that we are thinking of being more than silent dependents, that we are ready to give expression to our newly-stirred consciousness of nationhood. The part that we took in the war proved that we had reached a stage of development that should allow us some freedom in the management of our own affairs.

"This viewpoint is indicated, though not directly stated, in the report of the Deputy-Superintendent, for the year ending March, 1921, which appeared in the newspapers. Mr. Scott says: 'The Indian population appears to be fairly stable at about 100,000. They are becoming better agriculturalists.' He gives many figures to support this statement, and then continues: 'The Indian has justified the trust placed in him. His mentality and temperament and constitution fitted him for progress. ... Although there are reactionary elements among the better-educated tribes, and stubborn paganism even on progressive reserves, the irresistible movement is towards the goal of complete citizenship.'

"I would add this to the Deputy-Superintendent's words. It is not in the least surprising that the Indian should seek some form of self-expression. A time comes in a child's life when he begins to ask the reasons for the actions of his father; a time comes when he wants to know the 'why' of things. That may be a source of trouble and annoyance to the father, but not if he is wise, for he will know that it is in the nature of development and should be welcomed; he will do his best to guide this newly acquired curiosity. To check it is to hinder natural development.

"I hope that the Department will encourage what Mr. Scott has described as 'the irresistible movement towards the goal of complete citizenship.' The formation of the League of Indians of Canada is an expression of that movement; surely to encourage it is better than trying to help people who have no ambition, people who are content to live generation after generation with no interest or aspiration beyond the borders of their reservation.

"It was a Mohawk Indian who drew up the principles of the organization. He had been a lieutenant in the Canadian Expeditionary Force, who had the opportunity to talk to many Indians from all over Canada, and he saw the need for some medium through which the scattered tribes might be unified, with the view to securing a representative Indian opinion and some unity of action.

"The principal aim of the League, I would say, is equality for the Indian as citizen — equality, that is, in the two-fold meaning of privilege and responsibility; and to achieve this objective, our first emphasis must be upon improved educational and health programs.

"I was one of the large delegation that went from Saskatchewan to the meeting that was called at Sault Ste. Marie in September, 1919; I served on the committee that drew up a list of aims, setting forth the issues that concern us most, wherever we live in Canada. Those issues were discussed again at a meeting in June, 1920, in Elphinstone, Manitoba, for the Indians of that province and western Ontario, and at our own provincial meeting the same year.

"I don't suppose that every delegate would agree with what I say are the principal aims. That is why the list we drew up had to be a long one. And perhaps everyone would not agree with me again when I say that those who hold office in the League should make every effort to win the confidence and support of the Indian Department. I am not certain that the Indian Act in itself was unjust to the Indian as he then was, but things have changed. In one way or another, we have earned the right to have some say in the management of reserve affairs, in the disposal of proceeds from our own work. More particularly, the Indians of Canada should have a voice in the character of legislation that is passed in Parliament when it concerns ourselves, for that is the privilege of all under our flag — personal freedom.

"As an Indian, I am in sympathy with the idea of the League, not so much for what it is now, as for what it means. At last I see what I have always wanted to see — the Indians dissatisfied with themselves, hoping to better their condition, dropping that stoic indifference to their fate, showing practical interest in measures that affect their progress. ... For too long, we might have deserved — all of us together — the name 'Keyam'."

8.

Keyam knew that the discussion that had followed his talk that night had been good; the interest of the people in the work of the League had cheered him. He was in fine fettle when a request came from the Department for his services as interpreter at a conference on Indian education.

That so few of those responsible for education could speak or understand Cree was usually a cause for regret to him, but not when he was needed for the important service of translation. He knew that some of the Indian delegates found it most difficult to follow any involved discussion in English, and that all of them preferred to speak in their own language. With an interpreter of ability, they had the advantage of hearing the arguments twice, with time to marshal their own thoughts, and then express them readily in Cree. Keyam knew that he had that ability as translator, and he enjoyed demonstrating his skill

The experience gave him material for many talks, but it gave him also the diversion of attending the Fair with Chochena. The conference took place in a city about seventy miles from the reserve, and it immediately preceded the Fair, to which the Indians were always invited, with special camping privileges at the grounds. For years, Keyam had refused to attend, resenting the role that his people were expected to play in the eyes of curious spectators, sensitive to offence, however unintentional.

This time he decided that he would enter fully into the part, if for nothing else than the wry amusement it could bring him. Chochena had agreed to go with him, after much cajoling and reassurance, and it was her presence that restored simple happiness to Fair time. Usually those two or three paces behind him, she followed him with awe both for his masterful assurance and for the marvels to which he guided her, trepidation changing to an almost bemused state, until she was as enchanted as a child.

All winter long they would rehearse the wonders of the Fair, but that would be for their private entertainment. Old Keyam was well aware that many of the Indians attended year after year. His talks would deal with more serious matters, leading those others to believe, if that were possible, that for Old Keyam it was the meetings on education that had been the high point of the week.

When the people met to hear his report on the conference, he began with great cheerfulness. "Here we are again, my old woman and I. Being family people, as I like to think, we are naturally interested in any subject that has to do with the welfare of children. Chochena has become as keen as I am about schools, and she came to every meeting of that conference with me. I insisted on translating everything that was said in English into Cree, and that was not for her sake only. There were others there who understood Cree better than English, though she may have been the only one who spoke only Cree. At meetings that were called to discuss the education of Indians, I thought it was more important to translate from English into Cree, than to translate from Cree into English for the benefit of those who could not understand our fine language. Still, I did not fail to do that as well.

"I am sure that Chochena might repeat word for word everything that was said; she gave such close attention, and we have discussed it together many times. We are not in complete agreement, however. She agrees with the Chief who proposed that each reserve should pay something each year to the financing of schools; sometimes she has almost convinced me. His motion was defeated, although he spoke well. I think that the strongest argument against his suggestion is simply that it is many years too soon for that.

"The Chief who spoke in opposition was another fine speaker — a credit to us all. Now, I am not naming these Chiefs on purpose. It is not that I have forgotten their names, for I knew many of them before I went to the meetings. It is because I cannot mention all who spoke well, and review all their arguments; I would not slight any of those who represented our people at that conference. We can be proud of them. It is not easy to take the stand that some of them did, and to speak boldly.

"The Chief whom I support said that it was one of the principles of the Treaty that the Crown should be responsible for the education of the Indian — that that is part of the integrity of the Treaty. I agree, because it is important to hold to the Treaty, and we should not accept any divergence that is not in the spirit of that Treaty as we believe it was understood by the Chiefs who signed it.

"I am more than ever convinced that the foundation of progress, whether amongst Indians or other people, lies in the schools. The teacher who is of the right spirit and character can strengthen the very roots of nation-building. The clergy are not able to do this, for the hours of instruction of Sunday are too brief, and they have never been able to reach out to the entire adult population. A teacher instructs the children five days of the week, and they are the young of the nation, the rising generation. If the adults are to be affected, the time and place is with the young now.

"One of the aims stated by the League of Indians of Canada is the provision of 'improved facilities for the education of Indian children...the securing of qualified teachers'; and it urges that 'the prevailing school curriculum of the respective provinces be available for use in Indian schools.'

"The amendment to the Indian Act provides for compulsory education for the Indians. Some of us objected to that, some were thankful, but many more held that this could make no difference to the old state of affairs. When day-schools are closed for poor attendance, it is the Indians who are saddled with the blame. But were those schools operated by qualified teachers? If they were, then it is an open matter to blame the Indians. If not, then the Indians cannot be blamed for becoming indifferent to the attendance of their children.

"I — I, Keyam — was once an Indian Department school teacher. More than that, I received good reports. Well — I state here and now — for the life of me, I cannot understand why I was praised or commended in the slightest. No teacher could have been less qualified than I. No! No! Let us have no more Keyams in our schools, if the Indian is to make progress. The world around us is too far advanced for any such playing at education. Either close all our schools and let the children help at home and on the farms, or else supply properly qualified teachers.

"There are people who have come as immigrants to this land, who in their communities have no respect for the national life of Canada, who would in fact destroy it, and, during the dark days of its recent troubles, did all they could to embarrass the country. Yet the cry is to supply them with the best of educational facilities. That is a sound, protective policy, and it is worthy of our nation to try to make good citizens of these people. But, while these people are supplied with the best of teachers, is it justice that the weak Indian nation, which gave of its life blood to prove its loyalty, should have to be satisfied with teachers who seldom have any qualifications to teach? Is it because these others pay the school tax? The Indian has paid more than any school tax. The Treaty stands as witness to that.

"Schools, in the modern sense of that word, must have properly qualified teachers. If that is not so, then you may call the building in which the children congregate by any name you choose, but it is not a school.

"I get carried away by my own feelings, for this is a matter of life and death to us. Yet there is no need for me to speak loudly. I cannot hope to be heard beyond this gathering.

"I have seen the newly appointed Dominion Inspector of Indian Schools, and he seems to be a wide-awake young man. I may be no judge, but I think well of him. It is a newly created office, however, and if I were the kind of person who could meet him on equal terms, there are questions I would ask.[50]

"I think that I would ask first of all if he believes that Church schools have ever been truly successful, when he considers our record. Does their merit amongst us not lie solely in the fact that they voluntarily undertook work that no one else was willing to do?

"I wonder if he might not agree that the immediate and complete removal from the Church of all responsibility for Indian schools would be in the best interests of our children?

"Might it not be possible then to establish any boarding schools in cities, where our children could have the advantages offered in classroom and playground?

"And does he recognize that, in all the work of the Department of Indian Affairs, his particular responsibility in the field of education has the greatest possibilities?

"To bring that home to all of us, would he consider placing the education of our children where responsibility for the education of white children now rests: with the provincial governments — the Dominion Government subsidizing each province in proportion to its Indian population? If each reserve was a school district, and the teachers properly qualified, regular school attendance would be generally accepted at the local level, and the question of Ottawa's ruling in compulsory education would not need to be discussed and approved, or held in abeyance for Indian children, as it is now.

"Finally, I would ask the new Inspector of Indian schools for Canada if it would not be to the economic advantage of each province, in any case, with or without the subsidy from Indian Affairs, to undertake the education of all its children and so raise the productive level of its citizens?

"Perhaps I expect too much, for problems are seldom easily resolved; but I speak from our point of view, as an Indian — and that has its limitations, heaven knows."

9.

In the long summer evenings, when the weather was fine, Keyam often wandered to the sports grounds, to find an audience or to watch a football game (soccer). The field was in front of the farm instructor's house, near the centre of the reserve, and the young men would ride in from all directions to begin practising even before full teams were assembled. The older men came to sit in a group against the fence, talking and smoking.

Old Keyam smoked his pipe as contentedly as any of them, and rejoiced that he could still feel the twitch in his own toes when the ball soared, still recall the excitement of the games that he had played. It was white men who had taught them football, but the Indians had made the game their own, and these young men were good players indeed, making every effort to play as a team, resisting the strong desire for individual display — all except one whom he noticed — a tall slim fellow who raced about the field, shouldering others away, kicking the ball great distances, stopping often as though to make sure that his achievements were recognized. It seemed to Keyam that for all the display he was the least useful member of the team — and that here there was an example to support other ideas too.

"That young *Na-pwa-in*," he began, knowing that the others had been watching too, "he's the product of a boarding school — all show — speaks English like the preacher, writes a better hand than the Agent, figures like a Hudson's Bay Company clerk, knows a little about many things — and can't even play football unless there's someone right there to direct him and make him listen.

"I've watched men crank a car to make it start. They tell me that the new cars start without a crank, that something inside turns the engine, and the car goes. *Na-pwa-in* is not like that. He is not a self-starter. He needs a crank that will start him, and perhaps another to keep him going.

"Yet he knows how to do things. He can plough, he can harness a team of horses, he can run a mower, he can do anything that an ordinary farmer needs to do. He has a school diploma that says that, and another for being proficient in drill. But still he does not seem able to go. He stalls like those cars. The boarding school has taken from him all the initiative there may be in an Indian. He will work only when he feels like it. He will never take advice from his elders amongst us.

"Look at our other boys. They cannot talk as good English as he can, but they do speak it. They do not write with fine curves, but they write a readable hand. They cannot reckon the circumference of the earth, but they can measure the acres in their fields, figure the price of their grain at so much a bushel. They went to the day-school on this reserve, and every day of their lives they use whatever they learned there.

"Knowledge that is not used is abused. *Na-pwa-in* has become a useless fellow. If he had stayed on the reserve, he might have been as useful as his brother who stayed at home. The more I think about the education of the Indians, the more I think that it is wrong to take them away to make something like white men of them. You find such on every reserve.

"I've read about the colony at File Hills, made up of graduates from boarding school. They are said to be doing well. I have boasted about them myself when I had nothing better to do. But they are under the guidance of an official who has more authority than most, and he is an able man whose authority these young people accept in the way to which they became accustomed in boarding school. He is the 'crank' that makes the machine start and go. I do not think that if he were asked to do the same thing again, that he would be willing. That colony is a tribute to his own ability and to his strong desire to improve the Indian, but I do not believe that it is a natural development. It would not suit all Indians, nor is it necessarily an argument for boarding schools. I think that if those colonists had been hand-picked in the same way from day-schools, to work under the same guidance, there would have been the same success.

"This is what I ask: is it wiser to take an Indian boy away to civilization, or to bring civilization to him where he is in his natural surroundings? Civilization, I mean, as represented in education and training.

"A few years ago, you will remember, our minister went to the muskeg and brought back some young spruce trees that he planted in the light prairie soil along the fence at his house. He thought that they would grow tall and straight. All of them died, except one, though he tended them carefully. And that one is short and crooked. It is surprising perhaps that it lived at all. Yet the spruce trees in the muskeg from among which he chose those young ones are tall and straight. That is nature, which has had a million years to find its pattern, and will not be changed from its course by any passing thing.

"That is my parable. Human beings may adapt more readily than a tree, but something still happens to an Indian child when he is taken from his own life to another where he is caged within bounds and made to go through a sweating process. During the years when I worked, I came to know three boarding schools. These were no worse than their kind. I think they may have been better, for those in charge knew the Indians and they did their best.

"Now in a primitive society life expectancy can never be high; but the white men brought to us many diseases that have made us seem a dying race. Tuberculosis is everywhere amongst us, and in the past smallpox epidemics raged. These the white man dreads too, and has learned largely to control. There are others that he may regard less seriously — take even measles for instance, to which he is relatively immune. Any of these can be deadly to us, and particularly to our children.

"In boarding schools, the chances of infection are high; the life of strict barracks discipline, the thwarting of the most natural habits of the Indian child, the close confinement, the different food, the lack of outdoor life to which he has been accustomed through generations — all these serve to lower his vitality and make him still more susceptible, certainly to tuberculosis. Again and again I have seen children come home from boarding schools only to die, having lost during their time at school all the natural joys of association with their own families, victims of an educational policy, well-meant but not over-wise. Their parents' sense of loss, and their grief, I need not dwell upon here, nor use it to support my contention.

"As for those who do live, who survive and who graduate from the school at the age of eighteen, during every day of their training they have acted under orders. Nothing they did was without supervision. They did not sweep a floor, wash dishes, clean stables, without first being told to do so, and always there would be a member of the staff to show them each step. They never needed to use their own minds and wills. They came to think that it could be wrong if they went their own way. Now discipline and expediency in life are good, but will and initiative are better.

"Is this schooling the preparation for life and the fight that one must wage? It is but the making of machines. What are young Indians to do when they have no supervisor? They are like children, and when suddenly given their freedom they do not know how to use it. Their initiative is lost. They do not seem to know how to begin, and they lose heart quickly. This has been the story of most pupils when they leave these schools.

"To make matters worse, they have just enough learning to think themselves a plane above the rest of the band. They are not ready to take any advice from the older members, and though at first they are received joyfully, this feeling of superiority becomes evident and arouses ever sharper criticism. The young person is in a totally false position. He does not fit into the Indian life, nor does he find that he can associate with the whites. He is forced to act a part. He is now one thing, now another, and that alone can brand him as an erratic and unreliable fellow.

"His values too are false. He may glory in his football achievements, in his smart English, in his ability to adapt himself among whites; but he finds that these do not earn him a living. He is like a bird without tail-feathers in steering his course. He has had knowledge pumped into his head, but he has not the wisdom to use that knowledge in a practical way, nor the will and initiative to begin and to keep at one thing.

"Take *Na-pwa-in* again. He learned to milk cows that were not his, to plough land that was another's, to raise crops that brought no spending money to his pocket. True, there was payment in training, but not in the direct way that he could understand and see. To him, the work seemed to bring no reward; the pride of ownership was never his; he could never say, 'This is a fine heifer that I have, and if I care for her I shall have more in time.'

"That is all a mistake. The pride of ownership, the desire to improve and to develop what he has, should be encouraged in a boy while he is young. Things in school can come too easily for him. He never has a chance to learn that success in life is a matter of developing, of growing day by day. When he leaves school, he thinks that his diploma will in some way make life easy for him, and then he finds that it has no real value in itself.

"You may say that the boy in boarding school has the chance to learn more about the white people's world. That is not so. He comes to know only the members of the staff, and boarding school life has little contact with the world outside. His brother on the reserve may see more of that.

"Look now at young *Na-pwa-in*, wiping his face after all that racing about, while he sits on that fence dividing the farm instructor's grounds from ours. That is what he may be said to do all the time — sit on the fence between the whites and the Indians, belonging to neither, fitting into neither world. That is not his fault. He is the victim of a system that meant well. If he had never gone to that boarding school, he might be just a plain Indian, doing something useful now and again. You cannot make a white man out of an Indian. It is much better to make our children into good Indians, for we *are* Indians in our persons and in our thinking. Nature says that loud enough for all to hear, but the Indian's well-wishers do not listen."

Keyam stopped to fill his pipe again, and to assure himself that the attention of his audience was still his, before he went on.

"I would not say that there should be no boarding schools. In the north, where the Indians travel about their hunting grounds, the children need such schools. Even in this area, it might be well to have them for boys and girls at perhaps the age of fourteen — schools where they could learn more about farming, or train for some other vocation; where they could prepare to go to university. But for most Indian children, I hold that boarding schools are unnatural, that they are contrary to our whole way of life.

"The Treaty stated that a school should be given to a reserve at the request of the Chief and his band. This meant a day-school, and it could bring civilization to the reserve. The Indian cannot withstand a continued and heavy siege. He must give way. Now schools, if they are good schools, do bring civilization to besiege him.

"I know that in the past day-schools have had little success. The reason is as clear as the nose on a moose. They have never been given the chance to succeed. The teachers have been too often of the poorest type, and those who were good seldom stayed long, for they could always find more congenial work and higher pay elsewhere. The children made little progress in these day-schools; the hours were often irregular, the work unplanned, and the parents never insisted upon attendance. You could scarcely blame them, yet they are always blamed.

"Now, at last, the Department of Indian Affairs is beginning to provide properly qualified teachers, though many of them still lack the ability to rouse the parents' interest or to enlist the Agent's support. Yet, that can be done, and I have seen it proved in one school,[51] which had been closed as unsatisfactory, for a year or more. The missionary who sponsored the school and for a year paid the costs to prove his case, was a man of great ability and wisdom in Indian affairs. He found the right teacher and matron, and they won the support of the Indian Agent and of the reserve. The Chief, who is a young man, makes sure that the children are never absent without cause, and will accept no pleas from the parents. The Indians see the results even now, and they are doing their part.

"There has been indeed surprising progress in that school, and the Inspector says that. It can prove that day-schools that are properly run are the best way of dealing with the educational problem of the Indians. Not that it will ever be easy, but the way is now indicated — get the right people to handle the school and pay them a living wage in order to keep them, have the Agent back the school with all the resources of his position and personal force, give the Chief the authority that is really part of his office so that he can enforce attendance.

"The children will do the rest, for as they come into contact with the day to day life of the school and its teachings, they not only learn themselves, but they explain what they have learned to their interested parents at home. Even the required bath at home is a lesson in cleanliness for the whole family, and proper clothes for the child lead the others to dress properly too.

"It is true that there are local conditions on some reserves that can affect the success of the day-school, but the Indians are awakening to the value of education. Good schools are needed, good schools in our midst."

A sudden exclamation from those around him, a quick shifting of their attention brought Keyam just as swiftly to his feet — "Ah-hai!" he was the first to yell, "Let the game begin!"

10.

An Indian from another band wandered to their reserve that summer, visiting his relatives. He was a much disturbed man, and his story aroused so much feeling that the Chief called a meeting to hear the man give his own account of what was troubling him.

He told the people that during the winter he had narrowly escaped death while hunting, and to show his thankfulness to *Ma-ni-to* for his deliverance, he had vowed a solemn vow that when spring came he would "make" a Sun Dance. Even before the leaves appeared he had begun his preparations, inviting the people to come and pray with him. When the lodge had been erected and the dancers were ready, the police came to forbid the dance. That was the law they told the people, and serious trouble was averted only because the police were tactful, even sympathetic. But the man's vow remained unfulfilled and he was deeply troubled.

The Chief and others spoke of incidents of which they knew, though it had been many years since the last Sun Dance on their reserve. Nothing seemed to be resolved, or perhaps ever could be, and Old Keyam held his silence until the Chief asked him to speak.

"Like most of you," he reminded them, "I was brought up under Christian teaching and I have had little to do with any religious matters apart from that faith. Yet I believe that I am free of prejudice against any sincere form of belief that may be in the heart of my fellow man. I would never come between him and what he holds to be his God, except with kindly advice, carefully and prayerfully considered.

"I think that I should tell you the legend of the Sun Dance. I suppose that many of you know it, but these legends need to be told again and again if the Indian is not to forget them entirely. Legends of *We-sa-kā-cha'k* are not supposed to be told in summertime, but I am not superstitious, and besides we have no harmful snakes here, nor teepees into which they might crawl.

"This is how the legend of the Sun Dance goes:

"It seems that *We-sa-kā-cha'k* was walking along one day when he heard the sound of singing and the beating of drums. To appear at his best, he hurriedly painted his face with vermilion and arranged his garments to be as presentable as possible. Coming over the crest of a hill he looked down upon what seemed to be a great encampment, with a lodge of some kind in the centre.

"He approached with caution and stopped at a respectful distance to await as a stranger the offer of hospitality from one of the people; no one paid him the least attention, everyone moving eagerly about.

"*We-sa-kā-cha'k* was always curious, and he went on through the crowd, though he had to elbow his way at times. Finally he came to the lodge, and looked into it. On either side, he could see small booths, each one just large enough to hold one dancer, and from these booths, men and women advanced as soon as the singing began. They were dressed in their best garments, with beadwork and feathers, their faces painted with gay colours; they looked very fine to *We-sa-kā-cha'k*. He watched them as they danced solemnly to the singing and the drums, without leaping or any exaggerated steps, blowing little whistles as they moved. There was no evidence of mirth or frivolity. They were deeply serious.

"Between the two lines of booths, at the far end, there was a beautiful robe, and on it a painted buffalo skull. The singers were seated before this, a great drum in their midst. One who was evidently acting in a special capacity would pray at times, or would ask one of the Old Men to pray. They expressed in eloquent words their prayers to *Ma-ni-to* for health and peace and for love towards their fellow men. They prayed above all for rain to refresh the land, to bring to life again what had lain dormant all winter, that there might be plenty for man and beast. And all these needs, they presented earnestly and humbly in general intercessory prayer.

"*We-sa-kā-cha'k* was most interested. He pushed his head farther into the entrance so that he could see better, and he became so absorbed that gradually the chanting lulled him and he fell asleep in that position.

"Under the spell of the dancing and the drums it had all seemed sublime to him; when he wakened, it was only absurd. He found that it was not a dance-lodge into which he had thrust his head, but an old buffalo skull, and that those who had appeared as human dancers were in reality ants that had made their home in and around the old skull.

"Added to his humiliation there was pain, for the ants had bitten his face and it was too swollen to withdraw from the buffalo skull. He had to leave with the skull over his own head, and his appearance was so alarming that man and beast fled at his approach, and no one would stay to help him. All the while the ants continued their feast, and his state became more and more pitiful. Then a great thunderstorm broke, a flash of lightning struck a tree beside him, and *We-sa-kā-cha'k* was thrown violently to the ground. It was a mishap that proved fortunate, for he fell against a stone that smashed the buffalo skull into fragments. He was free.

"In relief and satisfaction, *We-sa-kā-cha'k* stayed where he had fallen, pondering the misfortune, until a moment of insight brought him to his feet in awe. 'I know,' he declared, 'that the *Ma-ni-to* does not perform such deeds without meaning. He hears the smallest bird cry; he hears the prayers of man when he goes on the chase. This vision requires some form of worship.

"'What I believed I witnessed was a dance in honour of *Ma-ni-to*, and for the purpose of asking blessing to meet the needs of man and beast. I saw the leaves, and they were young and green; I saw the dancers in their booths, the painted skull, the singers, and the leaders of the dance; and as I saw it, let the ceremony be.

"'The Thunderbird with his flash of lightning released me from my predicament. It is by his agency as the ruler of the air, that *Ma-ni-to* waters the earth, in response to man's appeal. Only rain then can slacken the thirst of those who dance, as a sign of faith that the *Ma-ni-to* will send rain in response to prayer.

"'I suffered distress, though it was not from a dangerous source. So must man sustain trials to open himself to the store of mercy that is in *Ma-ni-to*. In days to come, when the earth is well-peopled, at the time of year when the leaves are first out, let mankind as a whole perform this great act of prayer, the dance that shall be known as *Nē-pa-kwā-se-mo-win*.' (All-night-thirst-dance.)

"This is our legendary story to show the origin and meaning of the religious dance against which the white man has set his law. I am not criticizing the motives of those who made this law, nor those whose influence brought that about, but I do not think it altogether wise.

94

"One of the reasons given for the law is the self-torture that was inflicted in the dance, and which was mis-named 'the making of a brave.' This was practised to some extent long ago, more in the Blackfoot confederacy than amongst the Cree, but its aim was to bring down the compassion of *Ma-ni-to* and to mortify the flesh to subdue it to his will.

"This desire is common to the religions of all races. I have heard of such mortification of the flesh among Christians — of a man, for instance, who vowed to roll a pebble with his nose from France to Palestine, as an outward sign of penitence, seeking spiritual grace; of other holy men who dressed themselves in sackcloth and endured filth and vermin to prove the reality of their spiritual purity.

"As for the charge that the Sun Dance is a 'give-away' dance — from the economic point of view, I admit that such a ceremony may not be wise; but as a part of a religious act, giving in order that the poor and the destitute may have, then it is in line with the offerings taken for the poor, for the widows and orphans, in the churches of the Christian world.

"To my mind, the strongest objection to the Sun Dance is the time wasted by the Indians who often go to other reserves to take part in these rites, when they might be far better employed doing their work at home. And yet every year other Indians go on long pilgrimages to Roman Catholic shrines; they too leave their work, and no one can convince them that they do not receive benefits that more than balance whatever may be their material loss in being absent from their work and homes. Certainly, the worthy fathers of that Church would object strongly if their adherents were told that they might have to serve time in jail for going on a pilgrimage to Lac Ste. Anne or some other shrine. I am not saying that the two religions are on the same plane, but to the Indian who takes part in the Sun Dance it is as real as the pilgrimage is to his fellow Indian.

"Freedom to worship as one's conscience dictates is a British principle. I do not believe that the law against the Sun Dance is so wise or so necessary as to warrant the contradiction of that principle. If its aim is to make Christians out of all Indians, that is absurd, for that cannot be forced. Legislation that would suppress the Sun Dance is only keeping alive what would almost certainly die a natural death in a few years if left to itself. The ministry of the Christian Church must be one of love, of sympathy, of understanding, of tolerance where that is necessary, and of wisdom. Representing the Government, the Indian Agent should be equally understanding, not acting more strictly than the law warrants when he passes judgment under that law.

"This man who has come to us in his trouble belongs to a group of Indians who are still in the grip of the past. They have not the power nor the will to rid themselves of superstition. But that will pass. Is it right to put down by law that act of worship on his part, imperfect as it may be, when it is one which is free of any vice, and one that has guided the Indian in his relation to his God through countless years? Why should individuals be forced to give up what they consider to be a means of reconciliation with the author of their being?

"In my own heart, I long for the day when the Christian Church will be strong on every reserve, and when in the hearts of all Indians the homage to the Supreme Being will take no other form than that given to us by the Saviour; I believe that through the influence of Christian work these other forms of worship now legislated against will pass of their own accord into oblivion.

"This is a time of trouble for the Indian that will not end in my life-time nor during the lives of the youngest here. It is a time of change, when all that made our lives secure is going from us, and we have not yet learned the new ways, nor can we understand why these things should be.

"Once we depended upon medicine-men and conjurors to cure our sickness of body or of mind. Now some of us know that they deceived themselves and us; others still cling to those old beliefs. I think that often the Indian, groping in his darkness, found what the white man is compelled to scoff at because it does not always fall within reason.

"That is how it is with conjuring — and I say 'is' because the art still persists on some reserves. I shall tell you two stories, one that was told to me by the Old Man who witnessed it, and another that is much older, for it happened to that Old Man's father, to *Ah-tah-ka-koop* (Chief Starblanket) in the days long before he signed the Treaty at Fort Carlton in 1876.

"Now *Ah-tah-ka-koop's* son, Basil Starblanket, was a strong hard-headed man, a stalwart defender of the Christian religion. He was visiting a heathen reserve when he learned that a certain Old Man was going to conjure, to find out what had happened to a young man who had disappeared a few days before that. Starblanket knew about the ceremony of 'the shaking of the lodge,' the conjuring up of spirits, and he thought that this would be an opportunity to prove to himself and to all the others that there was nothing in it.

"He offered to help those who were building the conjuring tent, and was given the job of supervising. The men brought about twenty young trees, strong ones, yet slender enough to bend without breaking. They marked out a circle, and at intervals of two to three feet around this, they dug deep holes for the trees to stand in, digging not straight down but at an angle so that the trees would slant out from the centre. Then they placed the trees and packed earth solidly around each one. One tree they placed upright at the centre of the circle, and it was stronger than the others, which they bent in and lashed to this centre pole.

"The structure was firm and none of the men could move it, but Starblanket was not satisfied and he called for lariats of *shagganappi*, strong twisted rawhide, to tie from the centre pole to pegs driven into the ground outside and around the circle. Not until then was he convinced that no human force could move what had been so strongly erected. He watched while the men tied a bell to the centre pole and threw tenting over the whole structure.

"The conjuror had been bound securely too, even his fingers laced with thongs. It seemed to the men that it would not be possible for him to free himself for a long time, if at all. They placed him within the structure and closed the opening. No one else went in, and the men stood around the tent.

"First, the conjuror chanted a song that he said the spirits had taught him; then other noises were heard, and the bell high on that centre pole began to tinkle. Suddenly the ropes that had bound the conjuror were thrown out, in a bundle, the knots intact; while the people watched in awed silence, the conjuror walked out of the tent. He told the relatives of the young man who was supposedly lost that there was no cause for concern, that the young man was simply visiting at another camp. This turned out to be true.

"Basil Starblanket said that the poles were loosened, the holes in which they stood so enlarged that the whole structure leaned. He asked, 'How can you explain that? The Old Man was alone in the tent, and we all stood at a respectful distance. Yet I saw what happened, with my own eyes.'

"The other story happened in the long ago days when the fur-brigades from the Churchill would come by Frog Portage to join the Saskatchewan boats at Cumberland House, and continue the long journey to Fort York on Hudson Bay.[52] *Ah-tah-ka-koop* was in charge of one of these boats.

"Now there was an Old Man at the Bay, well-known to the Indians of that area and greatly disliked, and feared as well, because he was strong in spirit help. When the ships from England came to Fort York, no other Indian dared to buy rum until the Old Man had his keg. *Ah-tah-ka-koop* did not know of this custom, and when the others saw him bringing his keg of rum to his camp they were amazed at his hardihood. 'The Old Man will never forgive you, and he can harm you,' they warned him. 'If you have any spirit help that you can trust, make ready for him!'

"*Ah-tah-ka-koop* waited in his camp, and when the Old Man came he said courteously to him, '*Ta-waw* — there is room,' and motioned to a place in the tent. But the Old Man would not enter, and said angrily, 'I see that you have a keg of rum. It is the custom here that I get the first keg.' *Ah-tah-ka-koop* was always a peaceable man, and he answered calmly that he had not known of the custom, and offered him a drink. The Old Man refused. 'I have come only to warn you. Take care of yourself.' And he walked away.

"He returned late that night however, and he was drunk. He began to mock the prairie Indians, insulting *Ah-tah-ka-koop* who was their fur Chief. *Ah-tah-ka-koop* told him to leave, and when he would not, *Ah-tah-ka-koop* seized a smouldering stick from the fire and struck him across the head with it, and left him lying stunned on the ground. When morning came, the Old Man was gone.

"As the York boats were leaving with trade goods for the inland posts, *Ah-tah-ka-koop* received a message, 'Watch yourself. I have not forgotten.' He knew what that could mean, and he said to his men, 'Be ready to obey me at once, whenever I give the warning.'

"The long hard journey began; work for strong men only, poling those heavy boats up river, tracking them over rapids, carrying packs by long portages. Then one day, *Ah-tah-ka-koop* knew that the moment of danger had come, and the men pulled at their oars, tense with waiting. 'Down,' he shouted suddenly, and as they fell forward, something whirled over their heads to stick quivering in the mast. It was a hatchet, daubed with red. 'Take it, anyone who needs an axe,' the Chief said. 'It is no longer dangerous. But he will try again, for he knows that he has failed this time.'

"Days later, *Ah-tah-ka-koop* had the same foreboding, and gave the same warning. When he shouted, "*Ta-pā-cheek!*' the men dropped, and this time it was a knife, daubed again with red, that flashed past their heads and stuck in the mast. One of the men took it and sheathed it. 'He will try again, but not in the same way,' *Ah-tah-ka-koop* warned.

"They came at last to Lake Winnipeg, and could sail the heavy boat; but the waters became suddenly rough when they were far from the shore, and the Chief knew that his enemy had contact with the spirit of the wind. Now, *Ah-tah-ka-koop* was high in the secret society of medicine-men,[53] but he had never had this power. 'We are done for,' he said to his men, 'unless there is one of you who has the protection of the spirit who rules the wind.'

"Then a great Swampy Cree, whose name was *O-mu-skā-ko*, said, 'I shall try.' And he sang a song and chanted words that the others could not understand. After a few minutes, he told them that all would be well, and the force of the wind did abate. They were saved once more. 'That was the Old Man's last try,' *Ah-tah-ka-koop* said. 'The curse that he tried to put upon us will go back now upon himself.'

"The next year when they made that long journey again to York Factory, the Bay Indians greeted *Ah-tah-ka-koop* with joy. 'You have defeated him, friend,' they shouted. 'He is only skin and bones and must soon die.' Before *Ah-tah-ka-koop's* men had finished making camp, the Old Man's messenger came, imploring the Chief to restore his health, offering him packs of goods as peace offerings. But *Ah-tah-ka-koop*, so the story goes, answered, 'I can do nothing for him. His spirit has already gone from him, and the body must die soon.' And that is what happened, and the Indians of the Bay rejoiced, for they had been too long enslaved by an Old Man who used the spirit power in a way that was wrong.''

Keyam waited for a moment before continuing. ''I tell you these things that you may remember how our people once thought; I do not try to explain them. We who have gone to school know that such things are not always as they appear, but there are still Indians who believe as in the past our fathers believed.

''One of the greatest forces in maintaining this ignorance has been the influence of the medicine-men, particularly the one who professes the miraculous skill of conjuring. By song and dance, he tries to prevail upon some spirit to cast its influence in a healing way on the sick person; he sings and blows his breath of life on the unfortunate one, shaking his rattle all the while. His art is a combination of religion and medicine, and faith in him still persists on many reserves. In days when the Indian was strong in body, ignorance and such primitive ways of doctoring may not have harmed many, but they do today. Perhaps when the troubles were of the mind, these conjurors and medicine-men did help; some of them were skilled in herbs and could cure wounds and certain sicknesses of the body. Now most Indians turn to doctors and nurses for such help, and the power of the medicine-man is passing.

''There are other habits from our past that do us more general harm and that undermine the health of the Indian. In the old days, the Indian's outdoor life gave him pure air to breathe. He was always moving to fresh camping grounds, and dirt and refuse could not contaminate his dwelling place and the ground around it. His clothing too was simple, and easily renewed. Now, he has adopted the white man's clothing, without his cleanliness; he cannot move his dwelling, but he disregards sanitary ways; he eats food that is most readily procured and prepared, and it is seldom the best for his health's sake.

''Then there are diseases that the white man brought amongst us. For the dreadful scourge of smallpox, we have accepted vaccination with thankfulness; the cure for tuberculosis is harder and longer, while typhoid and even worse communicable diseases find their breeding ground in our living conditions. Our ignorance of the simplest rules of health has made all these a menace to life on the reserves; the factors that worked for our well-being formerly were the natural accompaniments of a free life, not the deliberate precautions that we must now take.

''The settled life imposed upon the Indian demands a complete change of habits. He has exchanged the teepee for a shanty of logs, mud-chinked, badly ventilated, poorly lighted, and over-crowded. He has lost his freedom to roam, and never thinks to remove the refuse that collects about his dwelling. Over-crowded conditions discourage any cleanliness; ignorance contributes to his children's malnourishment. The old life developed gregarious customs. Now on reserves, two or three families will often crowd into a dwelling not large enough for one family, sleeping and eating in the same room, keeping the door and the windows shut against the cold.

''When constant danger menaced us from every side we accepted the uncertainty of life with a stoic fatalism that carries over now into our disregard for the simplest rules of health. I have seen a consumptive person dying on a shake-down on the floor, the can into which he spat emptied just outside the door, and flies swarming everywhere. I remember a typhoid case where the patient would have recovered had he not been given a hearty meal of meat. But to me, the saddest of all deaths are those of small children and infants, where ignorance has been the murderer; the saddest of all sounds the lament of an Indian mother for her child. It has a wailing tune and the words accord, but both are the spontaneous outcry of human anguish, the cry of the race.

''I cannot believe that ignorance is without hope. I have seen the change that can come on a reserve, under the wise direction of a field matron, a trained nurse who went about her work with sympathy and assurance, kind but firm. The Indians must be educated to work faithfully with those who mean well, instead of working against them. Appropriate means must be taken to help us see the fallacy of old ideas on one hand, and on the other the efficacy of the white man's methods in simple health principles. We must learn to do things for ourselves, intelligently, for we cannot afford to trifle with our health. We have a hard fight to wage before we are again a strong people.''

11.

The resentment that had been roused by the incident of the forbidden Sun Dance was relieved only slightly by Keyam's talk on regulations necessary for their welfare. He took the first opportunity to return to the subject.

"Many of you wonder if we ever had our own form of law, or any government beyond what could be imposed by the will of a Chief through the force of his own personality. You ask, have the Indians ever enforced regulations by the will of the people? The answer to that is 'Yes.' There were two strong laws that were fundamental to the well-being and safety of the band. The first, that no family should separate itself from the band without permission; the second, that no individual should begin a buffalo chase until all the hunters were ready.

"The effect of that first law is known to many of us in the story that Thunderchild told of his uncle *Ē-pay-as*, who was the nephew of *Mis-ta-wa-sis*. The reason for the law was that every hour was full of danger, and the enemy could attack at any time and place. When he secured a scalp, it was not simply an individual disaster, it was a tribal disgrace — a temporary defeat at least, that had to be avenged speedily, always with additional loss of life. So it was accepted that no family or small group of families should separate themselves from the band, for trouble too often came from that, and could involve many others.

"The second law also protected the band. Those who were able hunters looked after many, and were known as Providers. They took charge of the buffalo chase, in which great skill and daring were needed. It had to be carefully organized so that all who were good hunters could take part, and no one individual alarm the herd; for, when frightened, the buffalo were known to migrate to safer country, and the hunters and the band then would have to travel much farther, sometimes dangerously close to enemy territory. The law rose from necessity again, and the Indians consented in council to curb their individual freedom for the good of the band.

"To make certain, however, that the laws were enforced, there had to be something like a police system. The men who were appointed by the council of headmen, to enforce the common will of the people, were those whose courage had often been proved, and who had influence for that reason. They formed the society of Dancers, and the name *Ō-ke-che-ta-wuk* (Warriors or Heroes) was also used for them. There were different orders, the Buffaloes, the Wolves, and so on — each order having its peculiar ceremonial and dance, representing the characteristics of the animal after which it was named.

"In addition to enforcing these two laws, their duty was to preserve peace among the members of the tribe, to right all wrongs as far as possible, to lead in battle, and to prevent others deserting in times of danger. They ate dog meat in their feasts, and they were both feared and respected, their authority being seldom questioned.

"Should an Indian break one of the two laws, the leading Warriors would summon the others of the society, and they would destroy that person's belongings and kill his dogs.

When the law-breaker submitted and showed by his behaviour afterwards that he was repentant, a time would come when the Warriors would assemble again, and from their own possessions make up the equivalent of what had been destroyed, or give even more to the man whom they had first punished.

"These were laws made by the Indians and obeyed by the Indians. When they infringed upon the liberty of the individual, he knew that it was for the good of the tribe or the band. The laws that we must now obey are made by the white man and enforced by his police; as well there are all the regulations of the Department of Indian Affairs, which are enforced by the Agent. Many of these are even harder to understand. Here is an example. I am an old man and these regulations no longer affect me much, but I read this in the paper a few days ago and I showed it to Angus Bird. I think we would all agree that he is one of the most progressive and hardworking fellows to be found on any Indian reserve. Well, he laughed when he read this. He did not say what it was that made him laugh, but perhaps you will know when I read it. It is from one of the high officials in the Department, and it says: 'A kindly supervision over sale of the Indian's produce is exercised by the Department in order to insure his getting a fair deal.'

"This 'kindly' supervision is the 'permit system.' I think that word 'supervision' in English implies a kind of higher vision on the part of the supervisor. That is why it is hard for the Indian to accept. I can admit the need for the permit system in a general way, and that it would be foolish for any thinking Indian to want it entirely abolished. It is a protection, and it shows that the Department is determined that its wards receive fair play from those who might be disposed towards taking advantage of them. We must not be blind to that. Many Indians do need this supervision or they would sell everything that they have.

"Certain abuses, however, make it most offensive. Such a regulation need not be applied to every case, or it does great harm. How far the Agent is allowed to use his own judgment, I do not know, nor have I any way of knowing. Perhaps the Indian is not given his rights when the Agent likes to feel important. But the fact is that every man on the reserve must go begging for a permit every time he wants to sell even a load of hay.

"This may be 'kindly supervision,' but it is most wretchedly humbling to many a worthy fellow to have to go, with assumed indifference, to ask or beg for a permit to sell one load of hay that he has cut himself, on his own reserve, with his own horses and implements. I say again, it may be right for some, but that is no reason why those who try to get on, and who do get on, should have to undergo this humiliation.

"I suppose some white people might say — 'What has an Indian to do with self-respect? How can he be humiliated?' I answer that the Indian was deservedly self-respecting at one time, that those who fought for their country are, and their families have some claim to be. Anyway, what kind of policy is it that aims at bringing a people to a point of self-respect, and then by the nature of its regulations destroys the very thing for which it works?

"For myself, I think that I would rather starve than go to beg for such a trifling thing as a permit to sell one load of hay, while I am trying to make every hour of good weather count. To sell ten loads might be different. From the standpoint of the Government it may seem good, a kind of drill or discipline. But who on earth wants this when he is busy, in a hurry, and needs to get food for himself? I have seen with my own eyes, Indians wasting a day, even two days, trying to get a permit to sell, when they are short of food. The Agent cannot always be at home, the clerk may be away, or busy, and the Indian must wait, though he may have to drive to the Agency from another reserve.

"That is not good, whatever the benevolent intention. It comes to this, that the Agent — whoever or whatever he may have been himself before he was appointed — has complete control over the business transactions of every Indian in his Agency. You might think that every Agent had been chosen for his sound business ability, but there are all kinds of Agents, each with his own ability or training, each with his own particular interpretation of this 'kindly supervision.'

"If it can be assumed that every Agent is a capable man, at least approximately suited to the position that he holds, and that he is a man of judgment, then surely he can tell an industrious Indian from the one who is not, and encourage the industrious one by giving him more privileges? This would only make trouble, it is said. That need not be so. Let the other Indians know that when they make a good showing they may have the same privileges.

"As for our cattle — there again, they are not ours. A white man, owning cattle and having no ready money, draws up a plan for himself which includes selling. An Indian may have more cattle than that white man has, but do you think that he can plan in that same way? No. He is told that the commissioner has said that no cattle are to be sold until the fall. It is useless to plan under this system, yet planning is what successful work requires. He does not get the chance to practise the adjusting of his work to his means, and in the light of all this 'kindly supervision' does it not seem premature to talk about compulsory enfranchisement?

"I think that rights in regard to what is surely his personal property should come when a man has shown ability through hard work. Why should he not own that which he has bought? I have known Indians who wanted to buy cattle when they had money after a successful hunt, but they would not because the ID (Indian Department) brand would be put on the cattle, and that would be the end of any say they had in the matter.

"Could there not be some limit set, within which the permit system would work? For instance, could not the first twenty head of cattle come under its operation, and the rest belong to the Indian, to do with as he chose? I am sure that many Indians would work far harder than they do now to try to graduate from the shadow of the permit system into the light of this new dignity. ...

"Two years ago, we had a very hard winter, and many cattle died, because of a general shortage of hay. Now, supposing that the people of the reserve had foreseen this in advance, and after meeting in council decided to sell the cattle that they would not be able to winter, the money to be banked for the purchase of more cattle the next year. Well, the Agent could refuse the necessary permit. The loss would be all the more discouraging, if they had foreseen the difficulty, and found a solution, but had been refused by 'kindly supervision.' Is it any wonder that the Indian does not appreciate the permit system?"

Old Keyam paused to let his words sink in, and before he could continue, a young man spoke. "I have something to add to that. Sure, we all like the farm instructor. He's good-natured, teases us, doesn't mind when we tease him. Well, we were branding cattle last week, and he asked in his joking way what we thought ID meant. Old Knife was there, and he's smart. He gave quite a speech about it, said that it stood for our chief source of light in the darkness, a sort of half-moon — only the outward curve with its full true light shone towards Ottawa in the east, the other part to the west, and that it was hollow, not giving much light, and doubly barred at that. Whoever planned that brand, he said, knew the whole business well.

"The instructor laughed with us, and he asked the rest of us for our ideas too. Some of us could think of words in English, which we probably spoke better than he did, but they didn't translate readily into Cree. Maybe we went a bit too far with some of those English words. Anyway, he stopped joking and changed to that self-important way he has at times, telling us that ID is a symbol that should make us proud, that it could be said to stand for *In Defence*, and that the Department does just that for the Indian — stands in defence as his guardian. We were to look upon that brand and be thankful for what it represented, just as we should be thankful that we were under the flag. Then he pointed to the flag, and said, 'I fought for that flag.'

"That was all I could take. I said, 'So did I, and I'm half-dead today because of it, even if I do have a military medal to show. I sniped more of the enemy than you ever saw in the forestry corps. And I still don't know what liberty under the flag is. I've never known it.'

"'I'll say for him that he did look a bit ashamed. Thought he could smooth it over a bit, I suppose, because he said, 'I know. You're a good boy, Jim. Come up to the house and I'll give you a pound or two of bacon.'

"What did I do? I went, of course. It's good bacon.''

12.

When Keyam's next opportunity to speak came some weeks later, he began by recalling to his listeners the young man's words. "He spoke for all our men who returned from the battlefields of Europe. Many of these men have been given one right — the right to vote in their country's elections. Through them, the Indian voice can be heard, but it is a small voice. They won the right for themselves, the right to say what should and what should not be done — and it is safe to say that they will not be the most ignorant voters in the country. Neither will they be too easily influenced.

"But if these young men can vote, what about their brothers and fathers? What about those who were willing to serve but were not permitted, and those who made a good contribution to the war effort, here at home?

"Enfranchisement is offered to us all, but at a price that many of us do not want to pay, for it means that we must leave our reserves, cut ourselves off from our own people. Why should we leave Treaty in order to have a say in the affairs of the land? There is still room for us here. Could the Government not set a standard that would exclude the unintelligent and the non-productive voters?

"Instead, we have this strange situation — the Government offering the vote to the Indian, and the Indian saying, 'no, thank you.' The white man cannot understand. He thinks that it only proves that the Indian is a queer animal, who says that he wants the vote, and when it is offered to him, will not take it.

"There is this talk of 'compulsory enfranchisement.' As I understand it, the Department sees that a man is progressing, and to consider his case appoints a committee of three — two to represent the Department and one who is an Indian from the reserve to which the man belongs. These three then take stock of all that the man has and all that he is. When they have considered what they know about him, they make their recommendation to the Superintendent-General who decides whether or not the man should be enfranchised. The man's own willingness is only one of several factors in that decision. If the decision is in favour of enfranchisement, the next step is to give him a part of the reserve, where he puts in so many years of probationary work before he cuts himself away from his band. Only then does he receive the right to vote.

"To the Indian this seems to be a way of breaking up the reserves. He knows the unhappy condition today of those who are only part Indian and who have wandered from place to place because they sold their original homestead rights, their scrip.

"These reserves are ours. We made Treaty with Queen Victoria, and the idea was that we should have sufficient land to live quietly, unmolested, and molesting no one. Why break up the reserves? That is what it would lead to. Is it that the Indian is not developing the land? I have seen great stretches of land that is not Indian reservation and yet it is undeveloped — land that is not kept intact by any solemn treaty. Reserve lands are. Is not the land that we deeded to the Government rich enough without our miserably small remnants? Can it be said that the land really belonged to the Hudson's Bay Company by virtue of their charter from King Charles, and not to us? By all that is right and just in heaven and on earth, I cannot agree.

"I claim that many of us have now reached the stage where we have in truth won the right to some share in legislating matters that affect us. As it is now, we never know what is going on from year to year in Ottawa, or what the next sitting of the House may bring forth regarding us — not, that is, until some Indian finds that he has clashed with the new legislation, and is so notified.

"Let us stay on our reserves, and let the Government give to those of us who earn it the right to vote. Have a standard set that will be a stimulus to the young men to earn that right. But in the meantime, have the Government put into force a vigorous educational policy — and then talk to us in ten years' time about enfranchisement.

"It is not that we do not want the standing of first-class citizens. It is that we know that general enfranchisement is premature. We have been brought up as children, treated as children, made to act according to rules and regulations that are not our own, and at the command of officials whom we do not always respect.

"That is no preparation for the enfranchised state, where half the battle lies in initiative, in the wise conduct of business, in the responsible planning of work according to the means in hand. Moreover we should have some representation in Ottawa, or, failing that, we should have consultation at least with the committee of the House. This would give us a chance to register our approval, or to give the reasons for our opposition.

"The world goes forward. Indians here and there have made marked progress, and one of the signs of this is that the ones who feel that they are doing their share in the work of the land chafe under this system of 'kindly supervision'; a system depriving them of all responsibility in the matter of taking any risk — other than the risk of disobeying the Agent.

"The other day I read that comment to you about a 'reactionary element' among the better educated Indians, and I wondered if that applied to words of mine. If criticism of the Government is 'reactionary,' then the whole of the white population in this and almost any other country is guilty of the same. However wise and kindly the Indian Department might be, it is surely not reactionary when one who is an Indian chooses to draw upon his limited knowledge of things and talk to Indian listeners."

Old Keyam paused for a moment. "Sometimes, I talk too much," he mumbled. "If what I say appears like high treason, I merely put into words what many more of you are thinking."

When it seemed that the Old Man had ended what he had to say, the Chief turned to the main business of the meeting.

"It's this matter of the sale of land. It was discussed in council, and some of you — all of you, I thought — knew about it. Now I find when it is too late, that some of you are saying that we did not do what was right. I repeat, it was with the consent of the band that we sold part of this reserve. Some of the money from that sale has been distributed amongst us, and the rest is funded so that it may be there to the credit of this band until such time as we may disband for the purpose of enfranchisement. We ourselves will get no benefit from that part of the money. Our children in the fourth generation may. The money will lie there safely in trust. It is our contribution to the welfare of our descendants."

Old Keyam was upon his feet at once, and he spoke with vigour. "I used to think the same way. That was how it was told to me too, by somebody — I cannot remember whom. But when I was young I listened to the talk of the old Chiefs who signed the Treaty, when they discussed its terms so that everyone would understand. Those old Chiefs and all who listened to them believed, without a single exception, that these reserves belonged to us entirely. They do belong to us, but not in the fullest sense of that word.

"We thought that we would be taught to work our land, would be advised in the white man's ways. Instead we are under constant rules and regulations, and we must conform. The old Chiefs were promised schools, and it was understood that these schools would be paid for wholly by the Government, in return for our surrender of claims to the rest of this land. Now, it appears that we pay through these funds from the sale of reserve lands that are in trust. As for the advisors assigned to us — there again we must pay towards the cost. The Treaty talk sounded different when the old Chiefs signed.

"I talk as I do because I was reading the Indian Act[54] today on this matter of the sale of reserve lands. The Chiefs who signed the Treaty saw the Bible on the table and they understood that it was a symbol of everlasting faith. I ask, is it right to acknowledge a nation as capable of signing a treaty, and then take advantage of their ignorance by allowing them to believe one thing while another is meant — just because that will make matters easier? Is it right, even though the plea may be that the changes are for the best for the people so misled? Heaven knows that I do not want to seem one who is never satisfied. I look at the subject from all sides, as well as I can.

"Listen to this — this is from the Indian Act, Section 88: 'The Governor-in-Council may reduce the purchase money due or to become due on sales of Indian lands or reduce or remit the interest on such purchase money, or reduce the rent at which Indian lands have been leased when he considers the same excessive.'

"I do not understand this language of the law well enough perhaps. 'Indian lands' is said to mean those portions of reserves that have been surrendered to the Crown. It surely cannot mean that a bargain is made with us — we sign a paper — and then later the Governor-in-Council may change the agreement that *we* have made, and yet still we stand bound to fulfill our part. No, Chief. Perhaps it does not mean that we lose anything by such a clause — I do not know — and neither does any one of us here.

"Let me read another clause from the Act:

The Governor-in-Council may provide for the general management of such moneys and direct what percentage or proportion thereof shall be set apart, from time to time, to cover the cost of and incidental to the management of reserves, lands, property and moneys under the provisions of this Part and may authorize and direct the expenditure of such moneys for surveys, for compensation to Indians for improvements or any interest they had in lands taken from them, for the construction or repair of roads, bridges, ditches and water courses on such reserves or lands, for the construction and repair of school buildings and charitable institutions, and by way of contribution to schools attended by such Indians.

"And Section 90 has two parts that read:

(1) The Governor-in Council may, *with the consent of a band,* authorize and direct the expenditure of any capital moneys standing at the credit of such band, in the purchase of land as a reserve for the band or as an addition to its reserve or in the purchase of cattle for the band or in the construction of permanent improvements upon the reserve of the band or such works thereon or in connection therewith as, in

106

his opinion, will be of permanent value to the band or will, when completed, properly represent capital.

(2) In the event of a band refusing to consent to the expenditure of such capital moneys as the Superintendent General may consider advisable for any of the purposes mentioned in sub-section one of this section, and it appearing to the Superintendent General, that such refusal is detrimental to the progress and welfare of the band, the Governor-in-Council may, *without the consent of the band*, authorize and direct the expenditure of such capital for such of the said purposes as may be considered reasonable and proper.

"You see, Chief — 'with the consent ... without the consent' — I may not understand these matters any more than the rest of you do, but I look at all this in the spirit of the treaty that was actually made and signed with us. I was only a small child then, but I talked with the old Chiefs when I was a young man and first concerned about these matters. Most of you are too young to have had that opportunity.

"Sub-section (1) says 'with the consent,' and following that there are the usual modifications. The words 'permanent improvements' include Agency buildings, fences, schools, etc. All this is to be done with our sanction. But if we refuse that sanction, the expenditure will take place anyhow. That is the gist of it.

"I would ask all of you: when we signed that Treaty did we sign it with the understanding that we were signing away all freedom until such time as 'in the opinion of the Governor-in-Council' we should be ready to be enfranchised? Is it lawful to withhold the real meaning of a treaty from one party, when that party is not in a position to understand?

"Allowing that freedom is not good for us — and I do allow that it may not be good for all — was it fair not to mention this at the time of the Treaty? Freedom is the most precious thing on earth. God gave it to all men, without exception. Was it such a small thing that it could be overlooked in the discussions at the time of the signing of that Treaty, when the actual withholding of it from one party was at the basis of all the negotiations?

"Chief, I have talked enough on these matters. I am not going to say any more. It is no use. I have tried to express the feelings of us all, but how far my old ideas are prejudiced I cannot know. I may misjudge the minds and feelings of the new generation, and that too I do not know. Nor do I know how far the failing of my sight and my other faculties has led me astray.

"Advise your young men to look upon my views as those that belong to a passing generation. Tell them to try to climb higher themselves by doing the best that is in them to solve the Indian problem — not by talking as I have but by working early and late, by observing the white men as they go about the duties of the land. And tell them, above all, to get their children educated, as if life depends on that, for it does."

Keyam stopped, and the Chief, who had been listening intently, rose to his feet. "There are many times," he said, "when I wish that I knew as much as Old Keyam. He holds no office amongst us, yet when we want to say what is in our minds, we ask Keyam to say it for us. He is more important than any other one of us here, for he is our Voice, he is the Old Man of this band, in the finest tradition of Old Men of the past. Sometimes I think that when all the rest of us are forgotten, Old Keyam will be remembered. He thinks and says that he is old. I think that Keyam lives forever.''

His words surprised the Old Man, and Keyam dropped his head to hide his emotion. His hands fumbled at his belt, untying a leather pouch that glinted with new beads, the work of Chochena's old fingers in an old art. "There is something here,'' he said, "Something that I have wanted to show you.''

He held out an ancient red-stone pipe-stem.[55] "This was given to me many years ago by one who had been a great Warrior and a wise man, in the tradition of our past; one who spoke to us of courage and of mercy, of love for our fellow men and reverence towards God. These teachings are the heritage of our past. They are for all time; they belong to all ages, to all people.

"When he gave me this, he said, 'As long as you keep this pipe-stem, speak words of deep thought to my children. Be faithful to the trust that I place in you.'

"I have tried to keep that trust, but I am only an ordinary man, and I have often failed.

"You call me Old Keyam, and have forgotten any other name I might have had. I have accepted the name as my own. There was once a very wise man who said, 'He is wisest among you who has found out that in truth his wisdom is worth nothing at all.'

"Now our Cree language can say all that in one word, in the name that you have given to me: *Keyam.*''

Notes Relating to the 1973 Introduction

1. *Cree Trickster Tales.* These legends of *We-sa-kā-cha'k* were published in *The Journal of American Folk-lore*, Volume 42, October-December 1929. Three of them were reprinted in *Saskatchewan Harvest*, a Golden Jubilee selection of Son and Story, edited by Carlyle King, and published by McClelland & Stewart Limited in 1955.

2. *Big Bear* was a Plains Cree, one of the River People. He was born about 1825 near Fort Carlton, and in 1865 was headman of a small band in the Fort Pitt area. Not until 1876 was he recognized as a Chief, when his efforts to deter the other Chiefs from signing Treaty No. 6 earned him the respect of independent plains hunters who continued their nomadic life until the disappearance of the buffalo reduced them to starvation. One after another, Big Bear's headmen might capitulate and sign their adhesion to Treaty No. 6, as Thunderchild and Little Pine did in 1879, but others of more reckless spirit joined the Chief, making his band a hard core of the fearless and the disaffected, numbering from three to five hundred. In December of 1882, however, Big Bear reluctantly signed his adhesion, but refused to take a reserve. He brought his band from the Cypress Hills to winter at Fort Pitt the next year, and then to Frog Lake for the winter of 1884-85.

    Though he was stubborn in his demands for better terms, Big Bear did everything in his power to restrain the Crees in any encounters with government authority, as at Battleford in the summer of 1884 (see note 37 on Poundmaker). He did not want an Indian rising. He knew the power of the whites, and recognized that the Indians had all to lose and nothing to gain by fighting. His efforts were directed to bringing about an Indian union that could force concessions by a potential threat rather than by actual hostilites. Small and scattered reserves weakened that power.

    In the end, his peaceful ambitions could not restrain such reckless men as his war-chief, Wandering Spirit, or his own son, Imasees. When the news reached Frog Lake of the Métis repulse of the Police force at Duck Lake, all the resentment and smouldering hatred burst forth in the murder of eight white men and one Métis. Then came the plundering of Fort Pitt, the encounter with General Strange's column at Frenchman's Butte, and the retreat to Loon Lake, when the Cree force broke into small straggling groups.

    Big Bear made his own way to Fort Carlton and surrendered there. In the trials that followed, he was charged with treason-felony and was sentenced to three years at Stoney Mountain Penitentiary, though the jury recommended mercy, and Commissioner Dewdney requested the clemency of the Crown towards the Indians. No one appealed specifically for the release of Big Bear, as the powerful Blackfoot chief, Crowfoot, (see note 36) and Dewdney pleaded for Poundmaker's. Big Bear served two years of his sentence before he was released. A general amnesty had been declared in 1886, but his band had been the principal nucleus of agitation, and its remnants were dispersed, merging with other bands. Big Bear went to Little Pine's reserve. He no longer had the will to live, and in the winter of 1887-88, quietly died.

3. *Treaty.* In 1870, Rupert's Land and the north-western territory were transferred to the Dominion of Canada. In eastern Canada, settlement had advanced slowly over a period of two hundred years. In the North-West, the Indians experienced the full pressure of the white invasion within two decades. The Government was aware of the danger both to the Indians and to the peace of the country, and it followed the policy of acknowledging the Indian title to the land, and negotiating for its surrender. An important difference in the western treaties was provision for the instruction, health and civilization of the native tribes.

    The first official treaty with the North-West Indians was signed at Fort Garry in 1871; the seventh, with the Blackfoot, in 1877. Treaty Six is usually considered to have been the most important, involving the surrender by the Plains and Woods Cree of the North Saskatchewan region. The area was vast, the Indians wild, war-like, and determined to allow no white invasion, though settlement was already beginning. The Treaty was signed at Fort Carlton, August 23, 1876, and at Fort Pitt, September 9. (See Appendix.)

    By ceding 121,000 square miles of land and accepting reserves and the Queen's payment, the Crees practically guaranteed that their future status would be as wards of the government. Only such resistant "unco-operative" Indians as Big Bear understood this. For all of them, however, the idea of "ownership" of land was beyond comprehension. Land could no more be owned than could the air that they breathed. Surely, the white man was only "borrowing."

Treaty provisions allowed annuity payments — $25 for each Chief or headman, with a medal and a suit of clothes; $5 for each man, woman and child — agricultural tools, livestock, and practical assistance in helping the Indians to adapt to agrarian economy, as well as certain consideration for their general health and education.

Treaty Six also contained the clause providing for aid and rations in the event of "any pestilence or general famine" and this was to bring serious discord when the buffalo vanished in a few years. Then in 1883-84, the Government's cruel policy of financial retrenchment almost wrecked the whole Indian experiment, increasing their distrust and leading to their active participation in the Rebellion of 1885.

4. *The Reserve System* was a policy that met the needs of the moment and probably saved the Indians from the fate of the buffalo, for they could not have withstood the westward march of expansion. Placing them upon reserves was seen as the first step towards civilization; and a definite farming policy was adopted. It was not an unqualified success even at the start, nor was the promise of the first few years on "progressive" reserves borne out by subsequent developments.

The area of land granted for each family of five was set at 640 acres. In the case of Thunderchild's first reserve, seventeen miles north-west of Battleford, the survey of 1881 allowed only twenty-four miles for thirty-two families, and in 1884 an additional reserve of eight and a half square miles was surveyed on the north side of the Saskatchewan River.

5. *Edward Ahenakew's ancestry* is traced in the incomplete notes which were gathered together for publication in *Saskatchewan History*, Volume XVII, No. 1, (Winter 1964). (See chart.)

In reference to his surname, he wrote: "A scholar may manipulate a Cree word or words which have a similar sound and feel himself justified in giving some meaning to the name ... unfortunately, it has none."

The first Ahenakew was one of five brothers who hunted for the Hudson's Bay Company at Fort Carlton. *Ah-tah-ka-koop* and *Na-pās-kis* were most widely known.

Mandelbaum, in his study of the Plains Cree which was published in 1940, refers to *Ah-tah-ka-koop* (Starblanket) as an outstanding Chief of the House People (p. 166). Much earlier than that, in *Red Indians of the Plains*, published in 1915, John Hines tells of his meeting with *Ah-tah-ka-koop* in September 1874: "I never saw a finer built man. ... He stood over six feet high, and was well proportioned. ..." (p. 78) "The Indian who came to us at Whitefish Lake and who was the cause of our settling (at Sandy Lake) was *Ah-tah-ka-koop*, whom we found to be one of the most influential Chiefs in the Saskatchewan country ... a better Indian never roamed the prairies. ..." (p. 88) "His second name, *Mis-se-min-na-hik* (Big Pine), was given to him on account of his size and strength; the latter he displayed in carrying heavy loads across portages when in company with the voyageurs who used to fetch the Hudson's Bay Company freight from York Factory." (p. 117)

Ah-tah-ka-koop was over eighty years of age when he died. An article paying tribute to him appeared at that time in the Battleford Industrial School paper, *The Guide*, for December 1896: "He is said to have been the last surviving real Cree Chief — that is one appointed or elected by the Indians themselves under their own old system, which was very different from modern appointments. He was a man of commanding appearance ... intelligent, trustworthy ... a thoroughly loyal Chief. When the rebellion broke out in 1885, he was strongly urged to join but said, 'How can I fight against one whose medal I wear, and for whom I pray often? If I have to take up arms I will take them up to help her and not to go against her.' He was one of those who were taken afterwards to visit eastern Canada, and he was greatly delighted with the trip and the many wonderful things he saw."

Na-pās-kis was the youngest of the brothers. His death was worthy of his name, which denotes manliness, for he died fighting the avenging Blackfoot, after leading a successful raid into their camp to steal horses.

The incident appears in the notes of Thunderchild's stories, and in the Rev. James Settee's unpublished journal, dated at Fort Pelly in July 1861: "A young half-Cree, half-Saulteau came ... he is mourning the death of his uncle *Na-pās-kis*, who has been killed just lately in battle by the Blackfoot with twelve of his men. This *Na-pās-kis* was a noted Warrior ... the bravest of the little plain Fort Chiefs. ..."

Just two years before that, at Fort Carlton, the Earl of Southesk had noted "a very bold intelligent young man named *Napēsskes*." And then a few days later: "*Napēsskes*, that clever, good-looking Indian, accompanied us in the capacity of guide. By birth he was really of French half-breed origin, but having always lived with the Indians he completely resembled them in his looks and habits, and nobody much remembered his European blood."

Edward Ahenakew makes no reference to this French blood, though his father and his uncles were all given French names, and one of them took the surname Chatelain.

Plains Cree Ancestry of Edward Ahenakew
with names that are remembered in western history or occur in his stories

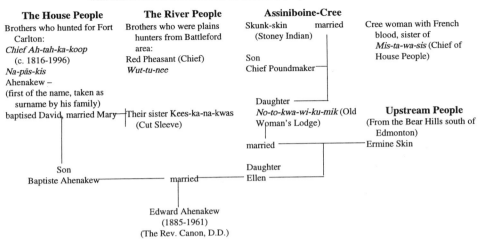

The House People	The River People	Assiniboine-Cree	
Brothers who hunted for Fort Carlton:	Brothers who were plains hunters from Battleford area:	Skunk-skin married (Stoney Indian)	Cree woman with French blood, sister of *Mis-ta-wa-sis* (Chief of House People)

Chief *Ah-tah-ka-koop*
(c. 1816-1996)
Na-pās-kis
Ahenakew –
(first of the name, taken as surname by his family)
baptised David, married Mary

Red Pheasant (Chief)
Wut-tu-nee

Son
Chief Poundmaker

Their sister Kees-ka-na-kwas
(Cut Sleeve)

Daughter
No-to-kwa-wi-ku-mik (Old Woman's Lodge)

Upstream People
(From the Bear Hills south of Edmonton)

married — Ermine Skin

Son
Baptiste Ahenakew — married — Daughter Ellen

Edward Ahenakew
(1885-1961)
(The Rev. Canon, D.D.)

He does not mention that his mother's grandmother had French blood. She was the sister of *Mis-ta-wa-sis*, a noted Chief to whom Thunderchild often refers. (See notes 16, 24). The names of two more Chiefs appear in the chart of Ahenakew's ancestry, brothers of his grandmothers, Red Pheasant on his father's side, and Poundmaker, his mother's uncle. (See note 37.)

6. *Emmanuel College.* In 1879, the Rt. Rev. John McLean, first bishop of Saskatchewan Diocese, opened a divinity school at Prince Albert, which he named Emmanuel College. Later he obtained a university charter but did not proceed with the plan. When the Rt. Rev. W.C. Pinkham became bishop of Saskatchewan and Calgary in 1886-87, he turned Emmanuel College into an Indian school, and allowed the university powers to fall into abeyance. Twenty years later, the Rt. Rev. J.A. Newnham made Emmanuel a divinity school once more, and in 1909 moved it to Saskatoon to affiliate with the new provincial university.

7. *John Alexander Mackay* was born at Moose Factory in 1838. His father and grandfather were officers of the Hudson's Bay Company. The boy was educated and trained in mission work under the Wesleyan missionaries and then under the noted John Horden of the Anglican Church, later the first bishop of Moosonee. After 1857, Mackay's training continued at Red River, and he was ordained in 1861 by the first bishop of Rupert's Land, the Rt. Rev. David Anderson. When the Diocese of Saskatchewan was established in 1874, Mackay was serving at Stanley Mission on the Churchill River. In 1877, he established the mission at Battleford, and in 1882 was appointed Archdeacon of the Diocese. He was a remarkably able man in every aspect of his work, and the Indians held him in great respect. After the Rebellion of 1885, the Government requested him to act as their Agent in the troubled Battleford area until the most pressing problems could be resolved. Then in 1887, he returned to his work for the Diocese, serving as principal of Emmanuel College for some years. He was noted as a Cree scholar, and he continued his work of translation until the very end of his life.

8. *Little Pine* had joined Big Bear in resistance to Treaty Six, reluctantly signing his adhesion in 1879. He and Poundmaker were granted adjoining reserves on the Battle River.

9. *School at Little Pine's.* Edward Ahenakew's account of this school was published in *Saskatchewan History*, Volume XVIII, No. 2, (Spring 1965). His incomplete notes, however, failed to give recognition to many who had contributed to the development of the school.

10. *Day-School at Thunderchild's.* The last entry in Ahenakew's ledger-book journal takes up five pages, and is un-dated, though presumably written in the early summer of 1923. It is the draft of a letter that he wrote for Thunderchild, translating the Chief's words into English. It is an earnest plea for the restoration of a day-school on that reserve; and it is signed:

> his
> Chief X *Thunderchild*
> mark

The appeal was successful, and the school re-opened in 1924.

Notes Relating to Part I
The Stories of Chief Thunderchild

11. *Everyone looked for old bones, to make grease.* It was part of the procedure after a successful hunt to split open the large bones of the buffalo and pound them with a maul. The crushed splinters were then placed in boiling water, and the grease that rose to the surface skimmed off and stored in buffalo paunches. It was called *oskanpimu* (bone grease). (*The Plains Cree*, p. 192.)

12. *Deadfall traps.* These were described to Mandelbaum (*The Plains Cree*, p. 199). One end of a heavy log was supported by a stick to which bait was attached. The lower end of this upright was set on a short stick which was displaced when the upright was moved.

13. *Stoneys.* The Stoney Indians are Assiniboines, a branch of the Sioux, and their Cree name is derived from their practice of using hot stones to bring the water in their cooking pots to the boil.

14. *The old Sun Dance place.* Ritualistic dances were held in the same place year after year; while ceremonial dances, which were simply community socials in which any dancer could join, were danced on any flat area that the tribe fancied.

15. *Dreams count, my son. ... The Spirits have pitied us and guided us.* In his outline for *Old Keyam*, Ahenakew planned a chapter entitled "Men Who Dream," but did not enlarge upon it. In chapter 4 of Part II, he speaks of "the spirit power given through dreams," and in the article he wrote about religious beliefs (See note 39) there is a reference to the power that a spirit indwelling in nature may give in a dream to a human being whom it "pities." This spirit power (*pu-wa-mi-win*) enhances and strengthens the one who is "pitied," man, woman or child, with that particular quality the spirit itself possesses.

16. *There were more than a hundred families in our band. ... Some families had horses, but only a few.* (See note 26.) The Chief of the band was *Mis-ta-wa-sis.* Mandelbaum (*The Plains Cree*, p. 166) speaks of him and *Ah-tah-ka-koop* as the two most important Chiefs of the House People in the mid-nineteenth century. Unlike *Ah-tah-ka-koop*'s people, the Indians with *Mis-ta-wa-sis* had left the forest life entirely and were living exclusively on the plains, hunting buffalo along the South Saskatchewan to supply Fort Carlton.

Thunderchild says that there were more than one hundred families in the band. Other reports (unpublished papers in Saskatchewan Archives) confirm that *Mis-ta-wa-sis* had a larger following than any other Chief of the Plains Cree, and took precedence over them, as in presentation to the Governor-General, the Marquis of Lorne, or in the signing of Treaty Six at Fort Carlton.

17. *Those who were great hunters, and could look after many were known as the Providers. ...* In the camp, the men who enforced law ... belonged to the *society of Dancers.* (See Ch. 12, Part II) The men who were appointed by the council of headmen, to enforce the common will of the people, were those whose courage had often been proved, and who had influence for that reason. They formed the society of the Dancers, and the name *Ō-ke-che-ta-wuk* (Warriors or Heroes) was also used for them. There were different orders, the Buffaloes, the Wolves, and so on. ...

Fine Day, who was Thunderchild's contemporary and Mandelbaum's "unexcelled informant" in 1934-35 (*The Plains Cree*), achieved the rank of "worthy young man" while still a boy, but was not yet a Warrior when he attended a meeting of the Rattlers. This required a formal invitation to sit in the Warriors' lodge in the centre of the camp circle when the band came together in the springtime. There he was taken to a place near the Warrior Chief, who might be the band Chief but was not the war Chief, though one of the boldest and ablest of the fighting men. Fine Day was told, "From now on your homes and your possessions are not your own." The important function of the society of Warriors, beyond dancing, feasting and providing for the needy, was policing the buffalo hunt. They also guarded the line of march when camp was moved, and hurried the stragglers. Usually the bravest men were taken into the societies, but a man without a war record might be asked to join if he proved to be a good hunter and had many horses. Worthy young men and Warriors maintained their prestige by demonstrating their detachment from the sentiments held by lower ranks. Often, their intercession averted disastrous blood feuds, as in the case of Ē-pay-as.

The story of Ē-pay-as is mentioned in *Old Keyam* and it appears again, though he is not named, in the account that Fine Day gave (*The Plains Cree*, p. 231).

18. *We could hear the wounded man singing his song.* In 1885, the eight Indians executed at Battleford for their part in the massacre at Frog Lake went to their deaths "singing their songs," as Almighty Voice did in 1897, a tragic outlaw, wounded and at bay.

In Ahenakew's account of the religious beliefs of the Indian (Note 39(b)) he describes how a boy attains his song: "All alone in the wild ... he senses influences that may pass, and he cries ... at times he sleeps ... exhausted because of thirst and hunger ... suddenly a spirit appears to him, speaking to him in great kindness and it promises him whatever power that spirit may have to give. It teaches him a song which is to be used when he wants to call upon the spirit ... in case of direst need."

19. *The Crees ... gathered there to take revenge against the Blackfoot.* Such vengeance raids, according to Fine Day (*The Plains Cree*, p. 301), often succeeded in recruiting large parties which set out against the offending tribe. It was only on such occasions that women accompanied the fighting expedition, to cook for the men. When the enemy was found, the plan was to annihilate their camp.

Fine Day lived until 1941 when he was said to be ninety-four years of age. That would have made him a year or two older than Thunderchild, whose date of birth is set in 1849. This story of Thunderchild's raises doubt as to Fine Day's actual age, for his account was that vengeance raids were no longer undertaken when he was a boy because the increasing use of firearms had terminated the custom. A few guns effectively used by the defenders could inflict great damage on a large number of assailants.

This effect of raids is proved in Thunderchild's story but the vengeance attack took place as late as December 1865 or 1866 (Thunderchild said January). Father Lacombe happened to be in the Blackfoot camp that terrible night and wrote his account in 1890. (Reprinted 1957, Historical Society of Alberta.) In that account he gives the date as 1866. In his biography (*The Black-robe Voyageur*, by Katharine Hughes) 1865 is the year given.

20. *... but the men said to us, ``You are not old enough to fight. ...''* Describing his first raid, Fine Day said, "Two worthy young men had seen me do these things, and that is why I became one of them. I was very young then, about *fifteen or sixteen.*"

21. *They gave her to Short Tail, the brother of Ermine Skin.* (See chart of Ahenakew ancestry.) The name Ermine Skin (*Ko-se-ko-se-wu-ya-new*) was given because he was uncommonly fair-skinned. He came from the Bear Hills, south of Edmonton, and married the sister of Poundmaker. Edward Ahenakew's mother was Ermine Skin's daughter, Ellen.

22. *This was Ma-che-num. ... Ma-che-num* was the father of *Mi-sa-ti-mois*, later of Little Pine's reserve, whose grandsons, the Venerable Archdeacon Adam Cuthand and the Reverend Stanley Cuthand were two of the first pupils of Little Pine School to continue their education through high school to university.

23. *Someone had found Father Lacombe's robes in a tent.* Father Lacombe's account of this raid was written in 1890: "In the year 1866, the third day of December, at one o'clock in the morning, at a place called by the Indians The Three Pounds, a war-party of Crees, Saulteaux, and Stoneys, about eight hundred in number, fell suddenly, without any warning, upon a small camp of Blackfoot, whose Chief was *Natous* (The Sun). I was at the time in the camp, receiving the hospitality of *Natous*. I had been sent by my superiors to pass the winter with the Blackfoot, to study their language and character, and to ascertain their disposition towards Christianity. On my way from Edmonton and Rocky Mountain House, I had joined a party of travelling Indians, and, after visiting many camps, had arrived at the last encampment, where it was intended to unite into one all the dispersed little camps, and so to pass the winter with the whole nation, that they might protect themselves against their enemies. The snow was pretty deep. The day before, Crowfoot, who was yet under the command of his old father (*A-kow-int-kas-tiw*, The Many Names), was visited, and he promised to join *Natous* as soon as possible; and so also did the Chiefs of other camps.

"Exhausted by fatigue, I was quietly sleeping in the tent of the Chief, and, when no thought of a war-party of lurking enemy was entertained, suddenly a dog put his head into the lodge. It was a Cree dog (*assinow emita*). The alarm was given. In one second, the Crees, who were watching about a hundred yards off, opened fire. In an instant some score of bullets came crashing through the leather lodge, and the wild war whoop of the Crees broke forth through the sharp and rapid detonation of many muskets.

"It is not my intention to give the awful details of that fearful night, when the groans of the dying, the yelling of the warriors, the harangues of the Chiefs, and the noise of dogs and horses all mingled, formed a kind of hell.

"I have only to say that at the most critical moment, when our little camp was half-taken by the Crees, and when the scalping and butchering were going on, the voice of Crowfoot was heard. He was rushing to our rescue. 'Take courage (*Ekakimak*),' he cried out as he came with a large party of warriors. We were saved. Crowfoot, alongside *Natous*, fought like a bear. ...''

24. ... *Then Mis-ta-wa-sis (Big Child) rode out from the line singing. ... This is no child.* "*Mis-ta-wa-sis* was a very little man,'' John Hines noted in *Red Indians of the Plains*, ''and had another name *Pe-wa-pisk Moos-toos* (Iron Buffalo) from the fact that when travelling hard with a herd of buffalo his horse stumbled and threw him onto the horns of a buffalo bull, which proceeded to throw him up into the air, but he eventually escaped ... and when his friends discovered that he was alive and unhurt they gave him the name 'Iron Buffalo.'''

25. *Afterwards we knew it was Gabriel Dumont.* ... (a) There were two Gabriel Dumonts, uncle and nephew, both of them noted buffalo-hunters, the elder notorious also for his violent temper. In his article (*The Alberta Historical Review*, Spring 1966, "Big Bear, Indian Patriot.'') William B. Fraser refers to the resentment roused in Big Bear, following a clash in 1873 over the two over their enforcement of hunt laws.

There are many references in western history to the second Gabriel Dumont, particularly relating to the Rebellion of 1885 and his military achievements as Riel's lieutenant, when he drove the Police back at Duck Lake, held Middleton at Fish Creek, and baffled overwhelming Government forces at Batoche for days.

One who paid somewhat surprising tribute to him was S.B. Steele (Sir Samuel Benfield Steele) who had come to the Territories with the North-West Mounted Police in 1873, and then, as Major Steele of the Alberta Field Force, led his scouts against Big Bear's Indians at Frenchman's Butte and Loon Lake. Later he was a superintendent of the Police and then a Major-General of the Canadian Army. In his book, *Forty Years in Canada*, Steele wrote of Dumont: "A remarkable Métis, who with careful and just treatment might have become one of Canada's most loyal citizens ... very much like a red man, far from faultless, extravagant, never looking to the morrow ... his good qualities far outweighed his bad, and he was a man whom many were glad to call friend ... one of the kindest and bravest of men. He was a great scout and knew the plains well. One might travel them from one end to the other and talk to Métis hunters and never hear an unkind word of Dumont. ... All turned to him when there was any grave crisis.''

(b) The term ''Métis'' was first applied to French half-breeds, descendants of Indian women and the *voyageurs* who came from Quebec in the days of the fur-trade, as distinct from the Scottish or English half-breeds who were descendants of fur-trading partners or the officers and Orkney boatmen of the Hudson's Bay Company. All of them might speak Cree. It was in the language of the father, in English or French, that the primary distinction lay — and in religion, even before the Roman Catholic or Protestant missions were established. The essential difference, however, was in the training and education that could be offered to them as children and in the opportunities for employment.

With such notable exceptions as Louis Riel, the French-speaking Métis had little or no education; and the choice for them was only between the free nomadic life of their mother's people, or the back-breaking toil of boatmen and labourers in the Company's service. They became unexcelled buffalo-hunters, living as the Indians did, resisting the efforts of their Church to hold them in permanent settlements, whether at Red River or later on the Saskatchewan.

As the buffalo herds drifted westward, the hunters followed. Fort Pitt became a centre for that trade, and Isidore Dumont, who was Gabriel's father, came from Red River as captain of a large party of Métis hunters, whose descendants still live in that area — Dumont, Nolin, Laframboise, Cardinal, Patenaude, Parenteau, Dufresne, Ladouceur — their names sounding a roll-call of *voyageurs* and buffalo-hunters of the nineteenth century in the territory of the Saskatchewan.

While the buffalo remained on the plains, the hunters followed the herds, or travelled back and forth with brigades of Red River carts along the trail that stretched a thousand miles between Fort Garry and Fort Edmonton, "the Carlton trail.'' They settled in casual communities along the River, often on the fringes of Indian reserves, near fur-trading posts.

In 1869-70 they had risen at Red River under Louis Riel as their leader, to claim their rights as a ''nation''; but neither that racial consciousness nor their primitive economy was strong enough to maintain a separate identity in the midst of overwhelming white immigration. Forced back into the valley of the Saskatchewan, they rose again in the Rebellion of 1885, "the last attempt of the primitive in Canada to withstand the inexorable advance of white civilization.'' (*The Birth of Western Canada*. Stanley.)

26. *I had only that one poor horse.* The Cree first became acquainted with horses (which had been introduced by the Spaniards in the south) in the early part of the eighteenth century, but even in the closing decades of the buffalo era they were poor in horses, compared to the Blackfoot and the Assiniboine. Only a few men owned horses that were swift enough for the chase and trained to hunt buffalo. The possession of horses made possible a rise in social prestige, and the most honourable and common means of acquiring them was by raiding the enemy camps.

Fine Day made this statement to Mandelbaum (*The Plains Cree*, p. 195): "My father came west as the

Blackfoot were driven back, because there were more buffalo. He died about 1860. In his time they had very few horses and used dogs more than we did."

27. *We built a lodge for him out of young green trees.* The ceremony of "the shaking of the lodge" is described in more detail in *Old Keyam,* chapter 11.

Mandelbaum (*The Plains Cree,* p. 261) writes: "Only a few *shamans* (a word of Sanskrit origin for a priest or conjurer — loosely, a medicine-man) among the Plains Cree could manipulate the conjuring booths ... Baptiste Pooyak, a well-read Indian and a devout Christian, told of a conjuring booth performance that he had witnessed in 1903. The *shaman* had made it to ascertain why a patient of his had fallen ill."

28. *Pu-chi-to now tells his story.* Pu-chi-to was a member of the band on Thunderchild's reserve, one of the Old Men who added his recollections to those of the Chief. The tone of this story differs from any of Thunderchild's.

29. *Wandering Spirit, who was always reckless.* ... He became one of Big Bear's headmen after Thunderchild signed his adhesion to the Treaty in 1879. At Frog Lake in the winter of 1884-85, Wandering Spirit was able to undermine the authority of Big Bear, and as War-Chief he precipitated the massacre when he shot Thomas Quinn, the Indian Agent. He was one of eight Indians hanged at Battleford.

30. *... carrying the bag that held the sacred symbols of his spirit power.* This "sacred bundle" might contain no more than a single article encased in many layers of cloth. The choice of that article and the ability to make this "sacred bundle" might be imparted in a vision; and it protected its owner through its "spirit power." (Mandelbaum, *The Plains Cree,* p. 258.)

31. *Sweet Grass was with them ... and Wut-tu-nee.* Sweet Grass signed Treaty Six in September 1876 at Fort Pitt but died not long afterwards and was succeeded by Strike-him-on-the-back. Fine Day was a member of this band.

Wut-tu-nee was Chief of his band in 1876 but did not agree to the provisions of the Treaty and withdrew in favour of his brother, Red Pheasant, who signed for the band. The reserve in the Eagle Hills took the latter's name when he became Chief. The name *Wut-tu-nee,* however, continues to be known. There is a lawyer and a writer of that name, and an artist. There are many others too, for the first *Wut-tu-nee* had two wives, who bore him six sons and many daughters.

The sister of *Wut-tu-nee* and Red Pheasant married the first Ahenakew and was Edward Ahenakew's grandmother.

Among the Ahenakew papers there are stories of the treachery and folly of women. Thunderchild, in one of the legends that he told, interjected, "How angry I am at all womankind when I tell this," and ended the story with the statement: "She was killed. Not a cry in the whole camp. The Cree is loyal and all must be loyal to remain Cree." The ending of story seventeen, of a faithless woman, is in the same tone: "He killed her. It is not only now that woman causes trouble. That has been since first man was."

In contrast to such accounts, there is this example of a woman's courage and endurance. It is Edward Ahenakew's own story of his grandmother, *Kees-ka-na-kwas,* the worthy sister of two Chiefs of the Plains Cree:

"When the Rebellion of 1885 broke out, she was visiting her daughter on Poundmaker's reserve in the Battleford country. All the others of her sons and daughters were in the Prince Albert area, and she was anxious about them. Her daughter's house had been looted. (Robert Jefferson, who was farm instructor on the reserve and Poundmaker's brother-in-law, speaks of the looting by the militia who remained in the West, in his article in *Canadian North-West Historical Publications,* Vol. 1, No. V, (1929).) There was no food for *Kees-ka-na-kwas* to take with her; spring had been late in coming, and Sandy Lake lay a hundred and fifty miles to the north-east.

"She had to travel through the Thickwood Hills, where snow still lingered, and there was no clear trail. Snaring a rabbit when she could and eating withered rosehips and shrivelled berries, she was able to keep alive and to go a few miles each day. Her moccasins she mended until it was no longer possible, then bound her feet with rags from her blanket; and every day she grew weaker. It was more than a month before she came to Sandy Lake.

"Fortunately the band had returned from its neutral encampment at Prince Albert; but when *Kees-ka-na-kwas* came within sight of her son's camp, it seemed deserted. She had to crawl towards it, for, in her stumbling weakness, it was too painful to walk on worn feet. Then at the door of the teepee, she knew that still more effort was required of her. My mother was quite alone, and it was the hour of my birth. Had my grandmother not come, had she not found still the strength to help, I might not be here to write this story."

32. *And he sang his song.* (See Note 18, story two).

33. *... down to the creek.* This was Cutknife Creek. Poundmaker's reserve was later at this junction of the creek with the Battle River, and it was here that the battle of Cutknife Hill took place in 1885 when

Colonel Otter unwisely attempted a surprise attack, on Poundmaker's camp. Ahenakew wrote in the story of his family (*Saskatchewan History*, Volume XVII, No. 1 (Winter 1964).): "For hours the battle went on, and then the soldiers had to retreat, their way to Battleford a country of rolling sandhills, ideal for ambush. The Indians ... might easily have waylaid and massacred the tired troops, carrying their wounded and their dead. Instead they followed them to the edge of the reservation and then allowed them to go in peace, Poundmaker restraining his angry and undisciplined men by the power of persuasion alone. Archdeacon Mackay ... said to me: 'Had Poundmaker not stopped his men, as he did, there would not have been many soldiers alive when that day ended.'"

34. *That was the grandmother of Moo-so-min.* Thunderchild and *Moo-so-min* had adjoining reserves in 1881 between the Battle and the Saskatchewan Rivers. In 1909, *Moo-so-min*'s was re-located on Jackfish Lake, and Thunderchild's at Turtle Lake.

35. *... he was protected by the spirits of small lice.* (See note 30(b), Ahenakew's account of belief in spirit power.)

36. *Se-po-mu-ke-se-kow* (Crowfoot) was born on the Bow River, about 1826. His mother was a Blood Indian, his father (The Many Names) a Blackfoot Chief, whom Crowfoot succeeded. According to Father Lacombe, this was not until after the father's death; in which case, Thunderchild's reference to "the Old Man who was his father" could be in the same tradition by which Crowfoot later made Poundmaker his son.

Lacombe described the Blackfoot nation of Crowfoot's youth as "a people of whom it may be truly said that they were against every man and that every man was against them." Crowfoot took part in nineteen battles and was wounded in six. His first war expedition had been when he was thirteen; but young bravery was the accepted norm in his "clan of nobles and brave warriors," and Crowfoot was forty years of age when his name "began to be proclaimed in the meetings of great men." That was when he led in the repulse of the Cree vengeance raid that both Lacombe and Thunderchild recalled.

It was from that shared experience that the friendship between Lacombe and Crowfoot grew, the latter saying of the courageous and unselfish missionary: "He is one of the greatest friends of our nation."

Lacombe's article of 1890, after the death of the Blackfoot Chief, spoke of his "great eloquence, savage pride, and wild love of freedom," and noted that he was "a skilled and astute politician who increased his power and influence by every possible means."

After Sitting Bull made his escape from the American Army and took refuge in the Cypress Hills, he had tried to persuade Crowfoot to join him in a raid upon the Americans at the border. Crowfoot refused. In 1877, he signed Treaty No. 7, insisting that the Canadian commissioners come to him at Blackfoot Crossing rather than that he should meet them at Fort Macleod; yet acknowledging in eloquent words the protection given to the Indian by the North-West Mounted Police.

In 1883, however, it was only through Lacombe's intervention that the Chief and his headmen agreed in council to permit the railroad to cross their land; then, two years later, when even greater disaster threatened and rebellion was being fomented, Crowfoot led the Blackfoot in declaring their loyalty and adherence to the treaty that they had signed. It was not unconditional loyalty though, as the Government was compelled to recognize in releasing Crowfoot's "son" when Poundmaker had served only seven months of his three-year sentence. Those months at Stoney Mountain Penitentiary had been too long, however, and Poundmaker died, Thunderchild recalling the heart-break of the old Blackfoot Chief at that time.

37. *He made Poundmaker his son.* Poundmaker was recognized as one of the most influential Chiefs of the Cree nation, yet he was actually only part Cree himself. His father was a Stoney Indian with such renown as a "maker" of pounds (see Ancestry of Edward Ahenakew) that he was entitled to give that name to his son. Poundmaker's mother was French and Cree, a sister of Chief *Mis-ta-wa-sis*, who as a head Chief of all the Plains Crees was the first to sign Treaty No. 6 at Fort Carlton, in 1876.

Poundmaker was then a man in his thirties, and present at the negotiations as one of Red Pheasant's headmen. When his Chief settled on the reserve in the Eagle Hills, Poundmaker remained on the plains. He had spoken twice at Fort Carlton, and to such effect that a number of young men chose him as their leader and joined the free Indians who recognized Big Bear as head Chief in resistance to the Treaty.

By 1879, Poundmaker, with Thunderchild, Little Pine and other headmen amongst those Indians, reluctantly accepted the change that had affected their whole way of life. He voluntarily settled on a reserve that adjoined Little Pine's, about thirty-five miles west and north of Battleford, where Cutknife Creek flows into the Battle River.

Poundmaker's band consisted of about 165 persons, most of them young men; he became almost at once chief spokesman for all the Indians in the Battleford area, for he was a man of impressive physical appearance and even more impressive abilities, distinguished in the arts of peace, oratory, and negotiation. Throughout the troubled years of his chiefship, he displayed remarkable judgment, dignity, and humanity.

At first, his band gave their efforts to farming, but the crops were poor, and assistance inadequate. By 1883, the Government's blind and even cruel policy of financial retrenchment had almost wrecked the whole Indian experiment, and had increased resentment and unrest to a point where unified action was clearly possible.

In June 1884, under the leadership of Big Bear and Poundmaker, great numbers of Indians assembled at Poundmaker's reserve for a Thirst (Sun) Dance. Then a desperate member of Lucky Man's band from the neighbouring reserve assaulted the farm instructor and the police came from Battleford to arrest him.

It had been the hope of the Chiefs that they could force concessions from the Government, not by actual hostilities but by the potential threat in such a large gathering of fighting men. The situation had become suddenly most dangerous, and Poundmaker and Big Bear had to use all their persuasive powers to bring it to an end without bloodshed.

The proposed council of Indians had to be moved to Fort Carlton, however, and their determination to achieve some better policy from the Government was minimized by those in authority, who held that the demands of the economic situation far outweighed any consideration of Indian grievances. Yet still the Indians made their plans for another council in 1885 — but 1885 brought the rebellion instead.

Circumstances involved Poundmaker's war-like band from the start, though he was to argue with justification at the time of his trial in Regina: "Everything I could do was done to prevent bloodshed. Had I wanted war I would not be here now. I would be on the prairie. You did not catch me. I gave myself up. You have got me because I wanted peace. I cannot help myself, but I am a man still and you may do as you like with me."

He was sentences to three years in the penitentiary at Stoney Mountain, and he said then: "Hang me now. I would rather die than be locked up."

38. ... *went out on horseback.* ... The leaders of the herd would always swing towards a rapidly approaching rider in an effort to head him off. A rider was able, for this reason, to make the herd veer towards him until they were racing between the lines of willows towards the gateway of the pound.

39. *The lodge for the Sun Dance must be built reverently.* ... (The term "Sun Dance" is not a translation of the Cree name *Nē-pa-kwā-se-mo-win*, which is "All-night-thirst-dance" or simply "Thirst dance.")

Thunderchild's talk emphasized its religious significance. There was no reason for him to describe in detail a ceremony familiar to his listeners.

(a) Ahenakew accompanied the notes with a sketch illustrating the completed lodge. In *Old Keyam*, chapter 11, he admits that the Sun Dance had never been part of his experience, yet he questions whether it was right to put down by law an act of worship that had guided the Indian in his relation to God through countless years.

In the story of his family (*Saskatchewan History*, Volume XVII, No. 1, (Winter 1964).) there is this reference to the Sun Dance, in the account of his grandfather, Ermine Skin:

"Before a Sun Dance, a structure of trees had to be built; and when these were cut and ready, there was a special ceremony to bring them to the site. Young women accompanied the men, and it was my grandfather's honour to select these women from the camp. Each horse carried a man and a woman. They would ride to the bush, tie a rope to a tree that had been felled, and then race back to the site of the Sun Dance, dragging the tree behind.

"The business of selecting the women was given to men who had taken women captives in raids. It seems that my grandfather had once captured a number of Blackfoot women. Single-handed! He had thought that it was secretly that he had helped an old Blackfoot couple and their daughter to escape when the Cree raided their camp; but other women learned of it and, afraid for their lives, gave themselves up to Ermine Skin. Most of these women were given to single men and they became Cree. Some may have had Blackfoot husbands before they were captured. I knew a woman who was the daughter of such a captive. She was married to one of our most influential Chiefs."

(b) Among Ahenakew's papers, there is a manuscript of later years — about 1950, it would seem — written for a Church publication, "on the Cree Indians and the work that has been done among them by our missionaries in Saskatchewan," reviewing the religious beliefs of the Indian.

"What religious beliefs had the Indian when the missionary came? He was a firm believer in the one, true, and all powerful God whom he called *Kessā munitō*. ... (Anglican Prayer-book spelling.) The word *munitō* means God, and the prefix *Kessā* is wonderfully apt.

"When you see a mother bird fluttering around, over its nest of young ones, anxiously trying to draw an intruder away, ready to lay down her life for her young, you say *a-kissāt* — which is the verb corresponding to the prefix in *Kessā munitō* — or *Kitche munito*, as the eastern Crees say it.

"To the Cree the word speaks of a being who hovers over his people as a loving father, anxious for their safety, looking after them as a bird mother does over her young ones.

"Old Men of the tribe who exercised great influence in the camp, who warned young men of the dangers of life, and who were as a rule very kind, were called *Kessā-yinewuk*.

"Because the Cree had the one over-ruling God, they were monotheistic, but there were other *munitos*. These were not tribal but were guardian spirits, in a sense, to individual Indians.

"The belief underlying this is that every phenomenon in nature has a spirit indwelling, which spirit has the power to give to any one it pleases the power to exercise that quality possessed by the phenomenon in which the spirit resides.

"For instance, *Pey-ā-siw*, the Thunderbird, may give to a human being whom it 'pities' (as the Indians say) its power over rain and lightning.

"As another example, the spirit residing in eiderdown, the lightest of almost anything existing, may give the power of lightness to whomever it 'pities.'

"A person sleeps, and in a dream some spirit comes to him and says that it has 'pity' on him. It calls him grandchild, *no-si-say*. The spirit promises him power such as it is able to give, which may be used miraculously when need arises. The man can use it for good or for evil. This gives a man standing in the tribe.

"Sometimes a father desires that his son should come into contact with a spirit who would have pity on him. He has a long serious talk with the boy. In a day or two, the boy disappears and no one looks for him.

"He goes up to the summit of some nearby hill — The Two Hills just west of Onion Lake were often used for this purpose. He takes off his clothes and lies down on the ground, covered with his robe or blanket. At times, he cries. Night comes, and he, only a boy, is alone in the wild. He eats no food. He may stay on the hill for two nights, and still no one comes to him. His nerves are strung tight. He senses all the influences that may pass and he cries. At times he sleeps; he is almost exhausted by thirst and hunger; the strain on him is great.

"Then suddenly a spirit appears to him, speaking to him in great kindness, promising him whatever power that spirit may have to give. It teaches him a song which is to be used when he wants to call the spirit to his aid, but only in case of direst need."

(See page 66, chapter 4 of *Old Keyam*; paragraph concerning the spirit power (*pu-wa-mi-win*) secured through dreams.)

"Many people had this kind of *munito* and often made dances honouring their particular one. Other people attended the ceremony, but even there prayers were said to the one, all-powerful *Kessā-munitō*.

"The highest act of tribal worship is the Sun Dance. This is held once a year, and great preparations are made for it. Small pieces of tobacco are sent far and wide, as signs of invitation to the dance. Usually it is held when berries are appearing.

"This is a worship primarily of *Kessā-munitō*, but through the Thunderbird, *Pey-ā-siw*, who rules the atmosphere. There is a large central pole in the lodge that is erected, and near the top of it a rude nest for the Thunderbird. Beside the pole, on a fine white cloth spread on the ground, is an old buffalo skull. This is painted with colours by a man who does it most reverently. It still is a sign of God's care when he fed his children on buffalo meat. Customs die hard, though buffalo skulls are not easy to find.

"I have been told that the prayers offered to *Kessā-munitō* are as beautiful as those of the Christians, only that they lack one essential, which is Jesus Christ and his redemptive work."

40. *Today, the dance is forbidden. ... Fine Day is one who is not permitted to make the Sun Dance that he vowed. ...* As early as 1882, efforts were made to suppress the customary dances of the Indians. It was held that they took the Indians off their reserves at times when the work suffered — that the dances were of "heathenish" origin and tended to create a spirit of insubordination among the young men of the bands. Gradually the traditional customs were losing their interest, discouraged by the Government, frowned upon by the missionaries, and shorn of their ancient glamour.

In 1895, Section 114 of the Indian Act was amended to read:

"Every Indian or other person who engages in, or assists in celebrating, or encourages either directly or indirectly another to celebrate any Indian festival, dance or other ceremony of which the giving away or paying or giving back of money, goods or articles of any sort forms a part or is a feature ... and every Indian or other person who engages or assists in any celebration or dance in which the wounding or mutilation of the dead or living body of any human being or animal forms a part or is a feature, is guilty of an indictable offence and is liable to imprisonment for a term not exceeding six months and not less than two months. ..."

The amendment of 1895 to Section 114 of the Indian Act was interpreted as forbidding the Sun Dance, but it was not rigidly imposed, for the Indians continued to "make" the dance, though under difficulties.

Mandelbaum gives an example of how Fine Day was able to secure permission to "make a Sun Dance" years before the incident related by Thunderchild and before the amendment to the Act.

118

A newspaper account from North Battleford to *The Star-Phoenix*, Saskatoon, August 10, 1936, speaks of Fine Day, supposedly ninety years of age, ''who was one of the most reckless of all the Battle River's fighting men. ... In his youth, his *Pu-wa-mi-win* (spirit power) had directed him to make eight Sun Dances as his span of life ran its course. ... To June of last year (1935) he had made seven. ... This year, he made his eighth and last Sun Dance, in tribal ritual. ...''

In June, 1961, an article in *The Free Press Weekly Magazine Section, The Prairie Farmer*, entitled ''Native Dances — Once Banned Indian Dances Now Return to Colour Heritage of Race,'' quotes Adam Cuthand:

''The Indians took on Christianity and threw away the drum. Dances can play a major role in bringing to the eyes of each new generation the cultural heritage that is theirs by birthright. ... In essence, the tribal dances involve both an inward and outward discipline. ... Peak physical condition is necessary for the vigorous and lengthy dances. Tenseness vanishes. ... The intelligence and co-ordination developed give as inspiring a picture of members of this noble race as do the members whose voices are heard in the arts, sciences and government.''

Pinned to the clipping of this article was a note from Anne L. Cunningham who was Adam Cuthand's teacher at Little Pine's school in 1923: ''The wealthy Poundmaker Indians (in contrast to those of Little Pine) came to Little Pine reserve each summer to a big Sun Dance. Adam was a small boy then, but would remember. Is that why he upholds it now? I felt that it was against all that we were trying to teach the pupils and their parents. Little Pine was a small and ignorant reserve — superstition was rife. When after a wonderful six months of school with happy pupils — came the other side — the feeling, that is. I have seen Edward Anenakew shrink when he translated for me, and Chief Poundmaker (son of the famous Chief) turned on him for not upholding the Indian side.''

41. *One of them was Father Delmas.* He was the missionary to reserves in the area of the town that is named for him, just west of Battleford, and who established an Indian boarding school there.

Notes Relating to Part II
Old Keyam

42. *... the young missionary*. ... John Hines came from England as Church Missionary Society worker to the Fort Carlton area in 1874. At the request of *Ah-tah-ka-koop*, he established a mission at Sandy Lake. He was later ordained and continued mission work in the diocese until his retirement in 1911. In 1915, his book *Red Indians of the Plains* was published.

Edward Ahenakew wrote of John Hines in a paper prepared for a Church publication about 1950: "He was a most practical man ... built his own house, then the church and a small school ... plowed a bit of land for his own garden and then went from place to place plowing for those Indians who planned to stay for the summer while the others hunted on the plains. He procured seeds for them so that when fall came they had a good stock of vegetables ... later they had small farms. ... As in a dream, I remember his departure from Sandy Lake to take up his work at The Pas. That was in 1888 when I was only three years old. His wagons were loaded, I remember, and the yard was full of kneeling people, while he stood, praying for them. It was a sad day for Sandy Lake, I have often been told.

"In his old age, John Hines lived in St. Vital, Manitoba. Archdeacon (later Bishop) Burd and I visited him there before his death in 1931. He was blind, and he told us that a small girl came in to clean and to cook a meal for him every day."

It may have been at the time of that visit that Edward Ahenakew was given the manuscript that is among his own papers. It is an account of the Indians who traded at Fort Ellice and Fort Pelly in the 1850's, and is based on the recollections of James Settee, "the catechist," as told to John Hines.

43. *Now the spirit power (pu-wa-mi-win) that is secured through dreams*. ... (See Note 39(b)).

44. *Now, when the Rebellion ended, the Indians accused of crimes were brought to trial*. Those tried at Battleford were given harsh sentences by Judge Rouleau. "The *Saskatchewan Herald*'s cry for vengeance was heard and heeded." (Bingaman) Dressyman (*Wu-wā-si-hoo-we-yin*) was sentenced to death, but this was reduced to life sentence, and he was released in a few years. He had returned to Frog Lake by 1892.

45. *François Ladouceur* — See note 25(b) about Métis.

46. *And he had given all this to people who were too improvident to give him anything of value in return*. Mandelbaum (*The Plains Cree*, pages 275-76) relates a similar incident in Fine Day's words: "If someone gives only poor little things for good gifts, he will generally not enjoy them. I was cheated like that once. But I didn't mind, even though afterwards I didn't even have a horse with which to hunt buffalo. The one who cheated me got a fast horse, but couldn't make use of it because he (the man) grew blind soon after. The old people said, 'He got blind because he cheated you. *Pah-ka-kōs* has strong power!' "

47. *... news from Duck Lake*. The encounter at Duck Lake on March 27, 1885, between Major Crozier's detachment of Mounted Police with some civilian volunteers, and Gabriel Dumont's Métis, cost the loyal force twelve dead and eleven wounded. They might have all been killed had Riel permitted Dumont to harass their retreat. The Rebellion had broken out.

48. *Just two old people who decided that life could be less lonely for them, together*. This is based on an incident at Onion Lake, and Edward Ahenakew was the young missionary who performed the marriage. Even the name Chochena is derived from the old woman's actual name, Georgina, for that is the only way she could pronounce the difficult consonants. The soft, sibilant language that she spoke is built around only nine consonants and five vowels. The story of her experience in the Blackfoot raid in her childhood, she herself told. Her first husband had been a Cree warrior, her son, Johnny Saskatchewan, a well-known guide. Her marriage in old age was to *Wēzo*, Thunderchild's contemporary, who had taken part in the encounter with the Blackfoot described in story four.

49. *A League has been formed*. ... In the plan that Ahenakew drafted for *Old Keyam* there was to be one chapter devoted to the League of Indians of Canada, and another to the Saskatchewan League Convention;

but his papers contain only five bedraggled pages of rough notes about the League, including a list of the aims in detail.

Amongst the papers of the Rev. Canon Edward Matheson, however, there was a printed copy of the address delivered by the Rev. E. Ahenakew at the annual meeting of the Woman's Auxiliary to the Missionary Society, which was held in Prince Albert on Wednesday, June 16, 1920. (Mrs. Matheson was diocesan president of the W.A., and had the address printed by the Battleford Press.)

Ahenakew's subject was the war record of the Indians and the formation of the League, and forms the material of Keyam's talk in chapter 7.

Amongst Canon Matheson's papers there was also a poem in his namesake's handwriting, signed by Edward Ahenakew. It was written in tribute to Chief Peguis at the time of the centenary of the Anglican Church at Red River in 1920. The paper carries the letter-head of The League of Indians of Canada. It names the following officers:

Dominion President, Chief, Lieutenant F.O. Loft, Toronto.
Vice-President, Rev. S.A. Brigham, Walpole Islands, Ontario.
Hon. Provincial President, Saskatchewan, Rev. E. Ahenakew.
Hon. Provincial Treasurer, Saskatchewan, James Wuttunee.

50. *... there are questions I would ask. ...* Ahenakew listed these questions in 1923. In 1963, Mr. R.F. Davey, Chief Superintendent of Indian education, presented a statement on behalf of Indian Affairs Branch to the standing committee of Ministers of Education, at the Canadian Education Association Convention, Sept. 15th. The statement concluded with "personal observations":—

1. What is now required, where it does not exist, is a common understanding at all levels of Government on attitudes towards the Indian problem and areas of responsibility and the necessary legislative machinery to carry out a programme which will eventually bring Indian education within the jurisdiction of the Provinces.

2. Legislation to permit the organization of school units or districts on Indian reserves under Provincial authority is required to extend the responsibility of the Indian in the operation of the local school.

3. Legislation to provide for Indian representation on school boards operating joint schools.

4. Increased Provincial control over the integration programme is essential to simplify administration. Federal financial support to the Province should replace tuition fees payable to local school authorities by the Federal Government.

5. The Indians must be recognized by the Provinces as residents with equal rights and privileges with respect to education.

51. *I have seen it proved in one school.* Little Pine's. Edward Ahenakew's account of the development of this school was published from his papers, in *Saskatchewan History*, Vol. XVIII, No. 2 (Spring 1965).

52. *... in the long ago days when the fur-brigades from the Churchill would come by Frog Portage ... and continue the long journey to Fort York on Hudson Bay.* After the union of the two fur-trading companies in 1821, York Factory on Hudson Bay was the great depot for imported goods and exported furs. Brigades of canoes, deep-laden with furs, landed there each summer from all the territory as far west as the Rockies, between Montana and the Arctic. About 1826, the York boat was developed by Orkney boatmen for heavy transportation on inland waters, "lineal descendants of the Viking galley" (*The Honourable Company*, Douglas MacKay, p. 249). Efficient freighters that they were, they replaced the great north canoes of lovely lines.

In the 1850's railroads in the United States were extending north-west, and St. Paul became a trading centre. Brigades of Red River carts from Fort Garry to Minnesota succeeded the more picturesque brigades of York boats to Hudson Bay. By 1859, Fort Garry was the distributing centre for the Hudson's Bay Company trade, and goods that had come by railroad to St. Paul and by steamboat down the Red River, went by brigades of Red River carts west along the trails that the buffalo-hunters had first marked, to Fort Carlton and on to Fort Edmonton for shipment by York boat to the Athabasca posts.

53. *Now, Ah-tah-ka-koop was high in the secret society of medicine-men. ...* Membership in the *Mitāwiwin* was made up of persons who vowed to join the ceremony in order to secure supernatural aid against sickness. Mandelbaum (*The Plains Cree*, p. 279-280) says that the ceremony was last given about 1875, and was always regarded with some suspicion by the Plains Cree because it dealt with the use of medicines which might be employed in sorcery. ... The novices were taught the use and manufacture of medicines which were wrapped in small packets and stored in the whole hide of a small animal. This hide was called *kaskipitakanan*. It was tied tightly and was the badge of membership in *Mitāwiwin*.

An old conjurer or medicine-man at Onion Lake, shortly before his death in 1913, gave his "medicine-bag" to Dr. Elizabeth Matheson. It contained or was contained in a weasel skin, which the old man "brought to life" so convincingly that both the doctor and her driver, James Buller, a well-educated

Indian, believed that they saw a live weasel run up the old man's arm to his shoulder, and that when he stroked it, it became a dry skin once more.

54. ... I was reading the Indian Act. ... The Indian Act of 1876, although changed and simplified by various amendments, remained the basic Indian law until 1951, when a new Act came into force. In keeping with the Government policy of encouraging Indians to take an active interest in their own affairs they were given an opportunity to review the proposed legislation and to make representation regarding its provisions. Also a group of representative Indians studied the provisions of the Act with the Minister responsible for Indian Affairs. (*The Canadian Indian*. A Reference Paper. Indian Affairs Branch. Ottawa, 1959.)

55. *He held out an ancient red-stone pipe-stem.* (*The Plains Cree*. p. 258-260. Mandelbaum.) "The Pipe-stem bundle was said to have been given by the Great Manito to Earth Man, the first human being. The successive owners of the bundle did not receive it through purchase or revelation but were chosen for the honour by the band council. Its ownership entailed obligations of fearlessness, liberality, and equanimity; men chosen for the office often ran away in an attempt to evade the responsibility. The bundle contained a pipe-stem three or four feet long, elaborately decorated with quills, beads, fur and feathers. The pipe-stem had no bowl; in fact, the stem was not used for smoking. ... No intemperate action could occur in the presence of the pipe-stem, and in this quality lay its peculiar potency ... the owner of the bundle had to intervene in all intra-tribal disputes, however hazardous ... could not engage in quarrels however provoked ... his conduct had to be exemplary. When he felt that he could no longer sustain the obligations incumbent upon him, he might, with the advice of the council, pass it on to a younger man. ... There might be as many as three or four such bundles in a band. One still (1935) exists on the Little Pine reserve. ..."

Ahenakew undoubtedly knew about that pipe-stem and had witnessed the unwrapping ceremony. In making *Old Keyam* the keeper of a sacred pipe-stem, he revealed the true character of the Old Man whom he had presented in the beginning as "poor, and inoffensive, and genial"; as one who had been defeated, and in disguising his bewilderment and hurt seemed not to care, but who did in fact bear the responsibility that the ownership of the sacred pipe-stem entailed.

APPENDIX
Account of the Signing
of Treaty Number Six:

"The site was about a mile from the Fort — on a rise of ground the Governor's tent — on a tree-dotted plain some 250 lodges of the main Indian camp. Between these and the Governor's tent was a clear space, and to the west the North Saskatchewan, its further shore fringed with timber. ... The Union Jack above the Governor's quarters ... beyond the Indian encampment, the tents of traders, assembled to do business with the Indians when the Treaty payments were made ... scarlet and gold of the Police Force ... colourful blankets of the Indians.

On the morning of August 18, the Governor (Alexander Morris), with Commissioners W.J. Christie and James McKay, with Dr. Jackes, Secretary, accompanied by Peter Erasmus (interpreter) were escorted by a detachment of Police, headed by a band, to the grounds. ... The Indians gave a simply magnificent exhibition of horsemanship, the whole band advancing in a semi-circle ... all were painted. ... The Governor, in cocked hat, gold braid and lace, represented the Queen. ... The Chiefs, with their headmen and councillors, advanced to within 50 yards and halted. ... Then began the dance of the stem (a long-stemmed pipe, gorgeously carved) to the accompaniment of chanting and drums. There was another exhibition of horsemanship, and then the whole party advanced to the Governor's tent. The bearer of the pipe-stem passed it to Morris and the entire party by turns, repeating the ceremonial of stroking the stem, as token of accepting the proffered friendship.

Peter Erasmus introduced the Chiefs and headmen, and before the terms of the treaty were outlined, the Governor delivered his address. ... The next day, the terms were stated again, and again the Chiefs asked for time to consider. ... The following day, Sunday, services were conducted by the Rev. J.A. Mackay and by Father Scollen from Bow River. The discussion continued for another three days. ... On August 31, the Governor's party left Fort Carlton and arrived at Fort Pitt on September 5. There the setting was not quite so picturesque, but the ceremonial proceedings were as at Carlton, the Indian display of horsemanship even better and more daring. ... Negotiations began on September 7, the Treaty payments were made on the 9th, and the Governor's party left Fort Pitt on September 13, arriving at Battleford on the October 6 — 1800 miles in all.''

The account of an eye-witness, John Andrew Kerr, (who was a driver with the Governor's party) written in 1936 when he was 87, and published in the *Dalhousie Review*, July 10, 1937. (Saskatchewan Archives)

The Treaty at
Forts Carlton and Pitt, Number Six.

ARTICLES OF A TREATY made and concluded near Carlton, on the twenty-third day of August, and on the twenty-eighth day of said month, respectively, and near Fort Pitt on the ninth day of September, in the year of Our Lord one thousand eight hundred and seventy-six, between Her Most Gracious Majesty the Queen of Great Britain and Ireland, by her Commissioners, the Honourable Alexander Morris, Lieutenant-Governor of the Province of Manitoba and the North-West Territories, and the Honourable James McKay and the Honourable William Joseph Christie, of the one part; and the Plain and the Wood Cree Tribes of Indians, and the other Tribes of Indians, inhabitants of the country within the limits hereinafter defined and described, by their Chiefs, chosen and named as hereinafter mentioned, of the other part.

WHEREAS the Indians inhabiting the said country, have, pursuant to an appointment made by the said Commissioners, been convened at meeting at Fort Carlton, Fort Pitt and Battle River, to deliberate upon certain matters of interest to Her Most Gracious Majesty, of the one part, and the said Indians of the other;

And whereas the said Indians have been notified and informed by Her Majesty's said Commissioners that it is the desire of Her Majesty to open up for settlement, immigration and such other purposes as to her Majesty may seem meet, a tract of country, bounded and described as hereinafter mentioned, and to obtain the consent thereto of her Indian subjects inhabiting the said tract, and to make a Treaty and arrange with them, so that there may be peace and good will between them and Her Majesty, and that they may know and be assured of what allowance they are to count upon and receive from her Majesty's bounty and benevolence.

And whereas the Indians of the said tract, duly convened in Council as aforesaid, and being requested by Her Majesty's Commissioners to name certain Chiefs and Headmen, who should be authorized, on their behalf, to conduct such negotiations and sign any treaty to be founded thereon, and to become responsible to Her Majesty for the faithful performance by their respective Bands of such obligations as shall be assumed by them, the said Indians have thereupon named for that purpose, that is to say:—representing the Indians who make the treaty at Carlton, the several Chiefs and Councillors who have subscribed hereto, and representing the Indians who make the treaty at Fort Pitt, the several Chiefs and Councillors who have subscribed hereto;

And thereupon, in open Council, the different Bands having presented their Chiefs to the said Commissioners as the Chiefs and Headmen, for the purposes aforesaid, of the respective Bands of Indians inhabiting the district hereinafter described;

And whereas the said Commissioners then and there received and acknowledged the persons so represented, as Chiefs and Headmen, for the purposes aforesaid, of the respective Bands of Indians inhabiting the said district hereinafter described;

And whereas the said Commissioners have proceeded to negotiate a treaty with the said Indians, and the same has been finally agreed upon and concluded as follows, that is to say:—

The Plain and Wood Cree Tribes of Indians, and all the other Indians inhabiting the district hereinafter described and defined, do hereby cede, release, surrender and yield up to the Government of the Dominion of Canada for Her Majesty the Queen and Her successors forever, and all their rights, titles and privileges whatsoever, to the lands included within the following limits, that is to say:—

Commencing at the mouth of the river emptying into the North-West angle of Cumberland Lake, thence westerly up the said river to the source, thence on a straight line in a westerly direction to the head of Green Lake, thence northerly to the elbow in the Beaver River, thence down the said river northerly to a point twenty miles from the said elbow; thence in a westerly direction, keeping on a line generally parallel with the said Beaver River (above the elbow), and about twenty miles distance therefrom, to the source of the said river; thence northerly to the north-easterly point of the south shore of Red Deer Lake, continuing westerly along the said shore to the western limit thereof, and thence due west to the Athabaska River, thence up the said river, against the stream, to the Jasper House, in the Rocky Mountains; thence on a course south-eastwardly, following the easterly range of the Mountains, to the source of the main branch of the Red Deer River; thence down the said river, with the stream, to the junction therewith of the outlet of the river, being the outlet of the Buffalo Lake; thence due east twenty miles; thence on a straight line south-eastwardly to the mouth of the said Red Deer River on the South Branch of the Saskatchewan River; thence eastwardly and northwardly, following on the boundaries of the tracts conceded by the several Treaties numbered Four and Five, to the place of beginning;

And also all their rights, titles and privileges whatsoever, to all other lands, wherever situated, in the North-West Territories, or in any other Province or portion of Her Majesty's Dominions, situated and being within the Dominion of Canada;

The tract comprised within the lines above described, embracing an area of one hundred and twenty-one thousand square miles, be the same more or less;

To have and to hold the same to Her Majesty the Queen and Her successors forever;

And Her Majesty the Queen hereby agrees and undertakes to lay aside Reserves for farming lands, due respect being had to lands at present cultivated by the said Indians, and other Reserves for the benefit of the said Indians, to be administered and dealt with for them by Her Majesty's Government of the Dominion of Canada, provided all such Reserves shall not exceed in all one square mile for each family of five, or in that proportion for larger or smaller families, in manner following, that is to say;

That the Chief Superintendent of Indian Affairs shall depute and send a suitable person to determine and set apart the Reserves for each Band, after consulting with the Indians thereof as to the locality which may be found to be most suitable for them;

Provided, however, that Her Majesty reserves the right to deal with any settlers within the bounds of any lands reserved for any Band as she shall deem fit, and also that the aforesaid Reserves of land or any interest therein may be sold or otherwise disposed of by Her Majesty's Government for the use and benefit of the said Indians entitled thereto, with the consent first had and obtained; and with a view to show the satisfaction of Her Majesty with the behaviour and good conduct of her Indians, she hereby, through her Commissioners, makes them a present of twelve dollars for each man, woman and child belonging to the Bands here represented, in extinguishment of all claims heretofore preferred;

And further, Her Majesty agrees to maintain schools for instruction in such Reserves hereby made, as to her Government of the Dominion of Canada may seem advisable, whenever the Indians of the Reserves shall desire it;

Her Majesty further agrees with her said Indians that within the boundary of Indian reserves, until otherwise determined by her Government of the Dominion of Canada, no intoxicating liquor shall be allowed to be introduced or sold, and all laws now in force or hereafter to be enacted to preserve her Indian subjects inhabiting the Reserves or living elsewhere within her North-West Territories from the evil influence of the use of intoxicating liquors, shall be strictly enforced;

Her Majesty further agrees with her said Indians that they, the said Indians, shall have right to pursue their avocations of hunting and fishing throughout the tract surrendered as hereinbefore described, subject to such regulations as may from time to time be made by her Government of her Dominion of Canada, and saving and excepting such tracts as may from time to time be required or taken up for settlement, mining, lumbering or other purposes by her said Government of the Dominion of Canada, or by any of the subjects thereof, duly authorized therefor, by the said Government;

It is further agreed between Her Majesty and Her said Indians, that such sections of the Reserves above indicated as may at any time be required for Public Works or buildings of what nature soever, may be appropriated for that purpose by Her Majesty's Government of the Dominion of Canada, due compensation being made for the value of any improvement thereon;

And, further, that Her Majesty's Commissioners shall, as soon as possible, after the execution of this treaty, cause to be taken, an accurate census of all the Indians inhabiting the tract above described, distributing them in families, and shall in every year ensuing the date hereof, at some period in each year, to be duly notified to the Indians, and at a place or places to be appointed for that purpose, within the territories ceded, pay to each Indian person the sum of Five Dollars per head yearly;

It is further agreed between Her Majesty and the said Indians that the sum of fifteen hundred dollars per annum, shall be yearly and every year expended by Her Majesty in the purchase of ammunition and twine for nets for the use of the said Indians, in manner following, that is to say:—In the reasonable discretion as regards the distribution thereof, among the Indians inhabiting the several Reserves, or otherwise included herein, of Her Majesty's Indian Agent having the supervision of this treaty;

It is further agreed between Her Majesty and the said Indians that the following articles shall be supplied to any Band of the said Indians who are now cultivating the soil, or who shall hereafter commence to cultivate the land, that is to say:—Four hoes for every family actually cultivating, also two spades per family as aforesaid; one plough for every three families as aforesaid, one harrow for every three families as aforesaid; two scythes, and one whetstone and two hayforks and two reaping-hooks for every family as aforesaid; and also two axes, and also one cross-cut saw, and also one hand-saw, one pit-saw, the necessary files, one grindstone and one auger for each Band; and also for each Chief, for the use of his Band, one chest of ordinary carpenter's tools; also for each band, enough of wheat, barley, potatoes and oats to plant the land actually broken up for cultivation by such Band; also for each Band, four oxen, one bull and six cows, also one boar and two sows, and one handmill when any Band shall raise sufficient grain therefor. All the aforesaid articles to be given *once for all* for the encouragement of the practice of agriculture among the Indians;

It is further agreed between Her Majesty and the said Indians, that each Chief, duly recognized as such, shall receive an annual salary of twenty-five dollars per annum; and each subordinate officer, not exceeding four for each Band, shall receive fifteen dollars per annum; and each such Chief and subordinate officer as aforesaid, shall also receive, once every three years, a suitable suit of clothing, and each Chief shall receive, in recognition of the closing of the treaty, a suitable flag and medal, and also, as soon as convenient, one horse, harness and wagon;

That in the event hereafter of the Indians comprised within this treaty being overtaken by any pestilence, or by a general famine, the Queen, on being satisfied and certified thereof by her Indian Agent or Agents, will grant to the Indians assistance of such character and to such extent as Her Chief Superintendent of Indian Affairs shall deem necessary and sufficient to relieve the Indians from the calamity that shall have befallen them;

That during the next three years, after two or more of the Reserves hereby agreed to be set apart to the Indians, shall have been agreed upon and surveyed, there shall be granted to the Indians included under the Chiefs adhering to the treaty at Carlton, each spring, the sum of one thousand dollars to be expended for them by Her Majesty's Indian Agents, in the purchase of provisions for the use of such of the Band as are actually settled on the Reserves and are engaged in cultivating the soil, to assist them in such cultivation;

That a medicine chest shall be kept at the house of each Indian Agent for the use and benefit of the Indians, at the discretion of such Agent;

That with regard to the Indians included under the Chiefs adhering to the treaty at Fort Pitt, and to those under Chiefs within the treaty limits who may hereafter give their adhesion hereto (exclusively, however, of the Indians of the Carlton Region) there shall, during three years, after two or more Reserves shall have been agreed upon and surveyed, be distributed each spring among the Bands cultivating the soil on such Reserves, by Her Majesty's Chief Indian Agent for this treaty in his discretion, a sum not exceeding one thousand dollars, in the purchase of provisions for the use of such members of the Band as are actually settled on the Reserves and engaged in the cultivation of the soil, to assist and encourage them in such cultivation;

That, in lieu of wagons, if they desire it, and declare their option to that effect, there shall be given to each of the Chiefs adhering hereto, at Fort Pitt or elsewhere hereafter (exclusively of those in the Carlton District) in recognition of this treaty, so soon as the same can be conveniently transported, two carts, with iron bushings and tires;

And the undersigned Chiefs, on their behalf, and on behalf of all other Indians inhabiting the tract within ceded, do hereby solemnly promise and engage to strictly observe this treaty, and also to conduct and behave themselves as good and loyal subjects of Her Majesty the Queen;

They promise and engage that they will in all respects obey and abide by the law, and they will maintain peace and good order between each other, and also between themselves and other tribes of Indians, and between themselves and others of Her Majesty's subjects, whether Indians or Whites, now inhabiting or hereafter to inhabit any part of the said ceded tracts, and that they will not molest the person or property of any inhabitant of such ceded tracts, or the property of Her Majesty the Queen, or interfere with or trouble any person passing or travelling through the said tracts or any part thereof; and that they will aid and assist the officers of Her Majesty in bringing to justice and punishment any Indian offending against the stipulations of this Treaty, or infringing the laws in force in the country so ceded.

IN WITNESS WHEREOF, Her Majesty's said Commissioners and the said Indian Chiefs have hereunto subscribed and set their hands, at or near Fort Carlton, on the day and year aforesaid, and near Fort Pitt on the day above aforesaid.

(Signed) ALEXANDER MORRIS,
Lieut.-Governor, N.-W.T.

JAMES McKAY,	
W.J.CHRISTIE,	
Indian Commissioners.	
MIST-OW-AS-IS,	His x mark
AH-TUK-UK-KOOP,	" x "
Head Chiefs of the Carlton	
Indians.	
PEE-YAHN-KAH-NIHK-OO-SIT,	" x "
AH-YAH-TUS-KUM-IK-IM-UM,	" x "
KEE-TOO-WA-HAN,	" x "
CHA-KAS-TA-PAY-SIN,	" x "
JOHN SMITH,	" x "
JAMES SMITH,	" x "
CHIP-EE-WAY-AN,	" x "
Chiefs.	
MASSAN,	" x "
PIERRE CADIEN,	" x "
OO-YAH-TIK-WAH-PAHN,	" x "
MAHS-KEE-TE-TIM-UN,	" x "
Councillors of Mist-ow-as-is.	
SAH-SAH-KOO-MOOS,	" x "
BENJAMIN, " x "	
MEE-NOW-AH-CHAHK-WAY,	" x "
KEE-SIK-OW-ASIS,	" x "
Councillors of Ah-tuk-uk-koop.	
PEE-TOOK-AH-HAN-UP-EE-GIN-EW,	" x "
PEE-AY-CHEW,	" x "
TAH-WAH-PISK-EE-KAHP-POW,	" x "
AHS-KOOS,	" x "
Councillors of Pee-yahn-kah-nihk-oo-sit.	
PET-E-QUA-CAY,	" x "
JEAN BAPTISTE,	" x "
ISIDORE WOLFE,	" x "
KEE-KOO-HOOS,	" x "
Councillors of Kee-too-wa-han.	
OO-SAHN-ASKU-NUKIP,	" x "
YAW-YAW-LOO-WAY,	" x "
SOO-SOU-AIM-EE-LUAHN,	" x "
NUS-YOH-YAK-EE-NAH-KOOS,	" x "
Councillors of Ah-yah-tus-kum-ik-im-um.	
WILLIAM BADGER,	
BENJAMIN JOYFUL,	" x "